Explorations in Theology 1

Explorations in Theology 1

D. E. NINEHAM

SCM PRESS LTD

334 01971 0

First published 1977
by SCM Press Ltd
56 Bloomsbury Street, London

Phototypeset by Western Printing Services Ltd, Bristol
and printed in Great Britain by Billing & Sons Ltd,
Guildford, London and Worcester

Contents

To my children
whose combination of sympathy and
frequent incredulity in the period
when most of these essays were being written
was both an encouragement and a stimulus.

Preface

It was the Rev. John Bowden who first suggested the publication of a selection of my essays and papers, and without his initiative and subsequent prodding, this book would never have appeared. My thanks are due to him not only for that but for the unusually large amount of assistance he and the other members of the staff of the SCM Press gave in the preparation of the material.

It would obviously be impracticable to list all the friends and colleagues on whose help and suggestions I relied in writing the essays which follow, but I should like them to know how grateful I am, even if they feel that I have sometimes misunderstood or misused what they said. A number of the pieces included were originally produced as lectures and I should like to thank the various bodies which invited me to lecture for the encouragement and stimulus their invitations provided. I have to thank Mr David Hart, and Miss Linda Foster of the SCM Press for preparing the indexes, and once again I have to express my deep gratitude to my wife not only for her patience and for her help with the proofs, but for her constant encouragement, both by precept and example, always to tell the truth as I see it.

Introduction

To reprint already published material – some of it written nearly a quarter of a century earlier – is decidedly a thing which requires justification. Any scholar who does such a thing, it might be said, has either let his brain go to sleep or else he is presenting what he no longer believes to be true. In fact, the alternatives are not quite so stark. Certainly, I should not express myself today quite as I did when some of these papers were written; but what they say still approximates pretty closely to the truth as I understand it today, and I see no prospect of treating most of these subjects entirely *de novo*. There is also, of course, the point that many of these articles appeared originally in publications to which most readers do not have easy access.

Perhaps, however, a rather fuller justification is called for. In a recent book ostensibly about the Bible I offered a fairly general critique of the present theological situation which made clear that in my opinion Christian thinking needs to change direction pretty sharply and to be predicated on significantly different premises. Naturally, I tried to give the reasons for my opinion in the book itself, but a far-reaching and fundamental conviction of that sort (and it *is* a conviction) is never simply based on reasons at the top of the mind; and it has been in the course of work in preparation for such essays as the following that I have come gradually to stand where I now do. A reader of these essays may thus find, not only that they sometimes make clear the detailed grounds for views only sketchily justified in the book, but that in seeing how I arrived at my position, he gets a clearer understanding of the position itself. That, at least, is my hope.

When, as a young graduate student, I first came to the study of theology from the study of philosophy and ancient history, it was no surprise to find that my interest was principally engaged by biblical studies, for I had long been fascinated by them, and in particular by the problem of Jesus and what can be known about him; even as a schoolboy, I had been deeply interested by the views of the Abbé Loisy.

In my student days New Testament scholarship in this country was dominated by three scholars of great eminence, none of them members of the Church of England, namely C. H. Dodd, T. W. Manson and Vincent Taylor. Ably supported by others, also mostly non-Anglican, such as W. Manson, A. M. Hunter and G. S. Duncan, they had contributed in their different ways to the emergence of something like a general consensus on New Testament topics. Although it owed something to continental neo-orthodoxy, it was essentially a home-grown product; and though it was very far from being fundamentalist, it allowed the New Testament to be used for purposes of doctrinal construction on *moderately* traditional lines. The New Testament writers were held to have been fairly close to one another on all essential points, and it was maintained that the picture of Jesus as messiah and once-for-all saviour of the world which they presented, went back in essentials to the teaching and self-consciousness of Jesus himself.

None of these men was in Oxford at the time when my theological studies began and I was taught, and deeply influenced, by R. H. Lightfoot, an Anglican scholar of a deeply devout, and fundamentally conservative, disposition whose almost paralysing modesty made him feel inadequate to enter into much open controversy with the scholars I have been describing, but whose equally intense honesty compelled him to disclose, in books but still more in conversation, serious doubts about the tenability of some of their conclusions. Like everyone else who knew him, I was deeply impressed by Lightfoot's integrity and painstaking thoroughness; so when I myself began to teach it was natural that I should feel compelled to explore further his doubts about the 'received' position. Work for an early article on form-criticism[1] convinced me that its implications were more significant than was generally believed in England at the time, and the preparation of the first essay in this book, and of another essay probing the views of Vincent Taylor, in a somewhat similar way,[2] further weakened my confidence in the received position. Increasing familiarity with German theology increased my suspicions, and the paper which underlay the three articles from the *Journal of Theological Studies* reprinted on pp. 23ff. was an attempt to subject one aspect of the English compromise position to a thorough test. By the time I had completed a commentary on St Mark's gospel in 1962 I was convinced not so much that the sort of position advocated by scholars such as Dodd and Taylor was wrong, as that it was incapable of proof, or even of being shown more probable than more radical interpretations of the evidence alternative to it. About one matter I became – and still remain – convinced that Lightfoot was right. New Testament scholars are seldom anything like ready enough to return a verdict of *non liquet*. 'They are so hot for certainties', Lightfoot used to quote from Meredith; and he would add 'If only they would freely admit: "We simply do not know"'. Some of the thinking which lay behind my agreement with that will be found in the papers on pp. 75ff. and 111ff. below and also in my contribution to the *Festschrift* for John Knox.[3]

If so, however, what were the implications for faith? Many German scholars had of course long since entertained doubts similar to mine, and indeed doubts much more radical, so it was natural to ask how they reconciled their views about the New Testament with a lively Christian faith; and I found much enlightenment in their writings, both those of Albert Schweitzer and those of Bultmann and his school. One thing they taught me which proved of lasting significance for my outlook. Our difficulties with the New Testament, whether considered from the historical or the theological point of view, are part of the wider problem presented by the fact that human culture is always changing and in the last two hundred years or so has begun to change at breakneck speed: 'The past is a foreign country: they do things differently there'. Indeed they do! They have different standards of accuracy with regard to the past and different purposes in writing about it, and they not only interpret, but actually experience, reality in ways extremely different from ours. Even a modest familiarity with the work of Ernst Troeltsch was enough to fix that in my mind for good.

But once again, what does it say about the relation between the New Testament and contemporary Christian faith? English theologians seemed strangely – I almost felt wilfully – blind even to the existence of the question. German theologians, while they were nearly all, including Barth, acutely aware of it, seemed to think that in one way or another they could exempt the New Testament from its scope – Barth by his 'positivism of revelation', Bultmann by the application to the New Testament texts of an appropriate hermeneutical procedure: there is 'an unchangeable fundamental structure of the human spirit as such' and if only the New Testament gospel is demythologized in the appropriate way, it will be found to have an abiding message exactly as relevant to us today as it was to the original readers. Increasing familiarity with the work of English-speaking sociologists[4] has made me suspicious of the theoretical basis of all this, and increasing familiarity with the detailed exegetical work of Bultmann's school has suggested:

(a) that texts are often wrested from their true meaning, and

(b) that even when the method makes them speak, it can only make them repeat endlessly the – admittedly vital – challenge to give up all the pretended securities derived from this world by which we try to bolster up the natural man, and to live entirely out of the future, out of God's resources.

The philosophical training I had received at the hands of W. G. de Burgh, D. M. MacKinnon and H. W. Cassirer would not let me surrender the problems of metaphysics, epistemology and natural theology as easily as most German theologians seem prepared to do, especially as I observed that the characteristic religious difficulty today is a metaphysical difficulty, at any rate in this sense: where men seem to need help above all is at the level of the *imagination*; they need some way of envisaging realities such as God, creation and providence imaginatively in a way which does no violence to the rest of what they know to be true. They need to be able to mesh in their religious symbols with the rest of their sensibility in the sort of way supra-naturalist and messianic imagery meshed in with the sensibility of first-century people. The later essays in this book see me wrestling with some aspects of the sort of question that raises, and gradually coming to feel that, *pace* the neo-orthodox, whether Barthian or Bultmannian, with their Lutheran belief in a Word of God which transcends all such particularities, in fact the future of Christianity depends on our taking with the fullest seriousness the existence of cultural change and its significance for man's understanding of, and relation with, God. We have to take Bonhoeffer seriously when he said that mankind has come of age and has a new relationship with the heavenly Father which, like a newly adult child, it must explore and express in its own way – of course without neglecting any help it can get from its predecessors' faith and experience, as witnessed in the Old Testament and the New Testament and later Christian writers.

Reviewers and candid friends often urge me to be more 'positive'. They want the new imaginative categories and symbols I desiderate spelt out for their inspection and judgment. That is fair enough and I can only reply – I hope honestly – that in a life which has brought many extra-curricular chores and concerns, I have gone as fast as I can. In any case, 'the Spirit bloweth where it listeth'. I am not sure that it is by taking thought that we can come by fresh vision and imaginative insight. Perhaps a sort of religious analogue to Keats's 'negative capability' ought to be a more prominent element than it is in the contemporary religious sensibility. In I Maccabees there were some priests who did not know what to do about certain things 'until there should come a prophet to show what should be done with them'. Perhaps we too must wait to be vouchsafed a prophet. I am fully aware, however, that even if so, none of us is exonerated from doing everything in his power to prepare that prophet's way before him; and I shall be more than satisfied if any of the essays which follow should prove useful contributions to that work of clearing the ground which almost always has to precede soundly based activity of a constructive and truly 'edifying' kind.

Keble College,   Dennis Nineham
Oxford

1

The Order of Events in St Mark's Gospel – an Examination of Dr Dodd's Hypothesis

In the *Expository Times* for June 1932, Professor C. H. Dodd published an influential article entitled 'The Framework of the Gospel Narrative',[1] in which he discussed the question on which principle St Mark arranged the order of events in his gospel. That the question is an important one does not need emphasizing; scholars have concerned themselves for several generations with it, and even now fresh answers to it are still being propounded. But in the last twenty years or so one particular answer, or type of answer, has been winning increasing acceptance, at any rate among English students of the New Testament. This answer is what might be called a modified 'form-critical' answer. It stands within the 'form-critical' tradition inasmuch as it accepts the thesis that the gospels can fairly be analysed into separate sections, or *pericopae*, which originally circulated independently of one another before their incorporation into the gospels. But it is a modification of the earlier 'form-critical' view in so far as it rejects the opinion of such scholars as Karl Ludwig Schmidt, Rudolf Bultmann and Martin Dibelius that the order in which the evangelist arranged these isolated *pericopae* was dictated solely by topical and theological considerations. This view holds rather that, along with the independent *pericopae*, the church preserved an outline account of the Lord's ministry and that this provided the evangelist with a historical framework into which he could fit the independent *pericopae* he found at his disposal.

It would appear that this view owes its origin to Professor Dodd, and in particular to the article in the *Expository Times* referred to above. Many subsequent writers who propound a view of this kind refer explicitly to the article,[2] and others, though they make no explicit reference to it, seem also to be indebted to its argument.[3] Since 1932 Professor Dodd has himself restated and extended the scope of the general argument in his two books, *The Apostolic Preaching and its Developments* and *History and the Gospel*, but on the particular point in question it does not appear that this treatment has anywhere been so full as it was in the article in the *Expository Times*, and indeed in his *Apostolic Preaching and its Developments* he himself refers his readers back to the article for a fuller treatment of the subject.[4]

In his book *A Study in St Mark*, Dr Farrer has subjected the whole position to hostile criticism from the point of view of his own argument. The aim of this essay is much more modest; it does not seek to advance any alternative hypothesis in the light of which Professor Dodd's view can be criticized, but simply to examine the argument as he presents it to see if it can be accepted as it stands and if it will bear the great weight of reliance that subsequent writers have placed upon it.

To begin with, it may be well to point out that Professor Dodd's conclusions, as he himself formulates them, are both more tentative and less far-reaching than those advanced by some more recent writers who champion a view similar to his. In particular he does not, like Professor Vincent Taylor, for example, argue to the substantial historical accuracy of St Mark's order on the grounds that St Peter and other eye-witnesses survived the Lord's death and must have remembered and spread abroad in the early church the knowledge of the exact order in which the events in fact occurred. Of this widely used argument there is no hint in the article;[5] Professor Dodd's own conclusions, as he himself expounds them in the last paragraph of his paper, are modest enough in their scope. He thinks of the evangelist as having had at his disposal:

(*a*) A skeleton outline of the Lord's earthly career. This was in some detail – longer and more detailed, for example, than the account of the Lord's ministry given in Acts 10.37-41, but still no more than a skeleton outline.

(*b*) A considerable quantity of *pericopae* relating to the Lord's ministry, some in isolation, others gathered into larger or smaller groups, usually according to similarity of subject matter, but none of them explicitly related to any particular place in the skeleton outline.

The task of the evangelist, on this view, was confined to fitting these *pericopae*, or groups of *pericopae*, into their proper place in the outline as best he could. The procedure he adopted for this purpose resulted, to use Professor Dodd's own words, in 'a compromise between a chronological and a topical order'. That is, where a *pericope* contained some indication of time or place which seemed to rivet it to a particular point in the outline, St Mark put it there. For example, *a pericope* which implied the use of a boat must belong to the point, or at any rate *some* point, in the outline where Our Lord was at the seaside, and so on. Where *pericopae* were already grouped on a topical basis the evangelist did not normally break up the grouping, but fitted the first *pericope* of the group into the skeleton outline by the method just described and allowed the remaining *pericopae* of the group to follow it in accordance with the topical principle on which they were already grouped. Where a *pericope*, or group of *pericopae*, contained no direct internal evidence as to where it should go in the outline, St Mark found a place for it as best he could, being sometimes guided by topical considerations and sometimes by a sense of the chronological stage to which a particular episode seemed most naturally to belong.

Before going further it may be well to ask what exactly has been shown about St Mark's order, if these conclusions are sound. If they are correct, St Mark's order is, as Professor Dodd himself says, 'in large measure the result of the evangelist's own work rather than directly traditional', and 'we shall not', therefore, 'place in it the implicit confidence it once enjoyed'. But he also says that St Mark did not do his work 'arbitrarily or irresponsibly, but under such guidance as he could find in tradition', and 'thus we need not be as scornful of the Marcan order as has recently become the fashion'. By 'placing confidence' in Mark's order and 'being scornful' of it, is presumably meant believing or not believing that Mark's order faithfully reflects the order in which the events he describes did, as a matter of historical fact, occur. Assuming that that is what is meant we shall proceed to examine how far Professor Dodd's arguments bear out his conclusion.

In the first place, the suggested outline, however accurate it may have been, must, in the nature of the case, have been very brief; it cannot have contained more than a minute fraction of all the things that the Lord must have said and done, even if we assume a ministry of only one year's duration. This is important, for it means, to take only one example, that the Lord may well have paid visits to the seaside on ten or twenty occasions not mentioned in the outline; and if, therefore, the evangelist dated a given *pericope* to a particular point in the outline simply on the basis of a reference in it to the sea or shipping, he may very well have put it in the wrong place, even perhaps at the wrong end of the ministry.

The next point we must notice is that very few *pericopae* contain internal evidence exact enough to tie them firmly to one particular place in the outline; more often it must have been, as Professor Dodd himself hints, a matter of 'suitability', that is, of where a particular *pericope* would fit into the outline most 'suitably'. But 'suitability' is a highly subjective category. For instance, Professor Dodd suggests that the first conflict story (2.1-12) was placed where it is because that seemed to the evangelist the most 'suitable' position for it in the outline. We may agree that it does fit very suitably in that position, but many people might feel that it would fit equally suitably, or even more suitably, elsewhere. What in fact this line of argument suggests is not that St Mark *knew* where the various events fitted into the outline, but that he fitted them in where he thought, on grounds of general probability, they were most likely to have occurred; and that is a very different thing. At the best this will have been inspired guesswork on the evangelist's part, and, unless we take the word 'inspired' in that phrase very seriously, we may be tempted to feel that our guess is sometimes as good as, or even better than, St Mark's.

Thirdly, we have to remind ourselves that, on Professor Dodd's own submission, a good half of St Mark's account of the ministry consists of *pericopae* which had been grouped together on a topical basis before ever they reached the evangelist, and have been left by him in the order in which he found them. In these cases, we may presume, St Mark cannot be held to guarantee any historical basis for the grouping. This last presumption, however, cannot be allowed to pass without further discussion, in view of an argument advanced earlier in Professor Dodd's paper. It runs as follows: the fact that a group of incidents as related in the gospel is dominated by a common *motif* does not by itself prove that these incidents have been artificially or arbitrarily put together; they may have occurred together in historical fact. The point is developed with special reference to two groups of *pericopae*, those in Mark 8.27-10.45, which are dominated by the thought of the approaching Passion, and those in 3.7-6.13 which, according at least to Karl Ludwig Schmidt, are dominated by the idea of the hardening of Israel's heart. About the first group, that concerned with the Passion, Professor Dodd writes as follows: 'Was there, or was there not, a point in the life of Jesus at which he summoned his followers to accompany him to Jerusalem with the prospect of suffering and death? Is it or is it not likely that, from that point on, his thought and his speech dwelt with especial emphasis upon the theme of this approaching Passion? Surely it is on every account likely. Thus, if one particular section of the gospel is dominated by that theme, it is not because Mark has arbitrarily assembled from all quarters isolated *pericopae* referring to the approaching Passion, but because these *pericopae* originally and intrinsically belong to this particular phase of the ministry.' Similarly with the other group, that concerned with the hardening of hearts, Professor Dodd takes as his starting-point the well-attested saying in Matt. 11.21 (cf. Luke 10.13) 'Woe unto thee Chorazin! Woe unto theee Bethsaida! for if the mighty works had been done in Tyre and Sidon which were done in you, they would have repented long ago in sackcloth and ashes'. This, he says, strongly suggests some particular incident as the occasion of its utterance and looks back to a period of unfruitful work in Galilee, now regarded as closed. What more natural, then, than that in this period and mood the Lord should have uttered a number of sayings about the hardening of men's hearts?

As a corrective to exaggerated scepticism about the general picture of the Lord presented in the gospels, the value of this contention may be conceded at once; but if it is used as an argument to support the historical accuracy of the order of events in St Mark's gospel, it seems to have serious weaknesses and limitations. They may be briefly set out as follows.

What the argument shows is that we know of two occasions in the life of the Lord which might well have given rise to such sayings and incidents as those described respectively in these two groups of *pericopae*; and therefore the attribution of those *pericopae* to those occasions is, from the historian's point of view, entirely plausible. But it must be emphasized again: it is one thing to claim that an account of the past is historically plausible and quite another to know it to be historically accurate. As far as the present case is concerned, must there not certainly in the course of the ministry – even if it lasted only for one year – have been numerous other occasions such as will also have given rise to sayings about the approaching passion and about the hardening of men's hearts? And may not sayings which were originally uttered on some of these occasions have been grouped together by the evangelist and attributed *en bloc* to the two occasions under discussion because he elected to treat these two as typical, and either could not, or did not care to, tell us about any of the others? Given the known habits of ancient writers, such a procedure seems highly probable; by ancient standards it would certainly not have seemed 'arbitrary' or 'irresponsible'. Indeed, if Professor Dodd's account of the matter were right, would it not be very odd that so much of what the Lord said on *these two* occasions about his coming passion and the hardening of hearts should have been preserved, while almost everything he said about these subjects on *other* occasions should have been lost?

It may seem then that the hypothesis of a traditional skeleton outline of the Lord's career preserved by the the early church will do even less to guarantee the historical accuracy of St Mark's order than Professor Dodd's very modest claims might suggest. We must now pass to an examination of the hypothesis itself.

Professor Dodd recognizes right at the beginning of his article that many scholars before him had rejected the idea of such an outline on the ground of its 'intrinsic improbability'. His reply to this is to point to evidence that, however 'intrinsically improbable' it may seem to us now, such an outline did in fact exist. He points first to two passages in Acts 10.37-41, part of St Peter's speech to Cornelius, and 13.23-31, part of St Paul's speech in the synagogue at Pisidian Antioch. He then shows that these passages, and especially the former, give, in brief compass, an account of the Lord's earthly career which tallies more or less exactly with the account underlying St Mark's gospel.[6] But does not this line of argument prove either too little or too much? On the one hand, if the speeches in the early part of Acts reflect genuine historical reminiscence of what was said by the apostles, then they can afford no evidence for the existence of a formal outline account of the ministry; for it can hardly be supposed that the original apostles were dependent on any such traditional outline; they had their own memories. If, on the other hand (and this seems more probable to many scholars), these speeches were produced by the author of Acts as a general summary of the sort of thing *likely* to have been said, after the Thucydidean model, then the outline of the ministry contained in them can have no independent evidential value; for it may have been derived by St Luke from St Mark's gospel, which we know him to have had before him. And this point is not affected if it be conceded that St Luke used sources in the compilation of these speeches, for it still remains true that, *in the form in which we have them*, these speeches have passed through the medium of St Luke's mind, and St Luke intended Acts to be read as a complement to the gospel he had just finished writing. To put the matter on the lowest plane: is it likely that St Luke, having just completed a detailed account of the Lord's ministry in the gospel, would then, in his second volume, ascribe to the original apostles accounts of that ministry inconsistent with the one he had just given? Whatever sources he may have possessed, this does not seem a very plausible suggestion.

We may conclude then that, whatever be the origin and status of the early speeches in Acts, they afford no clear evidence for the currency in the early church of a formal outline account of the progress of the Lord's earthly ministry. And we may add that, even if the two passages quoted from Acts could be taken as providing such evidence, they are so slight in content that they could afford only the most limited support to the historicity of Mark's order. It is true that, so far as they go, they are in agreement with St Mark's, or rather, significantly, with St Luke's account of the ministry, but even if their evidence is combined, it refers only to the lineage and baptism of Our Lord, and in general to a healing ministry in Galilee and a journey to Jerusalem; so that by far the greater part of St Mark's detailed account is unaffected by this agreement.

Two further passages from the New Testament are adduced as evidence for the currency of a traditional outline, namely I Cor. 11.23-25, St Paul's account of the institution of the eucharist, and I Cor. 15.3-7, his account of the crucifixion, resurrection, and post-resurrection appearances. It is true that in both cases St Paul seems to ascribe his account to church tradition,[7] but it must be pointed out that both these passages refer to events included in what is generally called the 'passion narrative'.[8] For it is generally agreed by students of the New Testament that, in respect of the matter under discussion, the *pericopae* which form the passion narrative stand on a different footing from the narratives recounted earlier in the gospel. There is general agreement that, for obvious reasons which have often been stated, the early church drew up an agreed, and more or less fixed, account of the events from the plotting of the chief priests and scribes to the resurrection of the Lord. The question at issue is precisely whether there was any such agreement about the events *preceding* the passion narrative, and to the settlement of that issue it will conduce nothing to cite examples taken from the passion narrative itself. These two passages cited from I Corinthians are not, therefore, relevant to the issue under discussion, and cannot be quoted as evidence for the existence in the early church of a skeleton outline of the Lord's ministry.

None of the evidence so far cited by Professor Dodd can be held to have weakened the contention that the existence of such an outline is 'intrinsically improbable'.

For the sake of completeness it may be well to emphasize just how strong this argument from intrinsic improbability in fact is. If the form-critics have shown anything, they have shown the essential importance of the factor they call *Sitz-im-Leben* in the preservation of the material included in our gospels; that is to say, no such material is likely to have survived for long unless it was relevant to *something* in the life, worship, beliefs and interests of the earliest communities. The question then is: what *Sitz-im-Leben* can plausibly be posited to account for the preservation of a skeleton outline of Our Lord's ministry which, on Professor Dodd's own admission, contained nothing of any hortatory or edificatory value? For it should be noted that the suggested outline was simply a bare chronicle of Our Lord's movements and activities, containing no material sufficiently detailed to be of any religious or practical value. Its only value could have lain in the satisfaction of historical curiosity, and all our evidence seems to suggest that historical curiosity, as such, was something in which the early church was conspicuously lacking.

The point may be put in the form of a question. What sort of people can be envisaged as having drawn up, memorized and preserved the suggested outline and in what circumstances and for what purpose are they conceived as having done it? If it were a question of the individual *pericopae*, no one who has heard the reading of the liturgical gospel at the Holy Communion need have much difficulty in answering these questions; but with the suggested outline it is a much more difficult matter. It is certainly hard to accept the suggestion that 'the simplest of the simple-minded early Christians' will have kept this outline in their minds, ready to fit any stories they might hear about the Lord into their appropriate place in it. Apart from this, the only answer to these questions suggested by Professor Dodd is contained in the following words: 'The outline which we have recognized as existing in fragmentary form in the framework of Mark may well have belonged to a form of the primitive *kerygma*'. But if *kerygma* means the preaching, or proclamation, of salvation, it is hard to see why, at any rate on ancient presuppositions, such a skeleton outline of events should have formed part of it. If we are to judge from the way St Matthew and St Luke felt free to alter and interpolate St Mark's order of events and the way the author of the Fourth Gospel treated the synoptic tradition, it does not appear that the precise order in which the saving events occurred seemed to the early Christian mind a very vital element in the saving proclamation or *kerygma*.

At this point it may be well to anticipate a possible objection. It may be asked: 'If it is generally agreed that the church from a very early period preserved a memory of the order in which the events of the passion narrative occurred, why should it be thought unlikely that a little later it should have taken the trouble to discover and preserve the order of events of the earlier period of the ministry?'

In reply three things may be said. First, the passion narrative is, on any showing, different from the rest of the gospels. It deals with a small and readily compassable number of events, and claims to give a more or less exhaustive account of them. The order of events is largely determined by the logic of the matter, arrest before trial, trial before crucifixion, crucifixion before resurrection, and so on, and is in any case easily memorable when the events are so few. To the earlier ministry none of these considerations applies.

Secondly, the reason for holding this view of the passion narrative is that the four gospels here display a closeness of approximation not found in their accounts of the earlier ministry. Thus the very evidence which suggests that the early church did preserve an account of the order of the events of the passion, suggests that it did not do so for the events of the preceding ministry.

Finally, the passion narrative does not really provide any parallels to the suggested outline. For what is claimed about the passion narrative is that the *pericopae* which make it up were themselves arranged in a fixed order; but the suggested skeleton outline is not a set of *pericopae* in a fixed order but a general historical outline of events with no *pericopae* attached to it, into which each man could fit such unattached *pericopae* as he could discover. Clearly the two cases are very different and no argument lies from the one to the other.

We seem driven, therefore, to agree with the scholars mentioned above that the existence of such an outline as Professor Dodd posits is intrinsically very improbable. What we know of the life and habits of the early church strongly supports their contention and, as we have seen, the passages adduced by Professor Dodd hardly appear to weaken it. We must now go on to ask what positive evidence there is to set against that improbability.

Professor Dodd throws the earlier part of his paper into the form of a discussion of a book published in 1919 by Professor Karl Ludwig Schmidt and entitled *Der Rahmen der Geschichte Jesu* ('The Framework of the Story of Jesus'). This book was one of the pioneer works of what is called the Form Critical School and its[9] 'thesis is that the gospel according to Mark is compiled out of separate *pericopae*, each transmitted as an independent unit in the folk tradition of the church. The arrangement of these *pericopae* is the work of the evangelist, who in arranging them has had little regard for chronology or topography, but groups them in the main according to the topics with which they deal, or the features of the ministry which they illustrate.

'Apart from the arrangement, and the insertion of such insignificant connecting words as εὐθύς and πάλιν the work of the evangelist himself is to be recognized in the composition of short, generalizing summaries (*Sammelberichte*), which punctuate the narrative, help the transition from one *pericope* to another, and remind the reader that the particular incidents narrated in detail are episodes in a widely extended ministry. These summaries can be recognized by their contrast in manner and content to the traditional narrative units. They lack the concreteness and particularity of the *pericopae*. They relate nothing which belongs to one point of space and time to the exclusion of all other times and places.' Their verbs, we may note, are usually in the imperfect, the tense of continuous or habitual action. While the *pericopae* possess a high historical value, these *Sammelberichte* are mere 'framework' and not to be taken seriously as a contribution to our knowledge of the course of the ministry.

With the main outlines of this view, the reducibility of the gospel to short narrative units and the imposition of a framework upon these units, Professor Dodd professes himself in substantial agreement; 'Professor Schmidt', he says, 'seems to have made out his case'. It is not within the scope of this essay to discuss the general question whether he is right in accepting so much of the form-critical position; we turn at once to the points on which he diverges from Schmidt's account. He doubts first whether the order in which the *pericopae* are arranged is entirely arbitrary – the work of St Mark – and he also declines to believe that the framework is nothing more than the artificial construction of the evangelist. He thinks that in arranging the *pericopae* Mark was controlled by the traditional skeleton outline and that the so-called *Sammelberichte* are, frequently at least, parts of that outline.

He opens his case by emphasizing Schmidt's own conclusion that several of the collections of *pericopae* in the gospel were grouped as we have them before they reached St Mark. Examples quoted are the groups of *pericopae* which make up 1.23-38,[10] 4.35-5.43[11] and 6.34-53.[12] But no significant conclusion can be drawn from this until the further question has been settled on what principle these pre-Marcan groups of *pericopae* were collected together in the pre-Marcan stage. Professor Dodd does not explicitly raise this question, but a little later, when he is dealing with 2.1-3.6, which he regards as a pre-Marcan collection, he says that it was clearly put together on a topical basis. But if these pre-Marcan collections were themselves put together on a topical basis, they afford no evidence for the existence of any such *non-topical* basis of arrangement as the traditional outline. One contrary argument is indeed adduced on the basis of such verses as 7.24, 9.30 and 10.1 where a *pericope* begins with the words ἐκεῖθεν δὲ ἀναστάς or some similar phrase.[13] This, it is argued, implies the question πόθεν; and suggests a geographical and historical, rather than a topical, basis of connection. But if this line of argument is to have any cogency it must be assumed that these phrases had been an integral part of their *pericopae* from the beginning, and that must remain at best conjectural. Is it not more likely that St Mark, or some pre-Marcan compiler, added these notes of place as part of a plan to present his collection of *pericopae* in the guise of a peripatetic ministry such as he knew the career of Jesus to have been? After all, if Mark was to present the Lord's ministry as having been exercised in a number of different centres at all, he was bound sometimes to insert between one *pericope* and the next some indication that Jesus left one place and went to another. What better phrases for the purpose than 'ἐκεῖθεν ἀναστάς' or 'κἀκεῖθεν ἐξελθόντες' or the like?

Professor Dodd's next main argument against Schmidt's position is very weighty and must be considered in detail, especially as it is repeated in a slightly different form later in the article. It comes in effect to this. If Schmidt is right in claiming that Mark's order is exclusively topical, then it should be comparatively easy for him to expose the precise topical basis on which Mark worked, and to show, in the case of every *pericope*, its topical relevance to the position assigned to it in the gospel. This, on his own admission, Schmidt can by no means always do; he is often forced to admit the apparent irrelevance of a *pericope* to the subject matter of the part of the gospel in which it occurs. To quote just one example, Schmidt places the *pericopae* in 8.27-10.45 under the topical rubric 'The Thought of the Approaching Passion', but he is then forced to admit that he cannot see the relevance to this subject of the *pericope* 10.2-12, the discussion of divorce. His own explanation of this awkward phenomenon is that sometimes when Mark found material joined together in his sources he did not bother to disjoin it in the interests of complete topical consistency. Thus, finding the *pericope* on divorce joined in some source to other *pericopae* concerned with the forthcoming passion, he put it, *with them*, into the section of his gospel to which they, but not it, were relevant. To this Professor Dodd replies: why was the *pericope* on divorce conjoined with the other *pericopae* in Mark's source? Was it not because the compiler of the source knew that historically the two belonged together, and was it not for that reason that Mark respected the conjunction when he incorporated this material into his gospel? At least, it is argued, we have evidence here of non-topical grouping, and if not topical, then presumably historical.

On this argument two comments of quite different kinds may be offered. First, it must not too readily be assumed that because two *pericopae* seem to have on topical connexions as we have them in St Mark, their juxtaposition in Mark's source was due to purely historical considerations. It is always possible that in their context in the source some topical connexion was apparent between them,[14] or even that the source used by Mark at this point was simply a collection of disconnected sayings-units. And if then it be asked why Mark did not disjoin them and fit each one into a topically suitable context, it may well be replied that such complete topical consistency did not seem to him of sufficient importance to merit all the labour involved[15] or even that he had no other context in the gospel which seemed to him to be appreciably more suitable for the *pericope* in question. He might, for example, have felt inclined to leave the divorce *pericope* with its surrounding material because there was no other point in the gospel where a discussion of divorce was self-evidently in place.

The second comment is of a completely different kind. Professor Dodd's argument at this point is correlative to the particular account of the matter offered by Schmidt. That is to say, the argument rests on the failure of one particular scholar to furnish an exhaustive explanation of St Mark's order on a purely topical basis. But Schmidt was a pioneer in this attempt; since 1919 other scholars have attempted to improve on his appraisal of Mark's order, and perhaps some of them have succeeded. They may have shown that the lack of topical consistency lay not in Mark's order, but in Schmidt's *incomplete understanding* of that order. It may be that, in the light of a further understanding of Mark's mind and purpose, *pericopae* which seemed to Schmidt and Professor Dodd irrelevant to their context can be seen in fact to be highly relevant to it.[16] And even if as yet no attempt to explain Mark's order on a purely topical basis has proved wholly successful, it is always in principle possible that one may; and so Professor Dodd's argument, from incompleteness of topical connexion to the probability of historical connexion, remains, in the last resort, as inconclusive as *ad hominem* arguments must always be. To some it may seem absurd to suggest that St Mark's gospel is based on a single topical arrangement which has yet succeeded in eluding readers for nearly 2,000 years. To deal fully with that objection would take us far afield; here let it be said that critical scholarship has so far taken little account of typological and liturgical and other theological factors which were undoubtedly very important in the production of the gospels; and also, in general, that the more fully we realize the complexities and the richness of the minds of the Biblical writers, the more ready we shall be to believe that no one as yet has plumbed the full depths of this particular writer's mind, purpose and order.

There is one further line of argument in Professor Dodd's article. For the purposes of this the *Sammelberichte* or 'connecting summaries' which Schmidt believes to be the creations of the evangelist, are isolated from the rest of the text. Professor Dodd then writes them out as a continuous narrative, omitting the detailed *pericopae* which separate them in the gospel. He then comments: 'The striking thing here is the way in which the summaries fall naturally into something very like a continuous narrative. We have in fact obtained merely by putting them together, a perspicuous outline of the Galilean ministry, forming a frame into which the separate pictures are set. So continuous a structure scarcely arose out of casual links supplied here and there where the narrative seemed to demand it.' We must first comment on the last sentence of this quotation; for it is far from clear how the conclusion it states follows from the preceding statements. If St Mark sought, as we know he did, to represent the Lord's career as a peripatetic ministry exercised in Galilee and its environs, and culminating in a journey to Jerusalem, then, surely, on any reckoning, if we put together all his statements about the Lord's movements, we shall be bound to get a continuous narrative which conveys that impression. But this seems to be a truism; it surely cannot prove anything either for or against the historicity of the impression Mark sought to convey.

But the argument is developed further by Professor Dodd.

Having isolated the *Sammelberichte* and set them down one after another, he goes on to analyse the outline thus arrived at into three stages:

(a) Synagogue preaching and exorcism in Capernaum and elsewhere.

(b) Teaching, healing and exorcism by the seashore.

(c) Retirement in the hill-country with a small circle of disciples, who are sent on preaching and healing tours.

He then has no difficulty in showing that, if this is the framework into which Mark sought to fit his material, he has done it very badly. For example, although stage (a) is entitled: 'Synagogue preaching and exorcism', at least a third of the Marcan material which deals with synagogue episodes falls outside it; and likewise with stage (b). The question therefore arises: if Mark had constructed his framework on a purely topical basis would he not have taken care to devise one into which all his material would have fitted neatly without remainder?

Whatever exactly the implications of this argument may be, they seem to be very damaging to the hypothesis of a traditional outline account of the ministry based on historical reminiscence. Professor Dodd's contention is that Mark had such an historical outline and that he tried conscientiously to fit all his detailed material into it at the appropriate place. The first stage indicated by this outline was a period of activity centred on the synagogue at Capernaum and other synagogues. Yet Mark has, on Professor Dodd's showing, deliberately refrained from inserting no less than one-third of his synagogue *pericopae* into their proper place in the outline; and the same sort of thing has happened with the second stage in the supposed outline – the period of activity by the seashore. But if so, can Mark really have taken this outline as seriously as Professor Dodd suggests? Can he, as Professor Dodd would have us believe, have regarded it as the controlling factor in the arrangement of his material? Can he in fact have had any such historical outline at all?

In conclusion it may be well to do two things. First to emphasize again the very strict limits of the scope of this essay. The aim has been simply to examine the validity of Professor Dodd's argument. Accordingly, even if the arguments advanced in this essay should find any acceptance, they could do no more than throw doubt on the validity of Professor Dodd's argument. They cannot possibly *disprove* that Mark's order was historical, for there may be arguments quite different from Professor Dodd's for believing that it was. They cannot even disprove that Mark had a skeleton historical outline of the Lord's ministry if fresh reasons can be advanced for believing that he had.

And then it may be well to anticipate the possible objection that the whole discussion is 'much ado about nothing' by pointing to some of the reasons for thinking the subject of considerable theological importance. Professor Dodd himself emphasizes the importance of the subject at the beginning of his article and he hints at the grounds of this importance when he says that many modern 'Lives' of Jesus are based on the assumption that Mark's order preserves – or can be made to yield – an historically and chronologically accurate summary of the days of the Lord's flesh. The point may be considerably extended – not only are certain modern 'Lives' of Jesus based on this assumption; any possible life of Jesus *must* be based upon it, if, by a 'Life', we mean a biographical study which seeks, as it were, to penetrate inside the *psyche* of the subject and to trace his inner and outer development. Such a study can be written only if the writer has exact information about the order in which the various episodes in the subject's career occurred and a sufficiently detailed knowledge of them to be able to show for what reasons he felt and acted and developed as he did. Our subject therefore is closely linked with the question of the possibility of producing a 'Life' of Jesus in the biographical sense.

In many theological circles nowadays it is a commonplace that the gospels are not biographies, but it may be doubted whether even now the implications of that statement are fully appreciated and faced. To be sure it is no longer fashionable to regard Christianity as consisting *primarily* in a relation of reverence and imitation to the earthly Jesus. But many who would firmly reject any such view seem often to handle the gospels in their meditating, writing and preaching as if the order of events at least could be regarded as accurate in the modern historical and biographical sense. It is of practical importance, therefore, to discover whether or not this assumption is well founded and, if it is not, to address ourselves to the further questions: what considerations did control Mark in the ordering of his material and what sort of conclusions were meant to be drawn in detail from the way in which he arranged it?

If the gospels are not biographies and not to be regarded or approached as such, then what are the assumptions with which to approach them in seeking to define the life of the believer and his relationship to his Lord? These are clearly questions of vital importance, but their very asking presupposes an answer to the question discussed in this essay.

2

Eye-witness Testimony and the Gospel Tradition · I[1]

According to the form-critics, eye-witnesses played little direct part in the *development* of the gospel tradition, however much they may have had to do with its original formulation. The point is too well known to need elaboration, but it may be worth pointing out that this opinion is no accidental or peripheral feature of the form-critical position. For it is of the essence of the form-critical approach that it starts from the internal evidence of the gospels in their finished form; and the characteristics of the finished gospels to which it points as the key features for their proper understanding are precisely those which are incompatible with any theory of much direct eye-witness influence after the initial stage.[2] The formal, stereotyped character of the separate sections, suggestive of long community use, the absence of particular, individual details such as would be irrelevant to community edification, the conventional character of the connecting summaries, all these point to a development which was controlled by the impersonal needs and forces of the community and not immediately by the personal recollections and interests of the individual eye-witness. Indeed it would not be too much to say that it is the absence of the characteristics we should expect in eye-witness testimony – knowledge of the particular, inclusion of the merely memorable, as opposed to the edifying, exact biographical and topographical precision and the like – which forms the very foundation of the form-critical edifice. And so it is a basic article of belief with the form-critic that the gospel tradition owed the form in which it reached our evangelists almost entirely to community use and its demands, and hardly at all to direct intervention or modification on the part of eye-witnesses.

But this conclusion, though so basic to form-criticism, has met with a good deal of adverse criticism, especially in England. First, an argument from general probability is often advanced against it, which runs somewhat as follows: We all know how, after the death of someone who has influenced us deeply, we cannot help recurring to the events of his life and recalling them to ourselves and to others who may be interested; and this simply from the emotions of affection and respect, without necessarily any idea of encouragement or edification. Did the apostles, then, not recall and pass on their personal, eye-witness recollections of him who had influenced them so much, and about whom their fellow Christians would be so anxious to hear? To ignore this factor, it is argued, is a clear sign of radical error in any theory.

As an example of such criticism we may cite some characteristically trenchant words of Professor Vincent Taylor, taken from his book *The Formation of the Gospel Tradition:*[3]

> It is on this question of eyewitnesses that Form-Criticism presents a very vulnerable front. If the Form-Critics are right, the disciples must have been translated to heaven immediately after the Resurrection. As Bultmann sees it, the primitive community exists *in vacuo*, cut off from its founders by the walls of an inexplicable ignorance. Like Robinson Crusoe it must do the best it can. Unable to turn to anyone for information, it must invent situations for the words of Jesus and put into His lips sayings which personal memory cannot check. All this is absurd.

And again:

> However disturbing to the smooth working of theories the influence of eyewitnesses on the formation of the tradition cannot possibly be ignored. The hundred and twenty at Pentecost did not go into permanent retreat; for at least a generation they moved among the young Palestinian communities, and through preaching and fellowship their recollections were at the disposal of those who sought information . . . when all qualifications have been made, the presence of personal testimony is an element in the formative process which it is folly to ignore. By its neglect of this factor Form-Criticism gains in internal coherence, but it loses its power to accomplish its main task which is to describe the *Sitz im Leben* of the tradition.

These quotations are typical; Professor Taylor himself repeats the substance of them in later writings, Professor H. E. W. Turner echoes, and in part quotes, the words, and similar sentiments are expressed by Professor A. M. Hunter and a number of other scholars.

Nor will anyone be unsympathetic to Professor Taylor's point; indeed, it is difficult to see how anyone could be, for although the argument is an *a priori* argument about 'what *must* surely have happened', it can easily be supplemented by empirical evidence from the New Testament and elsewhere which seems to show that, at every stage in its history, the early church was in fact interested in eye-witness testimony about the Lord. At the very beginning, when a successor was chosen for Judas, we are told that what was needed was a *'witness* of his resurrection',[4] and the qualification for candidates was that they should 'have companied with [the Eleven] all the time that the Lord Jesus went in and out among them'.

Again, in his speech in the house of Cornelius, Peter emphasizes the importance, and even the providential character, of the position of the apostles as witnesses of the Lord's ministry, death, and resurrection.[5] And so more than once in the speeches in early Acts, particularly in relation to the resurrection. And if these passages be regarded, as perhaps they should be, as evidence for the period of Luke–Acts rather than of the earliest church, we have still the early evidence of St Paul, who at the beginning of I Cor. 15 is at great pains to adduce the evidence of specific eye-witnesses in support of his account of the resurrection, and who appears to suggest that he had done the same in his original preaching at Corinth. For a later period we have, in addition to the passages quoted from Acts, the statement in the preface to St Luke's gospel, in which it is explicitly claimed that the writer, and the predecessors of whom he speaks, derived at least part of their information from αὐτόπται. For a still later period we have the evidence of the Johannine writings – 'he that hath seen hath borne witness and his witness is true'.[6] And again from I John: '. . . that which we have seen with our eyes, that which we beheld and our hands handled . . . we have seen and bear witness . . . that which we have seen and heard declare we unto you.'[7] Whatever exactly is to be made of these Johannine passages (all of them perhaps a little mysterious) they testify to the importance attached in the church of the period to the testimony of the eye-witness. To complete the list we should perhaps refer to I Peter 5.1 and to II Peter 1.16 and also quote the reputed words of

Papias: 'And if anyone chanced to come who had actually been a follower of the elders, I would inquire what Peter said, or what Philip or what Thomas . . . for I supposed that things out of books did not profit me so much as the utterances of a voice which liveth and abideth.'[8]

More will be said about these passages later; but inasmuch as they support such views as those of Professor Taylor, they seem to produce a rather odd situation in the contemporary study of the gospels in this country. For we seem to have two lines of approach to the problem of the development of the gospel tradition, which clearly tend in rather different directions, but which never meet on common ground so as to be able to do battle with each other and hammer out the truth. On the one hand we have the form-critical approach, which is essentially *a posteriori*, starting from the characteristics of the finished gospels, and reaching, by what is generally agreed to be a fairly consistent internal logic, a view of gospel development in which eye-witness testimony played no very large part. On the other hand the argument of Professor Taylor and those who think like him is in essence *a priori*. It starts from certain general habits of men, and, with the help of some empirical evidence about the habits of New Testament men – and of evangelists in particular – it argues that the eye-witnesses of the Lord's life *must have* played a significant part in the development of the tradition about that life.

The position is clearly unsatisfactory; how are we to know which view to follow? The general tendency is to try to strike a happy mean, as Dr Taylor himself does, and allow some truth in both views. But we can hardly rest permanently in that position unless we can form at least a general picture of *how* the two forces – community use and personal testimony – combined to produce just the kind of writings the gospels are. What part did each play, and above all, how are we to conceive of the impact of the one upon the other? What *Sitz-im-Leben* can be suggested for the process whereby personal testimony intervened in, and modified, the development of the community tradition? It may be objected that to put the question in that form is already in a measure to beg it, for it is to accept the form-critical account as giving the basic truth and to assume that any other influences must be fitted into that. In support of such an objection it might be pointed out that Dr Farrer, for example, in his account of the origins of St Mark's gospel, is far from conceding such priority to the forces of community tradition. If it is legitimate to combine what he says on pp. 24-25 of his book *A Study in St Mark*[9] with what he says on p. 370, his view appears to be that though anecdotes such as the form-critics postulate were current in the primitive church, Mark did not base his gospel on them. Mark got his material direct from eye-witnesses, but wrote it down in anecdotal form because of the familiarity of that form in the church of his day. Such a view, if it could be accepted, would provide exactly what is needed, an historical reconstruction of just how community use and personal testimony combined to produce a gospel. The difficulty lies in accepting the view, and in particular the part it assigns to community tradition. If Mark's material was indeed 'straight-forward and first-hand memories of Christ; for example, St Peter's' (p. 370), can we believe that, merely because 'the anecdotal form . . . was the form in which the oral tradition already lived' (pp. 24-25), Mark carefully suppressed almost all the personal detail his eye-witness informants would have given him and wrote such a colourable imitation of a series of community traditions that for forty or fifty years now it has deceived even the elect? The present writer finds that hard to accept; a detailed examination convinces him that the *pericopae* in St Mark are not only *like* the anecdotes current in the community tradition, they *are* such anecdotes, however much rephrased and reformulated by the evangelist.[10]

This is also the view of Dr Vincent Taylor, and if it is sound, it is correct to pose the question as it was posed above: How and when did eye-witness testimony impinge on the developing community tradition? It may, of course, be that the evidence simply does not allow us to say, and that we must be content to remain agnostic in the matter. But that seems hardly likely; for if the gospel material derives from two very different types of source we should expect it to show signs of its double origin. It would surely be very strange if, though it had in fact a twofold origin, its formal characteristics all pointed exclusively to a single origin. As Professor Taylor says, we should expect 'the influence of eyewitnesses on the formation of the tradition' to be 'disturbing to the smooth working of theories', that is, the theories of the form-critics. So our task must be to search the text of the gospels for such 'disturbances' of the form-critical account. Are there passages or phenomena in the gospels where the form-critical theory in its present form breaks down and where the facts are more plausibly explained on the assumption of direct eye-witness influence? And if there are, what do they tell us about the period and circumstances in which direct testimony impinged on the developing tradition? It is the purpose of this essay to suggest, in the barest outline, the form such a search of the test might take.

The obvious point at which to intercept the line of tradition first would be the point at which the twofold tradition of Mark and Q developed into a fourfold tradition by the addition of Matthew and Luke. That would be the obvious place because there we know that individual, personal activity supervened on the tradition; and, since we have the tradition both before and after this intervention, we know exactly what changes and modifications it was responsible for. Are they then such as seem likely to be due to the direct testimony of eye-witnesses?

As far as material is concerned, neither Matthew nor Luke gives the impression of having had anything but tradition to draw on. Much the greater part of both gospels is derived from written sources, Mark and Q, and of the rest very little seems likely to have been derived directly from eye-witness sources. This is generally conceded in the case of the M material, and in general, the material of L and M bears the usual marks of community tradition. It is true that many older critics were disposed to see in parts of Luke's birth and infancy narratives transcripts from the life, but Professor Sparks's findings on the Septuagintal character of the Greek, and, once again, the traditional *pericope* form of the material make such a conclusion difficult to accept. Detailed points cannot be discussed here, but it may be said in general that if Matthew or Luke had access to direct testimony, it is difficult to imagine why they remained so faithful to traditional accounts.

And what is true of the material appears to be true of the arrangement of it. In general both evangelists are dependent on the Marcan framework, and such changes as they make in it, and their arrangement of their non-Marcan material, seem to be dependent on considerations of doctrine and literary aptness rather than on direct eye-witness testimony. Even if Luke had a continuous non-Marcan source for the passion narrative, it would appear to have been a traditional and not a direct source.

All this, if detailed investigation were to conform it, would be important. In the first place, it will be remembered that the New Testament evidence for early Christian interest in eye-witness testimony comes principally from this period, from the text of Luke–Acts. In the light of the above considerations we might have to say that, for all the importance Luke, as a hellenistic historian, attached to contact with eye-witnesses, it was a privilege he himself did not enjoy, at any rate so far as the events of the Gospel were concerned. The bearing of his texts about αὐτοψία would be altered accordingly, and we should have to say, with Professor Cadbury, that when he describes himself as writing καθὼς παρέδοσαν ἡμῖν οἱ ἀπ' ἀρχῆς αὐτόπται . . ., we have to give full weight to the word παρέδοσαν and to take it as covering a 'transmission in part at least oral and collective'.[11] So interpreted, the words would hardly occasion any 'disturbance' of the form-critical position.

A further point arises if we recall the words of Professor Taylor quoted above. When we remember the different contexts in which Matthew and Luke put much of their common material, it would appear that at this stage, at any rate, the church *did* have to 'invent situations for the words of Jesus', or at any rate chose to do so. It would seem in fact that at this, the point most completely open to our inspection, few, if any, of the additions and modifications introduced into the gospel tradition can be traced directly to eye-witnesses. They seem either to be due to literary and theological considerations or else to have been derived from other community tradition. Indeed we can go further and say that even where Matthew and Luke had clear accounts of the sayings and deeds of Jesus, and of their contexts, they by no means always followed them. For all their dependence on Mark, and their respect for him as their chief and indispensable source, they by no means follow him slavishly as regards either order or subject-matter; and sometimes their deviations are quite radical, as for example in the case of Luke's treatment of Mark 10.45 and 16.7. The late Professor Lightfoot examined in detail one such divergence of Luke from Mark and there is no reason to think he would have minded our generalizing his conclusions. 'With Mark before us', he wrote, 'we are likely to feel that St Luke's version deprives us of features of great value in the story; and certainly his version of it is not what we expect to-day from a writer of "plain history".[12] The importance of this for our investigation is that if Matthew and Luke were thus prepared to modify their chief and indispensable authority in a doctrinal interest, we cannot be sure that their attitude toward eye-witness testimony would have been different. If it be replied that they would surely have put direct eye-witness testimony on a different footing, that serves only to emphasize how far Mark was in their view from being, or directly reproducing, direct eye-witness testimony. At any rate it would appear that the attitude of early Christian writers towards eye-witness testimony was less simple and straightforward than their explicit statements about it might at first suggest.

Before passing back along the line to Mark we may perhaps go forward for a moment to the Fourth Gospel, if only because the Johannine writings, as we saw, are one of the chief sources of evidence for early Christian interest in eye-witness testimony. Two passages from St John were referred to above. The former (19.35), is curious because it seems meant to guarantee only one very specific incident in the passion – the effusion of blood and water. Of this more will be said later. The second passage, 21.24, raises questions of interpretation. If, as some scholars hold, it is meant to refer only to the immediately preceding section (21.15-23) then we seem to have found exactly what we are looking for – a piece of direct testimony from the pen of an eye-witness 'putting the tradition straight' on a matter over which it had run into puzzlement or error. If, however, we accept the more popular, and surely more likely, interpretation of 21.24, as referring to the whole gospel, then too it has significance for our inquiry, though of a very different sort. Few would deny that the Fourth Gospel is, from the historical point of view, a fairly free rendering of the tradition about the life and ministry of Jesus. If then an eye-witness handled the tradition in this way, or even was thought likely to have done so, that suggests that the high valuation the Johannine writers placed on αὐτοψία was of a rather different kind from the high value we today attach to the direct evidence of the eye-witness. Clearly, in their view an αὐτόπτης need not be concerned to give the precise contexts of the words and deeds of Jesus, or even to relate them with exact biographical accuracy as we today understand it. Once again we are brought to the conclusion that early Christian texts which deal with αὐτοψία need careful evaluation before they can be used in the context of our discussion.

Of this more will be said later; meanwhile we must travel back along the line to the point at which the tradition was first organized in the form of a complete gospel, or at any rate a complete gospel that has survived. This is clearly a crucial point for our discussion. It might be thought that the points at which we have so far intercepted the line were in any case rather late for the direct impact of eye-witnesses; but Mark's gospel was produced within the span of their lifetime, and in this case there is the second-century tradition which links Mark closely with St Peter. Here surely, if anywhere, the living voice of direct testimony broke into, and took control of, the developing tradition. Professor Taylor and Professor H. E. W. Turner both take the form-critics severely to task for their virtual ignoring of the Papias tradition. However, as they recognize, the form-critics are by no means without excuse; for all, or practically all, the material in Mark seems to be of the *pericope* form and so presumably has passed through the formalizing processes of community tradition, just like the similar material in Matthew, Luke and Q. Professor Taylor himself writes: 'With the Gospel of Mark before us it is impossible to deny that the earliest tradition was largely a mass of fragments.'[13] This fact needs to be borne in mind when we come to the important question, whether there is any evidence in regard to particular sections of the gospel that they emanate directly from an eye-witness. Two well-known arguments suggest that there is. It is often suggested that certain sections of Mark were derived directly from St Peter on the grounds that no one but Peter, or some other member of the inner circle, would have known of the events related in them, or dared to criticize the original apostles as freely as they do.[14] Such sections are 8.14-21, 27ff., and 14.66-72. This argument can hardly be sustained. For if the form-critical position is to be accepted at all, most, if not all, of the passages referred to have certainly passed through a stage of community tradition; they show every sign of it. It may well be right to think of St Peter as the ultimate source of many of these stories; that, for example, is the view of Dibelius, but Dibelius holds that in getting from St Peter to St Mark they passed through a process of community tradition, and in some of the cases at least he is almost certainly right. Nor is there any mystery about the community's 'daring' to preserve these stories; the difficulties and imperfections of the original disciples served both to set off the unique character of the Lord and to encourage their successors in the faith when beset by similar temptations and uncertainties. Anyone, for example, who reads the account of the upbraiding of the Twelve as a *pericope* will be impressed by its power and will readily understand why the church dared to preserve and retell, for its own edification, such a story of the imperfect faith of the great founder-disciples. These passages are thus no evidence for the intervention of direct testimony into the development of the tradition *at the Marcan stage*, which is what is now under discussion.

For the same sort of reason it is difficult to follow the other argument, advanced by C. H. Turner. He argued, it may be remembered, following Zahn and others, that in a number of passages in Mark (e.g. 1.21ff., or 9.33ff.) we can get back to Peter's very words by translating the *oratio obliqua* of the gospel into *oratio recta*.[15] The curiously detached 'they' of these passages then becomes the 'we' of Peter's reminiscence. But, on examination, most of the passages in question show clear signs of having passed through a stage of tradition; and it is surely difficult to believe that throughout that stage the precise form of Peter's wording was retained.

There may well be other arguments in connexion with other individual passages; each would have to be examined on its merits, but meanwhile we must turn to a rather different, and much more general, type of argument which is often advanced. Commentators often point to the presence of vivid, circumstantial details in St Mark's narrative and see in them sure signs that eye-witness testimony stands very close behind. Thus, for example, Schniewind's comment on Mark 3.5 may be (freely) translated: 'The mention of Jesus' strong emotion (as in 1.41, 43; 8.12, 33; and 11.15ff. not mentioned in Matt. or Luke) is all of a piece with the direct reporting and powerful character of Mark's narrative'[16] and Dr Vincent Taylor writes, apropos such details in Mark 1.40-45, 'the narrative still preserves the rugged form of early testimony',[17] and in relation to Mark 2.1ff., 'The vividness of 3-5a, 11f., including the references to the breaking up of the roof, the crowds and the house, suggests dependence on primitive tradition.'[18] These and similar comments may well be justified, but it must be pointed out that such an interpretation needs careful scrutiny in the case of each particular passage. In the cases quoted, for example, Lohmeyer and others hold that the emphasizing of the Lord's strong emotion at Mark 3.5 is *theologically* motivated, while Wellhausen and others have held that Mark's account of the breaking up of the roof, to which Dr Taylor refers, rests on a misunderstanding of an original Aramaic tradition. These examples may prepare us for the fact that the presence of these vivid details has been interpreted by many along very different lines. Such details have been regarded[19] as signs of the comparative lateness of the material in which they occur, as variations on an originally simple theme, attempts to lend greater verisimilitude to the very bare narrative of the traditional *pericope* or to bring out some theological point in it. It may well be that in some cases the one explanation is correct, the other in others – decision in each case would have to rest on detailed investigation. But so far as the general principle goes, two points should certainly be noticed. It is the apocryphal gospels that are the richest in such vivid touches and circumstantial detail, and secondly, if the sources of the canonical gospels were to be graded simply on this criterion, the M material would be shown to be at least as close to eye-witness testimony as any other, a surely rather paradoxical conclusion.[20] This, of course, is far from showing that an argument can never lie from the presence of vivid detail to the presence of eye-witnesses, but it does suggest once again that the matter is by no means simple, and that great discrimination is needed in the use of this argument, particularly as it would pose in many passages the difficult question why Mark took over these vivid details direct from eye-witnesses but preferred to take the story in which he incorporated them, not from those same eye-witnesses, but from the impersonal tradition of the community.[21] And that question is only a particular form of the general question why, if Mark had direct access to Peter's recollections, he did not prefer them, much more than he has done, to community traditions.

Perhaps, however, the commonest argument for Mark's direct dependence on eye-witnesses is one derived from his ordering of his material. This argument, it should be noted, goes beyond the second-century tradition, for in the statement of Papias, as reported, Mark's τάξις – which still seems most likely to refer to his ordering of his material – is expressly dissociated from the inheritance he received from Peter. But the divergence is not as wide as might at first appear, for it is agreed by most advocates of this argument that Mark's order is for a great part controlled by purely topical considerations. It is true that in certain subsections of the gospel, Mark appears to have respected and retained the order in which he found the events related in his sources, but that calls for no comment at this stage of our discussion, for, if it is evidence for eye-witness influence at all, it presupposes it at a pre-Marcan, and not at the Marcan, stage of the development of the tradition.

The core of the argument from arrangement is the contention that, when all allowance has been made for topical groupings and the preservation of pre-Marcan arrangements of material, the general story of the ministry as Mark presents it is a living picture of an actual historical development, such as must go back to eye-witness evidence. Thus, to quote Professor Vincent Taylor once again: 'Mark's Gospel is no formless collection', and after outlining how some of its key features fit into a coherent pattern, he goes on: 'These are some of the features which in the past have led critics of all schools to suppose that Mark had access to good tradition concerning the Public Ministry of Jesus.'[22]

In relation to our discussion the first thing to be said about this is that at most it proves that Mark had good historical knowledge behind him; it remains undecided whether it was direct from eye-witnesses that he obtained that knowledge.[23]

But a further and more far-reaching question must be raised about this argument. Essentially it is an argument to the historicity of Mark's order from the fact that a modern historian, working on the basis of it, can construct an account of the Lord's life and work which entirely 'makes sense' in the light of all we know about him, and is completely plausible from the historical point of view. That this can be done admits of no question; to go back no farther than the last decade or so, Professor Taylor,[24] Professor Hunter,[25] Professor Turner,[26] and recently Messrs Polack and Simpson[27] have all done it; and what is more their accounts, broadly speaking, agree together. But the question has to be faced how far their accounts may have involved reading into

Mark biographical interests he did not share, and therefore historical information he did not intend, and cannot really be made,
to provide. In particular much rests in all these accounts on the
assumption that Mark intended to portray the confession of the
disciples at Caesarea Philippi as an historical turning-point in the
ministry, at which for the first time the Twelve recognized Jesus
as the Messiah. But the late Professor Lightfoot, for example,
became increasingly reluctant to interpret the passage in this
way,[28] and he may well have been right. The point may be put in
this way: Dr Taylor is no doubt justified in saying that Mark's
gospel is 'no formless collection' but he does not go on to raise, or
argue, the question whether the pattern which informs it is
historical, and not rather topical and theological. Yet the answer
certainly cannot be taken for granted, for if it is possible to
place a plausible historical interpretation on Mark's account, it is
also possible, as has recently been shown yet again, by Dr
J. M. Robinson,[29] to place a doctrinal interpretation upon it. And
many feel that such an interpretation arises more naturally out of
Mark's own language, and involves less straining of the evidence. The relevance of this for our inquiry, though limited, is
clear; if the organization of the material and the connexions
between the incidents in Mark are *theological* in basis and intention, then they do not need the activity of eye-witnesses to
explain them. These are large and already well-known problems
which cannot be fully canvassed here; indeed, before concluding
this first part of our inquiry it may be well to recall the precise
object of our discussion and to emphasize its strictly limited
character.

The two most popular accounts of gospel origins now current
disagree sharply about the direct influence of eye-witnesses on
the tradition after the initial stages.[30] Both appear to have sound
reasons of different sorts on their side, and the question therefore
arises whether evidence can be found in the texts themselves
which will help to resolve the disagreement. The purpose of what
has been said above is twofold – to suggest lines of investigation
along which such evidence might be sought, and secondly to
examine critically evidence that commentators have already
deduced from the text. It must be emphasized that so far our
inquiry has been entirely confined to the period in which the
finished gospels were produced, and to the question whether

there is internal evidence for the impingement of eye-witnesses on the tradition *during the period when Mark was writing and later*. Conclusions, so far as they emerge, will be considered in the next essay, but it is perhaps already clear that the matter is a highly complicated one, particularly as regards the reasons for which αὐτοψία was valued in the primitive church, and the functions an αὐτόπτης would, and would not, have felt himself obliged to perform in respect of the tradition.

3

Eye-witness Testimony and the Gospel Tradition · II

According to the form-critics, the formal characteristics of our gospels are best explained on the supposition that the material reached Mark and the other evangelists in the form of separate *pericopae*, generalized and stereotyped by the pressures of community need and use. But if so, what becomes of the age-old tradition that at least one evangelist, St Mark, derived the substance of his gospel direct from an eye-witness? Unless the whole form-critical approach is radically unsound, this tradition can hardly be accepted as it stands, for no plausible reason can be given why recollections derived directly from the living voice of St Peter should have been cast in the stereotyped, impersonal form of community tradition.[1] So far most students of the gospels agree; but many attempt a compromise solution, holding that though the evangelists derived a great deal of their material from community tradition, they also had at their disposal direct eye-witness testimony, with which they supplemented, or at least modified and corrected, the tradition. In the last essay, lines were suggested along which the text of the gospels might be examined to see if they afford any empirical support for this hypothesis. So far as a preliminary, and necessarily very general, survey could show, the results appeared to be mainly negative; the phenomena in the texts which have been pointed to as showing the direct impact of the eye-witness *at the stage at which the canonical gospels were in process of composition* appeared to be ambiguous and at best inconclusive.

Before attempting to assess the implications of this, we may ask whether it is possible to carry back the same sort of inquiry into the period before the composition of Mark. As soon as we make the attempt, we find ourselves in a region where the evidence for our inquiry is extremely scanty and inconclusive; yet even here certain points can perhaps be made, and certain lines of inquiry suggested.

In the first place, we have to allow time for the material which in Mark and Q has a highly stylized form, to have acquired that form through community tradition. As far as formal characteristics can show, there is no sign of any individual influence modifying it during that process, though of course it may all the time have been under the safeguard of the eye-witness's watching eye. But at least one piece of evidence springs to mind which seems to imply that this was not always the case. If, as is commonly assumed today, the two accounts in Mark of miraculous feedings of a multitude are doublets of the same story, then, as Dr Vincent Taylor, for example, points out, we seem to have in the tradition alternative accounts of a whole cycle of events (a meal, followed by a crossing of the lake and a controversy with the Pharisees) which go back to a common original. But, as we have them, they are significantly different, and so one, if not both, must have developed in considerable freedom from eye-witness control.

However, another piece of evidence has been brought forward as pointing in the opposite direction. There are in Mark groups of *pericopae* which are held to have received their present arrangement in the pre-Marcan stage, and to have been incorporated exactly as they stood by Mark, who respected and preserved their order. Why did he thus respect them unless it was because he knew them to be *historical* unities? These groups of *pericopae* certainly offer scope for further investigation, for they raise a number of questions. Professor Vincent Taylor has broached the subject,[2] and of the first group he cites he writes as follows:

> the four stories of Mark 1.[21-39] form a historical unity. After the incident in the synagogue Jesus enters the house of Simon and Andrew; in the evening crowds gather at the door and many healings take place; while the following morning 'a great while before day' he goes into a desert place and resists the entreaties of those who urge Him to return to Capernaum. Such a closely articulated sequence obviously demands explanation. . . .

We may certainly agree that it does, but it is by no means self-evident that that explanation ought to be in terms of historical unity. We must bear in mind the explanation given at one time by R. H. Lightfoot[3] along the lines that the arrangement of these *pericopae* was the work of Mark himself, who, at the beginning of his gospel sought to introduce his readers to the ministry by putting together a series of episodes typical of it. Although Lightfoot later came on balance to prefer the other explanation,[4] many scholars feel that his first thoughts were preferable. The very general and conventional nature of the section describing the healings after sunset might well point in that direction.

Professor Taylor's next example is the group of controversy stories in 2.1-3.6. Here there is every possibility that the grouping is topical, and, if so, it would not be evidence of direct eye-witness testimony even if, as the present writer increasingly doubts, it goes back behind Mark. The third group cited by Professor Taylor is that constituting Mark 4.35-5.43, a set of miracle stories set in the context of a journey. Here again decision is difficult, but, in the precise form in which we have it in Mark, it can hardly emanate from an eye-witness, for it appears to pack a quite impossible amount into the period between the late afternoon and the ending of a single day. Moreover, we have to take account of the fact that, in *The Riddle of the New Testament*,[5] Sir Edwyn Hoskyns and Mr Noel Davey have pointed to an important *topical* basis of arrangement in this section.

All this needs further study from the point of view of our question; meanwhile it would be hazardous to assume that any ordering of material which took place in the pre-Marcan stage *necessarily* presupposes eye-witness authority. The evangelists' predecessors were presumably as capable as the evangelists themselves of topical and practical arrangement; and in some cases it certainly seems to have been their practice.

So in this sphere, too, it seems difficult to find conclusive and unambiguous examples of the kind of eye-witness 'disturbance' of the tradition for which we are looking. But even if that is true, it comes nowhere near proving the negative that eye-witnesses were not all the time present and active. What it does do is to make the *impasse* more complete by suggesting that the *a posteriori* evidence can *all* be interpreted as pointing in one direction, while *a priori* considerations appear to point the opposite way. For the argument from general probability so strongly urged by Dr Vincent Taylor has lost none of its cogency. As he puts it in his commentary on St Mark:[6] 'It seems reasonable to suggest that historical testimony would be preferred to creative invention at a time when eyewitnesses still lived.' Perhaps the way forward lies through asking: *On what assumptions* is such a suggestion 'reasonable'? And perhaps we may best approach that question by looking first at St John's gospel, which, of all the four, makes the most explicit claim to be directly based on eye witness testimony. If for the moment we disregard such direct claims and concentrate on the body of the gospel itself, what do we find? We find a recension of the tradition about Jesus markedly different from any known to have existed earlier; and if we inquire into the reasons for the differences between this and earlier recensions, they appear to have little, if anything, to do with historical detail or biographical accuracy, although the resultant historical picture is significantly different from that of the synoptists.[7] Dr C. K. Barrett writes of John:[8]

> He sought to draw out, using in part the form and style of narrative . . . the true meaning of the life and death of one whom he believed to be the Son of God, a being from beyond history. It is for this interpretation of the focal point of all history, not for accurate historical data, that we must look in John.

In other words, John's motives for his reformulation of the tradition were essentially theological and edificatory, in the broad sense of that word, even though it was a narrative tradition that he was reformulating, and it still retains its form as a narrative tradition in his hands. That means that, in order to develop the tradition in just the way he did, he will have had no need of recourse to eye-witnesses; despite its narrative form, his was not the *kind* of reformulation that needed fresh eye-witness testimony as its basis. All this will have to be borne in mind when we come to discuss the Johannine passages which deal with αὐτοψία. But the immediate question is how far John may be regarded as typical of those who handled the narrative tradition before him. The church has traditionally regarded his work as an εὐαγγέλιον, a gospel, in broadly the same sense as the other three, but the scholarship of the last hundred years or so has tended to distinguish him sharply from his predecessors. Is this distinction justified so far as the matter of our inquiry is concerned? In many respects, of course, John was far from typical, as is clear if we compare him with Matthew and Luke. He was completely master of his material in a way that they were not, and accordingly their handling of the tradition was very much less radical than his. Yet in the light of our previous discussion of Matthew and Luke, and when, to take just one example, we see Matthew gathering all his teaching material into the five great *pᵉragim* which illustrate his thesis of the new law of the new Israel, must we not say that, so far as these two evangelists do reformulate the tradition, the basic principle of their reformulations was the same as that of John's?[9] Their writings, being gospels, were designed as contributions to the church's task of proclaiming Jesus as the Christ. Accordingly, the motives which controlled their formulations of the tradition were not exclusively biographical and historical, they were also practical and evangelistic. They sought to present the truth about the life and death of Jesus Christ in the way that would most clearly confront their readers with the theological meaning and practical challenge of it.

The disturbing implications of all this could easily be exaggerated; however practical their concern, we know that it did not lead them into any wild distortion of the historical picture presented in the earlier tradition. On the other hand, have we any really cogent reasons for thinking that the motives and procedure they exemplify originated with them and were not shared by those who handled the tradition before them? When the question is approached from this standpoint, it may be felt that very compelling grounds are needed to justify us in any sharp distraction of Mark and Q from their successors in the gospel tradition. And so perhaps our earlier examination of the texts takes on a new complexion.

That brings us back to the words of Professor Taylor. In assessing them a lot will turn on the precise meaning to be attached to the slightly question-begging phrase 'creative invention', but at least it will now be clear that the matter is by no means a simple one. Did St John prefer 'historical testimony' to 'creative invention', and would he even – and this is the really important question – have preferred it had it been available to him?

All this, however, does not dispose of the vitally important point that lies behind Professor Taylor's words. For is it not paradoxical to suggest that the early Christians, who pinned all their hopes of salvation on the occurrence of certain specific historical events, should have sat so loose to considerations of precise historical accuracy when they were framing the tradition of those events? By our standards it *is* highly paradoxical. But then we have to recognize that by our standards a lot of what they unquestionably did is highly paradoxical. None of us, for example, if faced with Mark and Q, would have done with them quite what Matthew and Luke did; and certainly no modern Christian, given the pre-Johannine tradition, would have erected the Fourth Gospel on the basis of it. Nor would any modern Christian have allowed all details of the Lord's personal appearance and characteristics to be lost to memory, as the primitive church so early did. Clearly, arguments from what we should have done to what they 'must' have done have always to be treated with the greatest caution. And nowhere is such caution more necessary than in relation to this matter of historical narrative.

Can we pinpoint the difference between them and us in this regard? Once again the clue may perhaps be found in some words of Dr Barrett. He writes:[10] '. . . it is by no means necessary to suppose that he [sc. John] was aware of the historical problems imposed upon later students by his treatment of the traditional material. It cried aloud for rehandling; its true meaning had crystallized in his mind and he simply conveyed this meaning to paper.' And John, we may suggest, was not aware of the historical problems he was creating because he did not share a presupposition by which the thinking of all modern students is controlled, the presupposition, namely, that all serious writing which takes the form of historical narrative must, whatever else it does, convey as accurate as possible an impression of the outward course of the events related. For us, when it is a case of narrative about the past which is not professedly fiction, strict and detailed accuracy comes first, and edification nowhere. If, when historical truth has been accurately determined by all the methods of research, it proves edifying or otherwise valuable, so much the better; but the very idea of edification as a separate value in historical narrative is completely foreign to us. That means that, had we had the handling of the primitive tradition about Jesus, our constant concern would have been to check and recheck it for detailed factual accuracy; and any reformulations of it we attempted would have been solely due to, or at any rate entirely controlled by, that concern. Interpretation, of course, there would have had to be, but we should have done our utmost to see that it was presented for what it was, and that it nowhere led to the slightest deviation from the historical 'facts' as presented in our sources. For example, in his recent Gifford Lectures[11] Professor Hodgson suggests that, though Our Lord may not, in the circumstances of the incarnation, have believed or claimed that he was anything more than the Messiah, he was in fact much more, and ought to be recognized as such. But no one with a modern background and training like Professor Hodgson's would ever dream of expressing this by producing a version of the narrative tradition in which supermessianic claims were ascribed to the Lord. What needs to be recognized, however, is that this modern attitude rests on a very special view of the character and purpose of narrative writing. There would be nothing inherently absurd in an attitude which said: 'If Jesus was in fact more than Messiah, then a good narrative tradition about him will be one that brings out that fact as clearly as possible.' And if the tradition in question was designed for *practical* use in public worship, to provide the basis for the hearers' continuing understanding of, and relation to, the exalted Lord, then such an attitude may well have seemed very reasonable. Is it not in fact just such an attitude that Origen ascribes to the evangelists when he writes[12] that it was their purpose 'to give the truth where possible at once spiritually and corporeally [or outwardly], but where this was not possible, to prefer the spiritual to the corporeal, the true spiritual meaning being often preserved in what at the corporeal level might be called a falsehood'? We have no guarantee, of course, that Origen was right in attributing such a procedure to the evangelists, but at least his suggestion, advanced as it is without any hint of disapproval, shows that such a procedure seemed perfectly acceptable in Christian antiquity to a man of the greatest intelligence, learning, and integrity. Nor is there really any reason to think that Origen does in fact misrepresent the evangelists. As far as the general principle is concerned, J. P. Gabler wrote more than a century ago:

> It is part of the character of the oriental never to give a bare report of an event but to report it in such a way as to do justice to what, in his opinion, the attendant circumstances or the results must have been. A writer's reflection was always included in his narrative, and its conclusions portrayed as fact. For the oriental could never conceive that

anything could have happened save in the exact way in which he pictured it. For the easterner *the fact and the way of conceiving the fact mingle to form one inseparable unity.* . . . It was not the oriental's way to separate events from his own judgment on them; but the occurrence and his reflection on it united in a single whole in his narrative.[13]

Here again some of the phraseology may be question-begging, but the judgment, especially that expressed in the italicized sentence, deserves careful consideration. Few Old Testament scholars, surely, would deny the words all validity in relation to their subject. For among the Jews the historian wrote very much under the inspiration of the prophet or the priest; history was very much the handmaid of theology, essentially a practical medium, prized as a way of bringing home to the people the true inwardness of their present situation and of the events which had led up to it. Of course it would not have served its purpose if the events narrated had been wholly fictitious, but the point is that the Jews had criteria for framing and assessing narrative traditions other than that of strict and detailed conformity with the outward course of the original events. He would be a brave man who would venture to generalize about the precise interrelation of these criteria in practice, but we have only to notice what the Chroniclers, or their sources, have done with the traditions independently preserved in Kings to see the justification for Gabler's contention that things were very different for them in this respect than they are for us.

Is Gabler's generalization also applicable, as he thought it was,[14] to the writers of the New Testament? It has often been pointed out that the New Testament writers differ from those of the Old Testament in that the events they narrated were of such comparatively recent occurrence that there had been little opportunity for interpretation to mould the tradition. That is certainly true and important, but it is not the only truth that has to be borne in mind. We must also remember that, as Henry Scott Holland used to insist, when the early Christians wrote about Jesus they felt themselves to be writing about a living contemporary, and not about a dead figure of the past; and a living contemporary with whom they had the closest relations, whom they knew with an intimacy which in some ways contrasted very favourably with that 'knowledge at the fleshly level'[15] to which eye-witnesses had for the most part been limited during the incarnation. The Lord's earthly life was seen as the first stage of a compact drama in three acts, of which the second act was taking place when the gospels were being written and the third act, the *parousia*, was momently expected to begin. Given that, given the contemporary attitude to historical narrative, and given the essentially practical and edificatory purposes for which the gospel narrative was designed, is it surprising if it was moulded by forces other than conformity to historical testimony, even when such testimony was available? Indeed if the matter is to be seen in its proper perspective, we need to recognize more fully than we often do that the primitive Christian churches were 'enthusiastic' bodies in the sense that word bears in the history of religions. Not only did their members know the exalted Christ, they had his power, mind, and spirit and were inspired by him in all their activities. And if in their other activities, then surely in the preserving, telling, and hearing of the tradition of his earthly life, death, and resurrection, especially as that tradition was so closely connected with liturgy and cult. Probably in some sense most of the New Testament writers thought of themselves as inspired writers of sacred scripture; would not something of the same feeling attach to those who related and expounded the gospel tradition at Christian worship in the pre-gospel stage? Can anyone read about Christian worship in I Corinthians and doubt it? The form-critics talk of 'community tradition'; it was not so the early Christians thought of it. They saw it as *sacred* tradition, the gift of Christ to his church, the account of his earthly life and death illuminated by inspired narrators with its true meaning for his saints.

All this, if true, will obviously have a considerable bearing on our original question. In particular it will be important when we are trying to envisage the *Sitz-im-Leben* in which community tradition and individual testimony combined to produce our gospels. It would be a mistake to draw over-hasty or excessively sceptical conclusions. The issues are complex, and since they must be viewed in the light of what the early Christians themselves said about αὐτοψία, it has been decided to defer discussion of them to the next essay. Meanwhile, attention must be drawn to a rather different set of considerations which must also be taken into account if balanced conclusions are to be arrived at.

We have to ask ourselves what *opportunities* eye-witnesses are

likely to have had to influence and mould the developing tradition. We have no means of knowing where in the Mediterranean
world the main process of preservation and development took
place, but we are safe in assuming that the communities outside
Palestine took their full part; and thus the question of travel and
communications becomes important. Even today it is not always
fully realized how impossibly difficult these will have been for
poor and uninfluential folk such as the original disciples, even
when all allowances have been made for the amenities of the *pax
romana*. In this respect our working picture of the early church can
easily be distorted because our main sources of information are
the Pauline epistles and the Acts of the Apostles. Paul was clearly
exceptional; a Roman citizen, a man of widish education, bilin-
gual, if not trilingual, and, on Deissmann's plausible showing, a
man of considerable means. All this must have made it possible
for him to exercise a peripatetic ministry and to undertake 'the
care of all the churches' in a way quite impossible for the poor and
comparatively uneducated Galileans who formed the bulk of the
original eye-witnesses. It is true that Acts represents the nascent
churches as under constant supervision from the centre at
Jerusalem, but there we must not entirely forget the argument of
B. S. Easton[16] that Acts was influenced by its apologetic aim of
representing 'the way' as a αἵρεσις of Judaism and, as such,
entitled to the privileges of a *religio licita*. The point must not be
exaggerated, as is shown by such passages as I Cor. 9.5 and I Cor.
1.12; but the fact remains that, according to our sources, those
who chiefly moved about among the Gentile churches and
supervised their development were, apart from Paul himself,
such as Barnabas and Timothy, Titus and Tychicus, Priscilla,
Aquila, and Apollos, none of them eye-witnesses and one at least
not very well up in the tradition.[17]

And finally, when we try in this way to envisage the historical
situation, we find ourselves forced to a careful definition of
exactly what we mean by 'eye-witness' in this context. There is a
danger of using the word in a rather artificial way, as if there was
a class of persons who had so continuously enjoyed the Lord's
company that they were definitive authorities as to what had or
had not happened at every point in the ministry. But even the
Twelve were not always in the Lord's company throughout the
ministry, and the presence of others must have been much more

occasional still. Surely there must have been many occasions when even those who had known the Lord in the flesh were compelled to say of some piece of tradition: 'This did not happen – or happen so – while I was with him; but it may well have happened at some other time, and it is edifying; who am I to quench the smoking flax?'

4

Eye-witness Testimony and the Gospel Tradition · III

The main function of this essay is to comment on some of the
implications of the argument advanced in the previous two
essays: but first the argument itself must be extended in one
direction. What is to be said about the New Testament passages
cited in the first essay[1] as evidence that the early Christians did,
on their own showing, set great store by eye-witness testimony?
It should be noticed, first, that almost all these passages come
from the later books of the New Testament. The single exception
which proves the rule is I Corinthians 15, and that is a highly
instructive passage, for it deals with the resurrection of Jesus,
which was bound to be a case apart. If, as Paul argues, the
resurrection of Christ is the very keystone of the Christian faith, it
will clearly have been of the first importance to convince out-
siders of its historical occurrence. In the case of so unheard-of an
event, there could be no hope of doing that unless the event were
exceptionally well attested, and so in this case the early church
had an apologetic motive for preserving eye-witness testimony
which will not have applied with anything like the same force to
many of the earlier events related in the gospels. So far as these
latter are concerned, the Pauline epistles certainly do not suggest
any very strong interest in eye-witness testimony about them.[2] In
this connexion it is also noteworthy that in Luke–Acts the word
μάρτυς, when used of those who had seen Jesus, is almost always
associated specifically with his resurrection and risen appearances.[3]

Apart from this Pauline passage, all the relevant New Testament passages come, not only from the last part of the first
century or later, but, with one exception, from the writings of

Luke and John. This latter is surely a significant fact. Luke, it is generally agreed, was the first historian of Christianity; the first, that is, to set out the origins of the faith in a way that would commend itself to readers accustomed to reading history and weighing historical evidence; but the history to which such readers were accustomed was *hellenistic* history, and, according to its canons, *autopsia* was of quite cardinal importance, as the proem to many a hellenistic history book will show.[4] Reference to αὐτόπται was thus inseparable from the task which Luke had set himself, namely the exposition of the origins and claims of Christianity in a way likely to commend itself to the attention of cultivated people. John's interest is still more clearly apologetic. He was faced with those who were tempted to deny altogether that Jesus Christ had come in the flesh, and in particular to take a docetic view of the passion and to question the necessity of the sacraments which were dependent on it. To counter such 'gnostic falsehood, eye-witness testimony was the strongest weapon, and it is noteworthy that one of John's appeals to eye-witness testimony (19.35) is limited to a particular incident in the passion which would validate both the full reality of the suffering and death, and the efficacy of the sacraments based upon them. It would seem, therefore, that in the case of both writers their interest in eye-witness testimony was a specialized, reflective, and apologetic concern, related to their peculiar circumstances, and forced upon them, in part at least, by contact with sophisticated inquirers and opponents; and the same is obviously true of similar claims in later writings. It must not too readily be assumed that either Luke or John had, or even claimed, direct contact with the eye-witnesses whose existence at an earlier stage they regarded as so vital to their case; and it would certainly be hazardous to take their apologetic concern with *autopsia* as immediate evidence for the interests and practice of their predecessors in the faith.

If the thesis put forward in these essays is sound, the conclusion must be that, though certain passages in our gospels may still be formulated exactly as they were by eye-witnesses of the events concerned, we have no compelling *a priori* reasons for thinking that it is so, and, even if it is, no absolutely watertight criteria for establishing *where* it is so. Accordingly, the gospels must be treated in the first instance as so many formulations of the early church's growing tradition about the ministry of Jesus; the only thing for which they certainly provide *direct* evidence is the beliefs about, and understanding of, that ministry in various parts of the early church between the middle of the first and the early part of the second centuries.

Conclusions of this sort about the gospels have been frequently stated and defended, but, rather strangely, thorough discussions of their implications have been much less frequent.[5] To what extent, and for what purposes, do we *need* direct eye-witness testimony about the ministry of Jesus? What difference does it make if the gospels do not provide such testimony? Some brief comments on these questions may be useful, if only as being likely to stimulate further comment and discussion.

For a start, a point of primarily apologetic concern may be cleared out of the way. If our conclusion is set against the background sketched in the previous essay – the general attitude towards history among first-century Jews, the difficulty of communications in the Roman empire, and the rest – no suggestion need arise of any dereliction of duty on the part of the early Christians. Certainly there need not be the slightest suspicion that they deliberately suppressed eye-witness testimony for fear of its conflicting with the interpretation of the ministry they wished to put forward. Indeed, as we have seen, there need not even be any suspicion that their treatment of eye-witness testimony implied any failure on their part to take history seriously in connexion with their religion. The point is worth making because the behaviour of the early church in this respect is sometimes judged in the light of modern attitudes to historical matters, and a very misleading impression is created as a result.

When we turn to the more directly historical aspect of the matter, it is idle to deny that some real loss is involved in our conclusions. If they are right, it is illegitimate to press the details, and many of the personal traits, in the stories; yet it is precisely through dwelling on such 'human touches' that many Christians have felt themselves brought most vividly into contact with their Lord. And not only is it illegitimate to press these details in an historical interest, it is surely hazardous to press them for devotional purposes, or at any rate for devotional purposes not directly envisaged by the evangelists. A question-mark is clearly set against some forms at least of *imitatio Christi* devotion[6] and also against the practice, which still largely governs the life of the churches, of quoting individual sayings and incidents from the gospels as precedents. In general it may be said that if our conclusions were to prove justified, they would have significant implications for devotional and homiletic practice and for moral and ascetic theology, which the churches for the most part have by no means thought through.

A further consequence would be that certain quite important questions about the life and ministry of Jesus – for example the question whether or not he claimed to be Messiah – would become genuinely open questions. For instance, in the light of our discussion, the question just mentioned cannot be settled simply by pointing out that certain passages in the gospels state or presuppose that he regarded himself as Messiah; and as soon as wider considerations, such, for example, as psychological plausibility, are taken into account, the matter is seen to be a very difficult and debatable one, as witness the discussion by Professor John Knox in his recent book *The Death of Christ*.[7]

One further point is only really an extension of the previous points. If it is illegitimate to press the details within the gospel stories, or the connexions between the stories, as biographically accurate, and if there are a number of undecided questions about the claims and consciousness of Jesus, the *coup de grâce* is finally given to the attempt to write a 'Life' of Jesus in the modern sense. It may be doubted, however, whether this conclusion has any very momentous significance. It has been increasingly recognized for some time that the gospels do not in any case provide material of such quantity or character as to form a secure basis for a Life of this kind, and also that Christian belief is not, and never has been, dependent on the ability to produce such a Life. Attempts to reconstruct the general outline of the ministry and the ideas behind it, such as those referred to in the first essay,[8] still have their apologetic value as showing that a perfectly plausible historical sequence can be imagined which would account for the general picture presented in the gospels; and it is doubtful if any significance beyond that has ever seriously been claimed for accounts so general and so highly speculative.

Undeniably, in these implications there is much food for thought, particularly perhaps for those who have to deal with

congregations and assemblies accustomed to accept unques-
tioningly the precise historical trustworthiness of every detail
they read, or hear read, in the gospels. At the same time, it would
be a great mistake to exaggerate the significance which this
limited question of eye-witness testimony has for the wider historical question raised by the gospels. We may doubt whether the
verdict of the modern historian on the gospel story will be as
much affected by the question of the presence or lack of direct
eye-witness testimony in the sources as theologians sometimes
seem to think.

In the first place, eye-witness testimony no longer possesses
for the modern historian the unique status which, as we have
seen, hellenistic historians tended to accord it. They, and their
successors for many generations, regarded eye-witness evidence
as the ultimate datum of the historian, the bed-rock truth below
which he cannot dig; and history for them consisted largely in
discovering and stringing together such testimony. Marc Bloch
shows[9] that this attitude persisted down to and well after the
Renaissance; as part of his evidence he points out[10] how even a
sceptical thinker like Montaigne, when presented with an eye-
witness account of some marvellous manifestation, did not normally think of questioning the account itself, but confined his
scepticism to seeking some natural or ostensibly intelligible
causes for what he accepted as having happened. Similarly
'Pompanozzi, shining star of that Paduan school so opposed to
Christian supernaturalism, did not believe that kings, simply
because they were kings, even if anointed with oil from the
sacred ampulla, could cure sick persons by touching them with
their hands. Nevertheless, *he did not dispute the cures'* [sc. in view
of their attestation]. For writers such as these, eye-witness testimony was indeed the *sine qua non* of serious history; in fact they
came near to equating eye-witness attestation and historicity.
Theologians sometimes write as if they shared this uncritical
attitude towards eye-witness testimony, but as far as the historian is concerned, it is precisely its emancipation from such an
attitude which forms one of the basic differentiae of 'scientific'
history. Lucien Febvre and Marc Bloch both make this point and
Collingwood makes it repeatedly. Dr T. A. Roberts writes of
Collingwood:[11] 'Scathingly he denounces the attempt to reduce
history to the activity of stringing together statements derived

from documents proved to be authentic and therefore endowed with a kind of sacred veneration as unimpeachable and infallible sources.' And Collingwood himself writes about this outmoded approach to history: 'The method by which it proceeds is . . . to go in search of statements . . . oral or written, purporting to be made by actors in the events concerned or by eye-witnesses of them, or by persons repeating what actors or eye-witnesses have told them, or have told their informants, or those who have informed their informants, and so on. . . . History constructed by excerpting and combining the testimonies of different authorities I call scissors and paste history', and, as readers of Collingwood will know, the last phrase is with him a very strong pejorative indeed.[12] By contrast the procedure of the contemporary historian is an adaptation of Francis Bacon's famous dictum about putting 'nature to the question'. Whatever his subject, the modern historian's first step is to formulate certain questions about it, and he then considers whether there are sufficient data to enable him to answer those questions; if there are, he subjects them to all the questioning and analysis necessary to make them yield the answers he needs. Whatever the character of the evidence, it must go through the fine sieve of his critical techniques before he can use any of it as a basis for his final historical picture. His very integrity and autonomy as an historian prevent his taking his 'sources' at face value or allowing them to dictate to him what is evidence. Collingwood writes again:

> If anyone else, no matter who, even a very learned historian, or an eye-witness, or a person in the confidence of the man who did the thing he is inquiring into, or even the man who did it himself, hands him on a plate a ready-made answer to his question, all he can do is to reject it: not because he thinks his informant is trying to deceive him, or is himself deceived, but because if he accepts it he is giving up his autonomy as an historian and allowing someone else to do for him what, if he is a scientific thinker, he can only do for himself.[13]

Marc Bloch is making basically the same point when he writes: 'There is no reliable witness in the absolute sense. There is only more or less reliable testimony', and goes on to analyse the 'two principal sorts of circumstances [which] impair the accuracy of perception of even the most gifted person'.[14]

The relevance of all this to our inquiry will be apparent enough. Even if the gospels consisted exclusively of eye-witness testimony, they would still have to abide the historian's question. They would still only be for him what basically they are now, crude ore to which he must apply his proper, rigorous techniques before he can extract the precious metal of historical truth. And no doubt, since the eye-witnesses belonged to an age which had quite different presuppositions and standards of evidence from those of the modern historian, the residual truth would look as different from the uncriticized testimony as refined metal always does from crude ore. It will, of course, always remain true that the statements of an eye-witness have a greater *prima facie* claim to credence than statements which reach us through one or more intermediaries; but in the light of what has been said, it will be clear that, in the case of ancient works such as the gospels, the force of this distinction is very much diminished. Moreover, it is to be noted that even where the witness of our contemporaries is concerned, it appears to be true – and if it is, it is very significant in relation to the gospels – that the evidential force of direct attestation varies in inverse proportion to the intrinsic incredibility of what is reported. If a friend whom I have found generally trustworthy comes in from the street and reports that he has seen something unusual but fairly readily credible, I shall probably believe him – for example, if he says he has seen forty policemen walking in single file along the middle of the Strand. If, however, it is a thousand policemen he reports having seen, my credulity will be stretched, despite the eye-witness attestation; and if the number reaches fifty thousand, the fact that the report comes from an eye-witness will weigh not at all against the factors making for incredulity. The principles of evidence in this connexion deserve further study by theologians, whose attention may be called especially to the acute, though ultimately unsatisfactory, argument of F. H. Bradley's first published work, *The Presuppositions of Critical History.*[15]

A further, and allied, feature of modern historiography is also relevant, namely the historian's ability to win from the 'tracks' of the past[16] truths which they do not bear on their surface and which they were not designed to yield, or even were designed to conceal. Marc Bloch writes:

> Even when most anxious to bear witness, that which the text tells us expressly has ceased to be the primary object of our attention to-day. Ordinarily, we prick up our ears far more eagerly when we are per-

mitted to overhear what was never intended to be said. . . . Despite
our inevitable subordination to the past, we have freed ourselves at
last to the extent that, eternally condemned to know [it] only by means
of its tracks, we are nevertheless successful in knowing far more of the
past than the past itself had thought good to tell us.[17]

The significance of this for our discussion will again be obvious
enough. If historians can wring truth relevant to the history of
Jesus from the increasing stock of remains of the Judaism of his
time;[18] if they can extract such truth from statements in all parts of
the New Testament which do not purport to be direct eye-
witness testimony about his ministry, then their dependence on
eye-witness testimony for an historical picture of Jesus is clearly
diminished. Obviously, however, the force of such a point must
not be exaggerated; much will clearly depend on the *kind* of
historical picture the historian seeks to produce. There are indis-
putably certain types of detailed historical reconstruction for
which the kind of evidence produced by the eye-witness is virtually indispensable, and the nineteenth century was inclined to
think that only this type of reconstruction deserved the name of
serious history. At that time history tended to be modelled on the
natural sciences, in the sense that the establishing of casual
relationships and the classification of the particular in terms of
the general seemed all-important. Consequently, in the sphere of
biography, exact chronology, the detailed *curriculum vitae*, the
precise stages of psychological development, and the external
forces and circumstances which produced it, had a high premium
placed upon them; and as a result the greatest importance was
attached to the type of direct, detailed evidence which made
possible the establishment of such things. But at least since the
time of Dilthey, the exclusive rights of this view of history have
been increasingly questioned. Attention has concentrated more
on the individual *in his transcendence of his environment*; on his
intention and self-commitment, and on the meaning which he
finds and creates in the outward circumstances of his life. The
question is too large to be entered into here, and in any case it has
recently been raised in English by Dr J. M. Robinson in his book
A New Quest of the Historical Jesus.[19] It is, of course, true that
history, even in this new understanding of it, if it is to produce
any account of Jesus, must have sources from which the original
facts can be deduced; but since it is no longer so vitally interested

in the chronological framework, the causal connexions, and the pattern of psychological development, it is no longer so dependent on the precise biographical details which the eye-witness is peculiarly well able to provide, and which, on our view, the gospels cannot on the whole be made to yield. On the other hand, as Dr Robinson has pointed out, the fact that the early Christians' concern with Jesus was a *kerygmatic* concern, a concern with his religious significance and intention, may well mean that precisely the material preserved in the gospels 'is the kind of material which fits best the needs of research based upon the modern view of history and the self'.[20] Dr Robinson writes:

> Now that the modern view of history and the self has become formally more analogous to the approach of the *kerygma*, we need no longer consider it disastrous that the chronology and causalities of the public ministry are gone. For we have, for example, in the parables, in the beatitudes and woes, and in the sayings on the kingdom, exorcism, John the Baptist and the law, sufficient insight into Jesus' intention to encounter his historical action, and enough insight into the understanding of existence presupposed in his intention to encounter his selfhood.

Collingwood makes the point in *The Idea of History* that an historian should not ask questions unless he has reason to think he will be able to answer them; unless 'he has already in mind a preliminary and tentative idea of the evidence he will be able to use. . . . To ask questions which you see no prospect of answering is the fundamental sin in science.'[21] With that in mind, we can formulate what is the really fundamental question about the gospels, from the historical point of view: Is their content such as to justify the modern historian in asking the questions which must be answered if he is to make any responsible judgments about the historicity of Jesus, or to produce a genuinely historical account of him? Among the overwhelming majority of modern critics who answer that question in the affirmative stand many of the convinced disciples of the form-critics, and the reason for that should now be clearer. For it will be seen that for the modern historian, the question as we have formulated it is by no means to be identified with a question about the amount of unaltered eye-witness testimony the gospels contain.

If the discussion we seek to initiate is to be comprehensive, it will have to take into account a further set of considerations of a rather different order. For the question may be raised – and it is essentially a theological question – why the commemoration of the saving historical events in the sacred tradition should leave so much to be desired in certain directions, when judged by modern standards. To some extent, no doubt, the answer will lie in the self-limitation of the divine providence to the natural limitations of the human condition. Apart from miraculous intervention, it is very difficult to see how an historical tradition originating and spreading among semi-educated folk in the first- and second-century Mediterranean world *could* have been other than it is. But it may also be worth pointing out that there is a function which a tradition such as that enshrined in our gospels is admirably fitted to perform. The discussion may begin with a commonplace point which can be illustrated by an example based on one from Professor Pittenger's book[22] referred to above. If at the end of this century someone wishes to discover the 'real significance' of what happened at the Yalta Conference, which will he consult, an account written by a participant in the Conference, or an account written fifty years after the event by an expert in political history? If the choice is an exclusive one, he will no doubt opt for the second source, because not only will the political historian be able to see the wood for the trees, but he will have been able to relate what went on at the Conference to the political events which preceded it and happened contemporaneously with it, and he will also have been able to estimate its significance in the light of the situation which succeeded it and to which it contributed. It need hardly be added that, however able or knowledgeable the political historian, his account will have only interim validity, and may well require considerable revision after the lapse of a further century. It will hardly be denied that what religious faith above all demands of the sacred tradition is an understanding of the 'real significance' of the events which constituted the life and ministry of Jesus Christ. From this point of view it may seem providential that the gospels were written a generation or more after the events to which they refer, by members of a community which had striven continuously to relate the events to the revelation previously given in the history of the Jewish people, and to the life and belief of Jesus' contemporaries, who had reacted so ambiguously towards him. Above all, however, the gospels were written by a community which, since the end of Jesus' earthly life, had enjoyed a continuous and deepening experience of him as the risen and exalted Lord, and had achieved increasing insight into the connexion between that experience and the events of the days of his flesh.[23] Consequently its members were able to describe and interpret those events as *gesta Dei per Christum* with a fullness and a clarity which would have been impossible apart from that experience. Given the conditions of the time, the delay was bound to mean a diminished degree of biographical accuracy, and in any case the early Christians were no doubt very naïve by our standards in the way they set about their task. If, for example, their experience had convinced them that all that was significant in Jewish messianic expectations had been achieved through the ministry of Jesus and the situation to which it had given rise, they were quite capable of ascribing to Jesus explicit messianic claims which he did not in fact make. By our standards this undoubtedly appears strange; we should prefer double-column gospels, giving carefully attested and documented biographical data on one side, and interpretation on the other. On the other hand, we must beware of a *naïveté* of our own. Modern writers have sometimes come near to suggesting that all we need is the accurate biographical data; given those we could interpret them for ourselves. We must realize, however, that recognition of events as *gesta Dei*, and of their meaning as such, is something which no amount of historical research could achieve by itself. What we have, incorporated in the gospels, is the insight into the meaning of the events described which had been given and tested in forty or fifty years of the church's experience of Jesus as the living Lord. If we look at the matter in this way we are less likely either to fail to see the need for an authoritative, divinely given, interpretation of the events, or to take too rigid and absolute a view of inspiration. We shall realize that just as the political historian's assessment of Yalta may need reformulation later, so the early Christians' account of Jesus, for all its authoritative character, will inevitably need restatement after the passage of centuries. On an older. view, all the interpretative categories to be found in the gospels, or at any rate all the valid ones, went back to Jesus himself; they owed their validity to the fact that he had provided them once and for all as the absolute and timeless terms in which his person and work were henceforth to be understood. On our view, many of these categories may be the work of the post-resurrection church, but that does not necessarily impair their validity; such a position seems to be at most an extension of a view several times put forward in the Fourth Gospel.[24] The gospels were not meant to give us an uninterpreted picture of Jesus' ministry so full and detailed that we could interpret its significance for ourselves. They were meant to admit us to that understanding of, and relationship with, Jesus which was vouchsafed to the apostolic church. At the same time they make possible sufficient historical knowledge of the person and ministry of Jesus for us to assure ourselves that the early Christians were not making bricks without straw; and also for us to see the sense in which their interpretations were intended and were legitimate and to set about the task of reformulating them in terms of our own needs and experience.[25]

5

Wherein lies the Authority
of the Bible? [1]

I have sometimes offered my students an illustration of this matter along some such lines as these. Suppose that a friend of mine were entering on some vital business dealings with a man who was personally unknown to him. He would obviously want to know all he could about this man – and he might appeal to me for help. 'Do *you* know so-and-so?' he might ask, 'Can *you* tell me at all what sort of person it is that I shall be dealing with?' I might have to say that I did not know this person in the sense of ever having been introduced to him or admitted to his family circle, or even of knowing his personal habits and peculiarities. I might even have to say that I had never seen the man and did not know what he looked like. 'And yet,' I might say to my friend, 'I think I can help you, for I know certain things that this person has done which will give you quite a good line upon him.' For example, I might be able to tell my friend how this man had begun with a very small retail business and had gradually expanded it till he was one of the most successful manufacturers and richest millionaires in the country; that would at least show that he was no fool where business was concerned. But I might also know of an occasion when this same man had provided expensive medical treatment for one of his employees at his own cost, or of another occasion when he had provided a much needed holiday for the family of an old associate. Or again I might be able to tell how he had once financed out of his own pocket a whole programme of research upon some particularly stubborn disease, and then built a special hospital in which the fruits of this research might be made available in the form of medical treatment. All this would reveal him, not only as a man of vast resources, but as a man of great generosity and goodwill, deeply concerned about the needs and sufferings of his fellows.

In this way I might be able to help my friend; and it is important to see why. Not because I knew the millionaire personally; I might not even know more than my friend about the outward course of the actions which revealed his character. For example, my friend might live in the district in which the hospital had been built; he might have watched it going up; he might have been inside it and know better than I what kind and size of hospital it was. The point is that to him, looking at it from outside, the building of the hospital would have appeared just one more building operation like all the others going on in the vicinity, and the hospital itself just one more, added to all the others already existing in the area. What *I* should be able to do for him would be to take him behind the scenes, as it were, and to show him that, viewed from the inside, this ordinary building operation was entirely due to the initiative and generosity of the millionaire, and so constituted an act of his which revealed a great deal about his character and attitudes.

But then there is the question what exactly *did* it reveal about him? So far we have accepted his actions at their face value, as evidence of sympathy and generosity; but in fact we can all quite easily think of other possible interpretations of them. They might, for example, have been so many bids for a knighthood or a peerage, or they might even have been based on subtle calculations connected with tax evasion. My original interpretation may seem the most reasonable guess, but it is a guess, and no one can take us beyond the realm of guessing except the millionaire himself. If we are to *know* the purpose and meaning of these actions – what they reveal about him – the knowledge must come from the man himself, though it may reach us through one or more intermediaries.

Of course this analogy breaks down, as analogies always do, at innumerable points; but the general application will be clear enough. It is the basic assumption of the biblical writers – which normally they do not attempt to prove – that there exists one with whom we must all carry on a relationship of life-and-death importance both for ourselves and for the communities in which we live. They do not claim to have penetrated into heaven and seen God face to face; they make no attempt to give us an account of his home life. What they do is first to describe certain historical events, which from the outside usually look just like other past events and are fully amenable to critical study by the historian. But then the biblical writers claim to be able to take us behind the scenes and show us that seen from within these historical events were in a special sense acts of God – saving and self-revealing acts in which God broke through, as it were, to encounter and help certain of his creatures and through them to reach the rest.[2]

Since their ability to do all this can come, in the last resort, only from God himself, we are approaching here very close to the question of inspiration. 'Inspiration' is a word with innumerable associations in Christian theology, not all of them entirely desirable. In particular it has habitually been used in connection with what is known as the 'two-source theory' of our knowledge of God – the idea, that is, that we can know some things about God by our own unaided intellectual effort, while other, and more intimate, knowledge can come only by direct, and sheerly supernatural, revelation from God himself. This theory has been subjected to searching criticism by C. C. J. Webb, Dr Rawlinson, Dr Hodgson, and many others both here and abroad,[3] and I mention it now only in an attempt to make clear what I do, and do not, mean by inspiration. The church has always said, and will no doubt always want to say, that the biblical writers are 'inspired', in the sense that their knowledge of the status and meaning of certain events as acts of God is somehow derived from God himself. But the word need imply nothing, as I use it, about the *mode* of the derivation, and it certainly need not presuppose the traditional dichotomy between 'natural' and 'revealed' knowledge. I should not even want to rule out the possibility that in certain cases biblical writers may have derived their insights through human intermediaries; for example, the writers of some of the historical books of the Old Testament may well have derived their interpretation of Israel's history from the teaching of the prophets or priests whose disciples they seem, in some cases, to have been.

In any case, it is here, over the question of the *meaning and purpose* of the acts of God in history, that my analogy finally breaks down. In that analogy, what my friend and I were trying to read off from the actions of the millionaire was the character and purposes of a *fellow human being*. It follows that, however subtle and tortuous his character and purposes might be, they would in principle be capable of being completely understood by us, if only we took sufficient trouble, and were sufficiently imaginative and acute. But when it is the character and purposes of God we are dealing with, things must be very different, for at least two reasons. In the first place, no one could *fully* understand the character and purposes of the all-holy God unless he were himself completely holy and sinless; and we have no reason to think the biblical writers were sinless in that sense. And secondly, the purposes of God revealed by his acts in history must be all of a piece with his eternal character and being; and therefore no human being could fully comprehend or reveal the meaning of God's acts unless he were privy to God's eternal being, as no man in this world can ever be. We cannot take religious truth and cut it up into sections and then claim that to Moses section A and Elijah section B was perfectly made known, and so on with all the prophets, priests, and wise men. The truth of God must form an integral whole. Human beings who see but a fragment of it can at best offer a fragmentary and imperfect interpretation of what they see. And it is important to realize that this is not an accidental fact, but something which belongs essentially to existence at the level of the creature, for human language and thought-forms are essentially geared to the limited existence of this world.

Before attempting to assess the implications of this, we shall do well to notice another, allied, inadequacy in my analogy. According to the analogy, the man whose actions my friend and I sought to interpret was a contemporary. But change the analogy for a moment; suppose now that the man my friend was seeking to understand was not a contemporary, but, say, a wealthy philanthropist of the Egypt of the eighteenth dynasty; and suppose that his guide and informant was not I, but some Egyptian writer contemporary with the philanthropist. However full and precise the account given by this writer, it would surely present my friend with considerable problems of interpretation. For the rich man's intentions would inevitably be expounded in terms of assumptions, values, and customs quite unfamiliar to a modern Englishman. A good deal of learning, imaginative sympathy, and what is sometimes called 'translation' would be necessary before my friend could begin to feel that he was getting inside the mind of the original philanthropist or of his interpreter. Once again, it is important to recognize that we are dealing here with an essential and inescapable feature of life lived at the historical level. When all allowances have been made for the unchanging continuity of 'human nature',[4] the fact remains that no writer who lives in history can interpret anything – even the deep things of God – except in terms of the accepted assumptions, values, and decencies of his time. He may be, as we say, 'ahead of his time', but that is a relative thing; man in history must always be the child of *some* age and so he must always make things intelligible in terms of the culture of that age; the very phrase 'make intelligible' must always be relative to some familiar and accepted terminology. Put it like this: God himself could not have enabled Isaiah to interpret the divine activity in terms immediately appropriate to his own *and all subsequent* generations. For the Hebrew language of the period simply did not contain words to express many of the ideas in terms of which the modern Englishman interprets his environment; and in any case, had the necessary words been miraculously provided, the resultant message would have been unintelligible to the prophet himself and to all generations down to the twentieth century.

The point is familiar, and does not need labouring; we may pass to another. The biblical writers all belonged to what we call the ancient world, and, for a number of reasons, it is a fact about that world that people in it could not attain to the kind of scientific historical accuracy with regard to past events which is possible today. Indeed, such accuracy was so remote from them that, at any rate with regard to the distant past, they had no conception of it, or even desire for it. The relevance of that for our subject is obvious enough. Unless a supply of error-free historical information was miraculously piped into their consciousness, their account of the various historical events which they expound as revealing acts of God is bound very often to seem woefully unsatisfactory and inaccurate when judged by the standards of current historical practice. That must be true, unless, as I said, a certain amount of error-free historical information was supplied to them; but before we take up the challenge implicit in that last phrase, it may be well to pause and take stock of what has been said so far.

I have assumed of course that God *has* acted in history to reveal himself and to save the world, very much in the way the Bible presupposes. Granted that, I have hinted at an interpretation of the function of the biblical writers which would ascribe authority to what they wrote, and even claim inspiration for it, without claiming detailed inerrancy for it at any level. On this interpretation, we should expect not only historical and scientific error, but error in matters of religion; and as for the precise words of the biblical writers, we should expect always to have to apply to them the question so admirably formulated by Professor Hodgson: 'What must the truth be, and have been, if it appeared like that to men who thought and wrote as they did?'[5] In fact this is an account of biblical authority which leaves the whole matter very fluid and assigns a considerable role and responsibility to the modern interpreter in the process of getting to know God with the help and guidance of the biblical writers.

I make no apology for that; but I *am* anxious not to give the impression of limiting unduly the scope of what the biblical writers were concerned to do. They were not confined to describing and interpreting certain acts of God in history; to suggest that they were would be to disfranchise certain biblical writers almost entirely. They were in fact fully aware that this world-order, which formed the necessary context of God's redemptive acts, itself owes its origin to God, and is, and always will be, in relationship with him. Among the things they seek to do is to define that relationship and then to show what kind of conduct is appropriate to inhabitants of a world so related to God. Our thoughts turn naturally in this connexion to the Wisdom Literature, but in reading it, and still more in reading such books as the New Testament epistles, we cannot help noticing how the understanding of man's relation to God as creature to creator is constantly illuminated, deepened, and indeed defined, by the recognition of God's redemptive acts in history and so of man's relation to him as redeemed sinner to saviour.

But to these and to all the other things the biblical writers sought to do, the same general considerations seem to be applicable. Indeed it is in this sphere that some of the things I have been saying find their clearest exemplification. Consider, for example, the author of Genesis seeking to give expression to his conviction that this world is, first and last and always, entirely dependent on the freely-willed activity of God. Clearly the purpose of God in creating and sustaining this world must reach out into his general being and purposes, and so be incapable of being fully comprehended by any of his creatures. And the relationships of the universe as a whole cannot be *literally* described in language and thought-forms designed only to deal with the internal relations inside it. How then did the author of Genesis arrive at what he wrote? Must he not in fact have started from the world as he knew it, and its relationship to God as revealed in his own experience and in the experience and tradition of his people? And when it came to expressing this relationship, what else could he do but make use of the creation mythology current in the near East of his day, modifying it wherever necessary to make it a better vehicle for the special insights vouchsafed in his particular history and that of his people? It hardly needs to be added that the current mythology he used was itself distilled from innumerable individual experiences of God and his relation with his creatures. And clearly what is true of the mythology of the beginning is equally true of the mythology of the last things – of biblical eschatology. Of course I have grossly oversimplified my account of the origin of the first few chapters of Genesis and attributed an impossible amount to a single individual; but if my account is broadly true, at any rate in principle, you will see why I talk of the position being fluid, and plead for a certain flexibility in our approach to the Bible.

By us this fluidity may be seen as inevitable if there was to be revelation at all in a limited world subject to the laws of historical change and development; and we may welcome it in practice as giving us room for manoeuvre. But our predecessors in the faith have for the most part taken a different view. Traditional Christianity, both Catholic and Protestant, has made far broader claims for the Bible than I have been doing, in respect of both authority and inspiration. It has taken inspiration to imply inerrancy, and an inerrancy which has usually been held to extend even to detailed points of history and science. It must be conceded, therefore, that the sort of view I have been propounding can make no claim to be the full traditional view; but a number of other things must be said, if that concession is to be seen in the right perspective.

To begin with, the traditional belief in inerrancy is a matter of custom rather than dogmatic definition, and of custom which is

not itself based on any very clear biblical authority. Canon
Charles Smyth, writing of the period before the rise of modern
science, goes so far as to say: '. . . nobody really believed in the
verbal inspiration of the Holy Scriptures until the geologists
began to question it. Hitherto, broadly speaking, people believe
everything they read in the Bible, in the same way that some
people believe everything they read in the newspapers.'[6] The
Bible itself nowhere claims inerrancy nor is it by any means
consistently implied in the way the biblical writers treat one
another's texts. The church has always believed that the Bible is
inspired and authoritative, but it has never *defined* the inspiration
and authority, at any rate in any formularies binding on members
of the Church of England. Indeed, in so far as the Report of
Committee I of the recent Lambeth Conference constituted an
attempt to bring this matter within the sphere of dogmatic definition, it was undoubtedly something of a novelty, so far as the
Church of England is concerned.

Then there is a second point of cardinal importance. The general belief of earlier ages that the Bible was inerrant must always
be seen in the light of the methods of biblical exegesis current in
those ages. Passages of scripture were believed to have meaning
other than the literal, for example, allegorical or typological
meanings. In practice it was often in respect of those meanings
that a passage was claimed to be an inerrant source of divine
revelation. Origen indeed went so far as to deny that some
passages of scripture have any literal sense at all, or at any rate
any literal sense which is revelatory of God. In the light of these
facts, we can see that the sting of the doctrine of inerrancy was to
some extent drawn in practice. In fact Origen and scholars like
him were more than half aware of the problems I have described,
and their doctrine of the multiple sense of scripture was their
practical device for dealing with those problems and for creating
that room for manoeuvre to which I have referred. In practice,
therefore, the situation has always been more fluid than would
appear if we concentrated exclusively on the formal theory of
inspiration. Our modern fundamentalists usually ignore these
compensating factors, and as a result they are no more the direct
heirs of traditional teaching in this matter than I am. They are in
fact 'plus royalistes que le roi'![7]

As a matter of fact their view is read off neither from tradition, nor from the Bible itself. It is based on an *a priori* argument which would run, if it were explicitly formulated, something like this: 'We know that the Bible is inspired because we find God speaking to us through it. But the God who speaks through it is the God of truth, so it would be natural for him to secure complete freedom from error in the means of his communication with men. Moreover he is a God of love, and so it would be natural for him to be concerned about our fears, and to give us the security that would come from possessing an inerrant statement of the promise and conditions of salvation.' Anyone can see how natural such an assumption is, yet it *is* only an assumption, and it can never be too strongly stressed that where God is concerned, *a priori* assumptions are always hazardous. How can any theist say what God 'must' have done, or know what is 'natural' to him, seeing that he is speaking of a being *toto caelo* different from himself? And if every theist should hesitate before making such *a priori* statements about what God 'must' have done, how much more the Christian theist! For if there is one thing the Bible and the history of the church make crystal clear it is that our God is the God of the unexpected. Who dares to say what 'must' be natural for a God who chose to save through the chequered, and often ignominious, history of an obscure little people in Palestine and the criminal's death of his own Son? If the means of salvation involve the 'scandal of particularity', why not the means of publishing that salvation? And in the light of the Bible and of Christian history, what are we to say of the belief that God will surely be concerned to give us full security? Can there be any doubt what must be said?

But if all this is true, how came the church to maintain the idea of biblical inerrancy so long? That is a question which up to a point is readily answered, and the general lines of the answer are familiar enough. For a long time the customs and assumptions of Western European man were so like those of biblical man that the difficulties in the inerrancy position did not declare themselves with their full force. I do not want to traverse well-worn ground again, but I should like to emphasize how very recent are the really wide divergences from the outlook of the biblical writers, of which we are so conscious today. Professor C. S. Lewis has pointed out in his Inaugural Lecture at Cambridge[8] that it is in the period after about 1800, and not at the Renaissance, that we must locate the really major break in the cultural history of Europe. And Dr Charles Galton Darwin writes as follows in his fascinating book on the next million years:[9] '. . . during the last one hundred and fifty years, the whole manner of living has been more changed than in the previous fifteen hundred years. It is true that life in Western Europe in 1750 was very naturally different from life in A.D. 100 in Italy; . . . there were important changes . . . but, without belittling these changes, they were on an incomparably smaller scale than those witnessed between 1750 and 1950, in nearly all parts of the world. It would surely be just to say that London in 1750 was far more like Rome in A.D. 100 than like either London or Rome in 1950.' It is then only since the middle of the eighteenth century that we have begun to make really fantastic advances in knowledge to which we are now accustomed, and that Christians have found themselves holding views and presuppositions on almost every subject markedly divergent from those of the biblical writers. And there is another point at least equally significant. It was only with this rapid divergence of world-view that there came, really for the first time, the consciousness how unlike one another men of different epochs are. It was this realization that gave rise, and such wide currency, to the historical novels of Scott and to the work of historians like Lord Macaulay who were fired by them. We find it hard to realize, but up till the eighteenth century an almost completely static view of history prevailed, and much even of eighteenth-century thought was based on such a view. The theory of the social contract, for example, was formulated by men who took it for granted that human beings had always been rational creatures like themselves. And only recently we have been reminded that Coleridge was the first person to use the word 'anachronism' in its modern sense. The magnitude of the changes we all realize; for our purposes their novelty is also important.

These changes were enough in themselves to alter men's orientation to the Bible, but in fact of course they were reinforced by the conclusions of the growing army of biblical critics, armed with all the weapons and techniques of research that the new developments had put at their disposal. Specific inaccuracies in the received text were thus pin-pointed, and it became clear that, whatever the truth of the Bible, the terms and thought-forms in which the biblical writers formulated it were simply the common coin of the philosophy and religion of a particular age. All this is really of very recent occurrence, and that may help to explain why the general considerations I advanced in the first part of this lecture, although they applied just as much before 1750 as they do now, did not impress themselves on Christians of an earlier period. It may also prevent our being too worried by our divergence in this matter from traditional views. The revolution that began in the eighteenth century was fundamental and far-reaching. Its implications were bound to take time to seep through, so it is only to be expected that ours should be one of the first generations of Christians to be faced with the need for a reappraisal which may well be not only agonizing but prolonged; for certainly at the moment the modern revolution shows no signs of having spent itself. And, that being so, it is only natural that our attitude to the authority and inspiration of the Bible should be very different from that of the Fathers, the Schoolmen, the Protestant Reformers, or even the eighteenth-century Latitudinarians and their opponents.

What then should our attitude be? Certainly there is no lack of suggestions nowadays from theologians of every school. The position which most commended itself to the Lambeth Bishops seems to have been that which they describe as 'biblical theology'. Whatever precisely is meant by that term,[10] it clearly refers to a view which holds that, when all allowances have been made for the historical and theological limitations of the biblical writers, their accounts, even as they stand, enshrine a hard core of truth, both historical and theological. The key events of their story – the Exodus, the entering into the Promised Land, the apostasy under the kings, the consequent Exile and the rest – all happened substantially as the biblical writers relate; and if we follow the broad lines of their interpretation, we can trace a single line of devine policy running through these successive events, a coherent plan of salvation which culminated in the ministry of Christ and the foundation of the church. Sometimes the internal testimony of the Holy Spirit is invoked as the authority for selecting just *this* line of events as the key episodes in the biblical story, and the exponents of biblical theology usually suggest that, at any rate as far as these key incidents are concerned, the categories of the biblical writers themselves are wholly adequate for their interpretation, if not indeed the only ones legitimate for the purpose.[11] It will be clear from what I have already said how far I am in sympathy with this approach; yet I do not think it can be accepted by any means without qualification, particularly if it is offered as a total solution of the problem of the modern approach to the Bible. In the first place, as I hinted earlier, it is in danger of disfranchising large sections of the Bible; significantly, the exposition of it in the Lambeth Report has very little to say about the New Testament, and particularly about the New Testament epistles. The necessity of appealing to the internal witness of the Spirit suggests that this approach is in fact highly selective, and often it is not as true to the general proportions of the Bible itself as its exponents seem to suppose. All of which leads me on to a deeper doubt. Can it be that some, at any rate, of the exponents of biblical theology are motivated by the old longing for security? Are they perhaps trying to isolate *some* element in the Bible which can be shown to need neither historical revision nor theological reinterpretation? Any such attempt is surely doomed to failure, and even to make it involves serious temptations. With regard to the historical accuracy of the biblical narratives, some biblical theologians sometimes seem to me already to be on the verge of treating the problems *a priori* and sitting a shade loose to the empirical evidence. For example, I have sometimes heard it treated simply as a matter for derision that the historicity of Moses should be questioned; and the whole question is frequently shrugged off with the epigram: 'If Moses had not existed it would be necessary to invent him.' The biblical theologians may well be right about this particular issue, on the evidence at present available – I am not sufficient of an expert in Old Testament matters to know; but the question is not one which can be settled by any other method than the patient, detailed examination of historical evidence, in the full realization that subsequent discoveries and developments may compel a complete change of opinion. The point I want to make is that a search for final security in a sphere where imperfectly-attested historical events are involved is fore-doomed to failure.

As for the insistence on interpreting the biblical events exclusively in the categories used by the biblical writers themselves, such ancient Semitic and Hellenistic categories are not the natural ones for the modern European to use, and he can only confine himself to them at the cost of ignoring a number of questions which inevitably occur to him. Professor Cullmann and other exponents of biblical theology do in fact demand of us just such a self-denying ordinance, and as a result they are able to attribute to the categories of the Bible a more or less absolute validity. In this way they gain a confident security with regard to the biblical revelation – they know exactly what it means, but it is at the cost of writing 'improper' across a whole area of what is apparently perfectly proper inquiry and valid insight. Professor Hodgson has dealt very faithfully with this question in his recent Gifford Lectures,[12] so I will leave it with just one quotation from what he there says: 'It is, of course, true that the revelation given to us through the Bible comes through Hebrew minds, and that questions which troubled the Greek thinkers apparently never occurred to them. But to draw from this the conclusion that God wills us neither to raise these questions nor to seek to learn from those who have thought profoundly about them is ludicrously absurd. Why, in order to be a good Christian should it be more important to have a Hebrew type of mind than to have a Hebrew cast of countenance? If we must be limited to the Jewish idea of eternity, why not to the Jewish shape of nose?'

Biblical theology then, is a good servant but a bad master. As a suggestion of one very fruitful way of approaching the Bible, it has a lot to commend it; but when it claims a monopoly of the field, it reveals another side, on which it has some at least of the characteristics of a failure of nerve.

Much the same must be said about the approach to the Bible associated with the names of Dr Austin Farrer and Dr Lionel Thornton. These scholars rightly point out that Hebrew thought usually proceeded, not so much by way of systematic argument as by the accumulation of successive images which would suggest different aspects of the truth, and the interweaving of them in such a way as to preserve the balance and proportions of the whole. From this come most valuable insights about how at any rate certain biblical passages should be approached and unravelled. Yet here again we cannot allow such an appreciation to be converted into a total theory of biblical authority. Dr Hodgson writes:[13] 'There are passages in Dr Austin Farrer's Bampton Lectures[14] which seem to suggest that the presentation of truth in images is what constitutes the Bible a revelation of divine

truth. Taken by itself this book suggests . . . that it is the presentation in images that makes the Bible revelatory and that if we would
receive God's revelation we must think in images too.' I am not
quite sure that that does full justice to Dr Farrer's book; and I *am*
quite sure that I have not done justice to a way of approaching the
Bible which I myself have found very illuminating, and for which
I am extremely grateful. Yet I think I see Dr Hodgson's point, and
I sympathize with him. He is worried by the tendency to pin-
point the authority of the Bible in any one aspect of, or element in,
it. In the old days, if Christians were asked, 'Wherein does the
authority of the Bible lie?' they could answer, 'In the inerrant
truth of all its statements'. Now that that answer is no longer
possible, there is a natural temptation to try to find some equally
simple alternative answer. For example: 'Its authority lies in the
image character of its thinking and in the content and mutual
interplay of its images. Allow that hierarchy of images to condition your response to God and your neighbour and all will
certainly be well.' Or: 'Base your relation to God and the world on
the belief that the key incidents of the biblical theologian actually
took place and meant what the Bible says they did, and again all
will be well.' Of course I caricature, but you will see my point. The
question about biblical authority can be simply formulated, and it
is always a temptation to assume that questions which can be
simply formulated must have answers capable of equally simple
formulation. But that is a temptation to which we should not
always succumb. And in this case the very amorphous and
heterogeneous character of the biblical material might suggest
that it is not meant to yield up its secret in any one easily formu-
lable way.

So perhaps the best thing I can say in reply to your question,
'Wherein does the authority of the Bible lie?' is that it is a deceptively simple question. Beware of all who claim to have a simple
answer to it; they are almost certainly guilty of serious, and
dangerous, oversimplification. At any rate at the present stage
this is a problem which *solvitur ambulando*; obviously the clue
must be found in the figure and work of Jesus, on which all else
converges, but as we try to use that clue we shall become increasingly aware that the problem of biblical authority cannot be
cleared up in isolation. The authority of the Bible is inextricably

connected with other authorities – the authority of the church, of the saints, of the liturgy, the conscience, and the reason.

6

History and the Gospel

[What follows is the text of the major part of the Charles Gore Memorial Lecture for 1966 exactly as it was delivered in Westminster Abbey on 8 November of that year. Earlier in the year there had appeared a volume of essays by a group of Anglican theologians, edited by Professor A. T. Hanson and entitled *Vindications*.[1] I devoted my contribution to the John Knox Festschrift[2] to a detailed discussion and critique of Professor A. T. Hanson's own essay in *Vindications*, but I also spent the first few minutes of the Gore Lecture on some general criticisms of the volume as a whole. At this distance of time these remarks hardly deserve to be reprinted *in extenso*, but two points they made may be worth bearing in mind.

The first was that, though the *general* trustworthiness of the gospel records has withstood criticism in the sense that no serious scholar now doubts either that Jesus existed and was crucified by the Romans or that his previous activity as exorcist, teacher and controversialist was broadly as outlined in the gospels, the position is rather different when it comes to the individual details and incidents in the gospels. Here we do find repeatedly a wide measure of disagreement between reputable scholars about the historicity, or degree of historicity, of individual pericopes – a fact which is the more disconcerting to the preacher because it is with individual incidents and passages that he habitually deals.

Secondly, however, I urged that this degree of uncertainty is an inescapable consequence of the nature and origins of the gospels as we now understand them, and it is not to be attributed, as it was by some at least of the contributors to *Vindications*, to a sort of sceptical demon which has got inside one group of so-called 'radical' scholars. It is, I argued, a serious distortion of the real situation to invent such a demon and then suppose that if only it could be exorcised, many of the major problems on the historical front would disappear. I continued as follows] To that extent I want in this lecture to deepen disquiet and to broaden its base by suggesting that – radical scholars or no radical scholars – there are elements inescapably present in our situation which will continue to arouse disquiet until we have seen our way through them. To lay blame on a single group of allegedly radical, or sceptical, scholars, can thus be a way of obscuring the real situation which needs to be faced. Let me try to explain.

It is often suggested (e.g. in *Vindications*) that the trouble lies in what is called 'historical scepticism'. What would those who say this desire to see in its place? Not presumably 'historical credulity' – perhaps they would use some such expression as 'historical realism', or 'a sober historical approach'. What would that consist in? I imagine it would be said: 'in applying the historical method to the Bible in a reasonable way'. And what does that mean? In practice it often seems to mean believing what the biblical text says unless there are quite overwhelming reasons for questioning it. Professor John Knox has noted the frequency with which in writings on the gospels we meet such expressions as 'there seems no need to doubt what the evangelist says at this point'. But if this is how theologians understand the application of historical method, it must be said at once that it is not an understanding any competent historian would accept for one moment. The matter seems to me important and I should like to develop it a little. It is, I take it, beyond serious question that in the last two centuries or so Western Europe has been the scene of a cultural revolution – a revolution which has often been described, for example, by C. S. Lewis in his inaugural lecture at Cambridge,[3] where he showed that it quite dwarfs the so-called Renaissance of the fifteenth and sixteenth centuries in its scope and implications. Most of us probably think immediately in this connexion of the natural sciences, but, in fact, historical science and the transformation that has been produced in historical understanding are probably just as significant, and might, in the long run, prove even more important.

I say so much in order to prepare you for my conviction that the various historical problems which confront theology today are genuinely novel; and that, being part and parcel of an all-embracing and continuing cultural revolution, they have deep roots and wide ramifications, and so are likely to be with us for a long time, and to involve for their solution a great deal of thinking and rethinking on many topics. Any suggestion that biblical theology is now 'over the hump' or 'into a post-critical phase' is, I suggest, dangerous nonsense. One of the disturbing but stimulating things the cultural revolution has taught us, or should have taught us, is that there can never be definitive and timeless solutions of intellectual problems in the conditions of historical existence as we know it.

One outcome of the cultural revolution which is important for our subject is that historians have come to adopt a quite new – and still changing – approach to historical documents. No doubt, as Professor Herbert Butterfield insists, the roots of the new attitude go back a long way into the past,[4] but nevertheless he would be the first to allow us, or rather to require us, to see something distinctively, and significantly, novel in the modern historian's approach. Perhaps, at the risk of gross over-simplification – and greatly daring, for I am no historian – I could put it like this:

What any historian is concerned with is past events, but the modern historian emphasizes that once an event is past we can have no *direct* access to it or relationship with it. All we can have are data relating to it. These data may be of many different kinds: words, written or spoken, archaeological remains, later events needing earlier events for their explanation; in fact, vestiges of the past of any and every kind. But whatever they are, the historian insists they are never more than data. A sworn affidavit by an eye-witness of an event, for example, is only a datum; he may be lying or mistaken. A tape-recording of a conversation is only a datum; it may have been doctored or it may not be a recording of the particular conversation it purports to record. Even my own memories of an event at which I was present are only data, and the psychoanalyst is always on hand to remind us what highly selective, and often distorted, data our memories in fact provide.

I emphasize this matter of the status of data because it needs to be grasped before we can understand the historian's procedure in dealing with his data. Just as, in Bacon's phrase, the natural scientist 'puts nature to the question', so a historian puts his data to the question; as Collingwood strikingly expressed it, he 'tortures his evidence', that is to say, he sifts it, analyses it, compares it with all other relevant data, in fact does to it everything he can think of which will make it yield its secret, what it has to disclose about the event to which it relates.

Even were I competent, time would fail me to describe the historian's testing techniques in detail; but for our purposes it is not necessary because I rather *think* – and I speak as a fool – that in the last analysis they amount simply to a sustained and rigorous application of commonsense.

You have all read detective novels, so you know the sort of thing involved. At the beginning, the police detective, or at any rate the local man, gets it all wrong precisely because he fails to 'torture', or test, the clues in the way described. There is the suicide note, there is the gun found beside the dead man with his fingerprints on it; and there is the testimony of several witnesses that he had been unusually agitated and depressed for some weeks past. Taking all this at its face value, the local man concludes that he is dealing with a straightforward case of suicide. But then along comes Holmes or Poirot, Maigret or Inspector French. He insists on sifting the data minutely; on giving full weight to some small but vital clue which will not fit into the local man's reconstruction; he discovers the relevance as data of facts and events apparently quite unconnected with the case. And as a result of his collecting and thorough 'torturing' of all the relevant evidence, a quite different picture of the original event emerges; it was not a suicide at all, but a murder committed by someone totally outside suspicion on the basis of the data as naïvely defined and accepted by the local man. In practice, we may suspect, life is not often quite so complicated, but the principle stands. Data are nothing more than data. It is only by testing and sifting them in every possible way, and by refusing to take any of them at their face value, that a historian can arrive at a picture which deserves to be called a genuinely historical reconstruction and will win respect from his fellow historians.[5]

To convince you what great significance a modern historian attaches to this, let me quote you some words of R. G. Collingwood about a historian's obligation: 'If anyone else', he writes, 'no matter who, even a very learned historian, or an eye-witness,

or a person in the confidence of the man who did the thing he is
inquiring into, or even the man who did it himself, hands him on
a plate a ready-made answer to his question, all he can do is to
reject it: not because he thinks his informant is trying to deceive
him, or is himself deceived, but because if he accepts it he is
giving up his autonomy as an historian and allowing someone
else to do for him what, if he is a scientific thinker, he can only do
for himself.'[6]

The historian, then, must apply his tests in all their rigour; but
it is important not to misunderstand the nature of those tests. The
layman – and in this context theologians are laymen – has often
been misled through supposing that the historian's testing
techniques are like those of the pathologist in his lab. An historical report is brought in; the relevant tests are applied with
clinical objectivity; and in a few days we know whether the event
reported was historical or not. Some such conception seriously
misled more than one theologian in the nineteenth century. In
fact, the historian's procedure amounts, as I put it just now, to a
refined, sophisticated and rigorous application of commonsense;
that phrase, and the illustration from the detective novel, were
designed to bring out the great part played by the subjectivity of
the historian in the process. What seems perfect commonsense to
one person seems quite otherwise to another. That, of course, is
not to deny validity to what the historian does. Attempts are
continually being made to refine historical techniques so as to
minimize the effects of arbitrary subjectivity; and historians of
different views discuss and criticize one another's conclusions.
The fact remains, however, and seems likely to remain, that one
historian may feel bound to deny a statement in his sources,
because perhaps he feels that 'human nature just does not work
that way' or 'miracles don't happen', while another historian,
after equally rigorous testing, but judging from a different background of experiences and belief, may feel driven to accept it.
And the effectiveness of the check historians exercise on one
another's conclusions is limited by the fact that all share largely in
the common assumptions of the age to which they belong.

On the basis of his testing a historian may feel justified in forming
a picture of what happened, a process sometimes described as
'establishing the facts'. Such a way of referring to it is proper

enough provided it is borne in mind that the 'facts' as established by the historian can no more be identified with the original 'event' than the data can. An event is something which can never be compassed in its fullness even by those present when it occurs; and certainly no structure of words, whether those of the historian or his sources, can ever encompass an event. One historian's account will perhaps catch some elements of it, others will be caught in the reconstruction of another; but event and 'facts' remain separate. An event, once it has occurred, does not change, but it is quite otherwise with the so-called 'facts'. Rarely, if ever, do the facts as established by one historian commend themselves in their entirety to all his fellow historians, who insist on reformulating them in an amended version. And even if they should accept them as they stand, in a given instance, we can be quite certain that the facts about the same event as established by historians two centuries hence will look very different in certain respects.

On all this two further points may be made. First, if the account I have given of the historian's procedure is true at all, it is true for all historians and not just for some special radical or sceptical group. Thus, some such picture as I have given emerges, I believe, from the writing of such different historians as Collingwood, Professor Butterfield, and the Frenchman, Marc Bloch.

Secondly, it is important not to draw false conclusions from the distinction between the event and the facts as established by the historian. To insist on their being distinguished is not for a moment to deny that there is often a very close relationship between them. There are cases where the historian is convinced – and justifiably – that the facts as he establishes them correspond very closely with the event. 'We can be sure what happened.' Indeed Father Martin D'Arcy[7] argues that there are plenty of cases where the data are so numerous and so consentient, where so many things presuppose by their very existence that a certain event happened in a certain way, that we can properly talk of being certain of that event. Whether philosophers will allow the word 'certainty' in this context I am not sure, but neither they nor any other sane person will entertain the slightest doubt about the occurrence of certain events in the past and their having occurred in a certain way. As examples we might cite the battle of Waterloo or the reign of Queen Victoria; and I suggested just now that the existence of Jesus in first-century Palestine also belongs to this class of events.

Which brings us back to our central subject. The gospels, whatever else they may be, are historical documents, so the question arises whether they should be treated exactly as other historical documents are treated by modern historians. Christian opinion, with a few well-defined exceptions, appears to answer in the affirmative; but I sometimes wonder whether some people do not make rather serious mental reservations when they give their answer. If so, it is obviously a fact very germane to the disquiet about which I am speaking, and each of us should get quite clear in his mind where he stands in the matter. I shall say only this. If we do not unreservedly answer 'yes' to the question, then we surely forfeit any right to apply the word 'historical' to the contents of the gospels; or if we do apply it, it will not be in the sense the word normally bears nowadays. For what the word means, in the sense in which historians respect it, is that the fact to which it is applied has been declared factual on the basis of such rigorous 'torturing' of data as I have been describing.

If, however, we do answer the question with an unqualified affirmative, are we clear what is involved? First of all, it will mean that the gospels must be regarded as data, data which can never be taken at their face value from the historical point of view, but must be tested with all possible rigour before any picture which deserves to be called 'historical' can be constructed from them. If that were realized, at least one misconception would disappear. It would be recognized that there is nothing specially sceptical about scholars who at the outset refuse to take the gospel accounts at their face value, but insist on sifting them, raising awkward doubts about them, testing alternative constructions to the ones they directly suggest, and so on. In one sense, of course, this is sceptical, but then, as we have seen, at the first move the historian is *paid* to doubt – a controlled and reasonable initial scepticism is one of the most essential tools of his trade. He is only sceptical in any blameworthy sense if, after completing a reasonable process of testing, he always unreasonably refuses, like the famous Oxford don, 'to take "yes" for an answer'.

A second conclusion follows; or perhaps I am just restating

what I have been saying in other words. No one can have the right, whether in the pulpit or in his own mind, to call his picture of a gospel incident or saying 'historical' unless he has satisfied himself that a rigorous testing of all the relevant data has taken place and that his reconstruction is validly based upon it. At that point we are all, I suspect, sometimes tempted to give the gospel accounts the benefit of the doubt, or perhaps I should say to give *ourselves* the benefit of the doubt. Even to work through the tests carried out by others and to assess their various conclusions, to say nothing of doing it for ourselves, involves so much labour that we are apt to say: 'After all, it is the Bible which is speaking, I will trust it as it stands.' As I shall show later, I think in certain contexts such words may be fully justified, but at the moment we must recognize that we cannot use them and at the same time claim an historical basis for our account of a gospel incident. Maybe when you take this line you have some vague notion of biblical inspiration at the back of your mind. If so, bring it to the front of your mind and I think you will find it cannot do what you are asking it to do. Or perhaps on such occasions you say to yourself: 'The apostles and their followers were holy men; they would never have made up stories about our Lord which they knew to be false, so we can safely believe what they say.' As part of a general argument for the fact of our Lord's existence and his *general* likeness to the gospel picture of him, some such argument may have considerable force; but when we are discussing the historicity of individual stories and details in them, it will not take us very far. Whatever the precise rights and wrongs of form-criticism may be, it is now generally agreed that at any rate many of the traditions found in the gospels had a considerable pre-history before the evangelists wrote them down. They were passed from person to person by word of mouth, often in a context of public speaking and preaching where they were being used to teach a lesson or make a point. There is a good deal of evidence that when they changed hands they were liable to be modified in greater or less degree; indeed, we can now put it like this: those who handled the tradition, so far as their moulding of it was governed by historical considerations at all, were in their way true historians precisely in the sense defined just now; each received data from some fellow Christian and on the basis of it he constructed his picture of what had happened, until at the end of the process the evangelists committed their reconstructions to paper in the late first and early second centuries. We have already seen that one century's understanding of an historical event never commends itself in its entirety to the historians of the next century, so we should hardly expect the picture presented by the evangelists to approve itself in its entirety to us, seventeen or eighteen centuries later.

You may feel that all this is obvious to the point of platitude. If so, all to the good – there will be no danger of your supposing that it represents the view of some small radical minority among historical theologians. It certainly does not; much of what I have been saying is said in a not dissimilar way, for example, in the excellent, though professedly rather conservative, book on our subject, published not long ago by Professor H. E. W. Turner of Durham.[8] I venture to repeat it because I am not at all sure that we have yet really taken it into our systems. If we had, it would surely have driven out some of our disquiet, or at any rate transformed it into something from which we could profit and learn.

If you want to get it into your system, the only way is to try it out in practice. Take specific gospel passages and follow in detail as the various scholars who have written on them 'torture' the data. See *in detail* how they arrive at their sometimes rather different reconstructions. Anyone who does that will discover that, though sometimes different reconstructions simply rest back on the different assumptions of the scholars in question about general matters of principle, very often they do not. They are due to different ways of defining and testing the data, to the different data which seem relevant to the various scholars; to the different questions it has occurred to them to ask and the way they answer them; and to the different weight they attach to the questions they ask in common. In detective novels the reader is left in no doubt at the end which is the best reconstruction of the crime; but there the detective novel is not necessarily a good analogy. Imagine a novel in which Poirot and Miss Marple both play leading parts and at the end each advances a characteristically brilliant and cogent reconstruction of the crime which, however, is incompatible with that advanced by the other! Every serious student of the gospels knows this type of situation. Sometimes he may be convinced that A's reconstruction is distinctly more likely than B's, but he will nevertheless have to admit that B's picture also has elements of probability and cannot summarily be dismissed as impossible.

A somewhat similar situation can arise when the evidence is too scanty to allow of a firm verdict from anyone. In criminal investigations it often happens that the police find some clues as to what happened but they are too scanty and disconnected to provide the basis for an arrest and conviction; and no witnesses are forthcoming. The police may 'have their suspicions', but the clues are just not sufficient to justify a verdict one way or the other, so no case is brought. A comparable situation frequently arises for the historian. Data perhaps exist, which, taken at their face value, would suggest that an event of a certain sort occurred in a certain way. But they are very scanty and no other evidence is at present forthcoming to provide a basis for testing them, so the historian can only return a verdict of non-proven, or better still perhaps refrain from raising the question of historicity at all. The historian, writes Collingwood, should not raise historical questions unless 'he has already in his mind a preliminary and tentative idea of the evidence he will be able to use . . . To ask questions which you see no prospect of answering is the fundamental sin'.[9]

It so happens that the gospel material not infrequently gives rise to this sort of situation. Often it rests, in the last resort, on a single tradition, and we have not as yet data from outside to help us in assessing it. That does not, of course, prove it unhistorical or even prevent us from *suspecting* that it may be authentic, but it makes difficult any claim to historicity in the strict sense of the word. In such cases we do well to heed Collingwood's warning, and some of us can remember how R. H. Lightfoot was often to be heard lamenting that New Testament scholars 'are "so hot for certainties"; if only they would sometimes say, "we simply do not know" '.

What it comes to is that when we get down to the detailed, individual narratives in the gospels, the facts can often be established only with relative probability, if at all. This is no reflection whatever on the evangelists or their sources. They hailed from a period – and a comparatively unlettered community – which knew not the modern historian; and their concerns and purposes were in some respects very different from his.

But what of us, who share the modern historian's standards and attitudes? It is here that the rub comes. We have all been told times without number that 'Christianity is an historical religion' and that 'the revelation was given not through propositions but through events'. Yet now we are being told that these events are just what we cannot have; the most we can have are facts, facts established with a greater, or sometimes less, degree of probability. It is to the event that authority attaches, and if we cannot possess the event, are not our faith and preaching deprived of authority? Here it seems to me are questions far more taxing and significant than the alleged scepticism of one small group of New Testament scholars.

Solutions to this problem have been sought, along very different lines. Among our fellow Christians on the continent who have studied the question most intensely, one group, as you will know, is convinced that the authority of our preaching is not affected one whit. For they hold – on quite other grounds – that the only proper basis for preaching is not the Jesus of history but the Christ of faith, the Christ of the Christian *kerygma*; *he* is the one through whom God speaks and draws near to men in judgment and in blessing, and the demand is that we accept or reject him as he is proclaimed to us; *he* is God's word to man and it makes no difference what earthly events entered into the making of his picture; decision about him is a matter for faith, and historicity would not add one cubit to his stature.

I wish I had time to expound this position to you at length, for I believe there is more in it, and more to be learned from it, than is commonly recognized in this country; it cannot be dismissed as lightly as Professor Turner, for example, dismisses it. But I have no time, especially as I could not in the end commend it for your acceptance in anything like its full-blown form.

In this country, on the other hand, so far as our problem has been discussed, the general conclusion has been that we must confine our preaching to those elements in the gospels that can be established as historical with reasonable assurance.

For those who advocate some such view the present time is propitious. Scholars of very different sorts are increasingly agreed, not only about the fact of Jesus' existence but about the nature of his person and claims. With surprising unanimity, there comes from the pens of scholars in England, Germany, and

America an argument which runs something like this: None of the gospels provides a photograph, and the portraits in the various gospels, and principal gospel sources, differ a good deal. Nevertheless, these very differences, when combined with certain striking similarities, are of a kind which suggest a single figure, a single sitter of whom they *are* all portraits. And by studying minutely the technique and style of each portrait and the kind of impression it was intended to give, you can begin to build up a picture of the sitter in considerable detail.

In just how much detail is a matter of dispute, but so far as the reconstructions of the various scholars go, they are notably similar. Some, it is true, doubt if Jesus actually claimed, or used, messianic titles of any sort, but they agree that he did what amounts virtually to the same thing, claimed to speak and act directly in God's name. As one German scholar who takes this position puts it, 'His attitude is not that of a prophet or a sage; it is that of a man who dares to act in God's place.'[10] He claimed that people's relationship with God was essentially bound up with their relationship to him. His unconditional promise of love and acceptance was in fact God's promise made through him; and to accept his promise and follow him was already to be at one with God and to partake of God's kingdom.

Many people who cannot accept the non-historical position I mentioned just now are content with this; it satisfies their deep sense that he who demanded righteousness must have been himself the righteous one, that he who demanded faith must have lived the life of faith, that he who promised resurrection must have died and been raised from the dead; in short, that the word must have become real flesh in a genuinely human life and death.

It will be obvious, I hope, that nothing I have said rules out of court either this picture, or the process by which it is being built up. It is in fact the result of extremely acute and detailed work on the part of scholars who accept, and put into practice, all that I have been saying about historical method. Obviously, we must not exaggerate the unanimity of their conclusions, but with a lot that many of them say, and their reasons for saying it, I myself have considerable sympathy.

Nevertheless, it would be possible to pin one's faith to this reconstruction in the wrong sort of way. In the first place I must remind you that, however great the skill and scholarship that have gone into it, this reconstruction can provide us only with facts and not with the event itself. That means, as we have seen, that future generations are sure to want to restate these facts; and it is perhaps already possible to detect certain hair cracks in the structure of the current reconstruction which may indicate where parts will break off, so that the whole will have to be remodelled by our successors.

Secondly, if we attribute too vital a position to this reconstruction, is there not a danger that we shall lose our disinterestedness and objectivity in deciding what gospel material can properly be brought within the scope of it?

And thirdly, I suggest that if we concentrate exclusively on this reconstruction, we shall involve ourselves in an unnecessary and impoverishing self-denying ordinance with regard to those elements in the gospels which cannot be built into the reconstruction.

Where, then, do I stand? A great deal depends, it seems to me, on the perspective from which we view our problem, and I should like to conclude by suggesting a possible perspective to you.

To be a Christian is to be a member of the church.

No one joins the church, or at any rate no one remains a member of it, unless he finds in it, in large measure, what it claims to possess, peace and communion with God, community with one's fellows, the power to serve the world and the other elements of Christian faith and experience.

Anyone who does find those things in the church – any Christian – knows that the church must be a community created by God. Which is to say that whatever exactly the events may have been through which the church came into being, God was active in them. Now, as we have seen, it is as nearly certain as any historical fact can be, that the events in which the church originated were the life and activity of Jesus; so the Christian can be quite sure that in Jesus God was at work producing the community in and through which salvation should be available. Nothing the historian may show in detail can shake that conviction. Probably we shall not want to go all the way with Kierkegaard, but from this perspective we can at least see the truth he was trying to express in his famous dictum, 'The historical fact that God has been in human form is the essence of the matter; the rest of the historical detail is not . . . important. If the contemporary generation had left nothing behind them but these words: "we have believed that in such and such a year the God appeared among us in the humble figure of a servant, that he lived and taught in our community and finally died", it would be more than enough'.[11]

No doubt there is deliberate paradox in Kierkegaard's words, and certainly no modern Christian can leave it at that. In an historically-minded age to do so would compromise our integrity and would invite misunderstanding from our contemporaries; and also, of course, it has always been a conviction in the church that a knowledge of the original Christian event affords help and strength of many kinds for faith and life in the present.

However, as soon as we begin to investigate the event in detail, we are brought up against the fact that Jesus himself left no writings or other direct historical traces that have survived. Historically, we can know him only as he is mirrored in the response of his earliest followers to him, as that response is preserved for us in the New Testament and other early Christian writings.

Their response to him took many forms; one, for example, was the furious theological activity we find in Paul's epistles, but another was the telling of stories about the days of his flesh. The application of modern historical methods to these stories suggests that some of them may be inauthentic, in whole or part, and forces us to admit that about the authenticity of some others we have no means of deciding. But the point is that, wholly authentic or not, they are *part* of the earliest Christians' response and they are *evidence for* that response. We have only to ask how any inauthentic elements in these stories arose to realize that we are not dealing with any conscious attempt to deceive, indeed we are not dealing with any *conscious* process at all, but with an unselfconscious and entirely innocent (corporate) attempt by the early Christians to express something of the magnitude and significance of what they had experienced – in the earthly Jesus and no doubt in the heavenly Christ as well. If you suspect, for example, that the Virgin-birth stories are not wholly authentic, you can still see how they grew up in order to express the conviction of Jesus' followers that his fully human activity had been of more than natural origin, that God's initiative had lain behind it and God had been uniquely active in it.

It is this character of these stories as part of the earliest disciples' response to what had happened that we need to grasp; and I believe that if we could look at them from that perspective, we could be more relaxed about them and they would reveal profound truth we are at present missing. For while we ply them incessantly with historical questions and try so insistently to prove that this or that trait *could* have had its original in the lifetime of Jesus, we often miss truths which would become clear if once we related some of them to the period after Jesus and saw them as part of the response to him. If we were thus relaxed, perhaps we could sometimes let go the historian's hand and call in the psychologist, the poet, and the literary critic, who could help us to unpack the profound truth – often layer after layer of it – which stories of this sort can yield.

And this would be no 'flight from history'; for what we should be unpacking would be the full depths of the response which Jesus, the event of Jesus, evoked both during and after the days of his flesh. The real grounding of the truth of his resurrection lies here.

May we not even say that this response of the disciples was part of the saving event itself in which God was active? Dr John Knox has argued powerfully that it was,[12] and certainly it seems awkward to define the saving event as the life and activity of Jesus in artificial abstraction from the effect they had on those who witnessed them. It is no argument against God's having had a hand in the disciples' response that it involved the telling of stories not entirely accurate by twentieth-century standards, or even that it included moral and religious elements which do not commend themselves to the mature judgment of the church. We know, in any case, that God was content to entrust the treasure to earthen vessels.

In the field of Old Testament studies Dr James Barr has recently been warning us against the dangers of over-exclusive emphasis on historical categories,[13] and I am wanting to say something comparable about the gospels. Let me emphasize that I am *not* denying that many of the gospel stories may be substantially accurate and that this is important; but whatever the meaning and truth of the slogan that 'Christianity is an historical religion', it clearly does not preclude God's having used as *one* medium of revelation stories about his Son which may in a vital sense have been 'true' without being historically accurate.

I am not at all sure that my general position need involve this last suggestion about the response of the disciples being itself part of the saving event, and I know that if such a suggestion were accepted several important Christian doctrines would need to have their traditional shape recast. I am also aware that some scholars doubt if this could be done without vital things being lost, and indeed that they are unhappy about some aspects of the position I have been describing on other grounds. What I plead is that such scholars should formulate their doubts with all possible accuracy and precision so that the dialogue may go on from there. For only by such continuing dialogue can our disquiet on this score be creatively resolved, as opposed to being suppressed. And whatever may be true in other realms, in this one repression is of the devil.

7

The Use of the Bible in Modern Theology

Had the phrase been more informative, this essay might have been called 'The Dogma of Normativeness'; for that phrase from one of the later works of the American scholar Shirley Jackson Case[1] helps to define the sort of concerns with which we shall be dealing. The area in which these lie may be defined as follows.

If anyone asks about the distinctively Christian position or if a question is raised inside the church about the right belief or attitude in relation to some matter, the answer is almost always determined by reference of some sort to the past. Christians of different traditions and outlooks will define rather differently the precise area or aspect of the past to which they appeal, and correspondingly the form of their appeal will vary somewhat; but it is more or less unanimously agreed that Christianity is a historical religion in the sense implied.

For Anglicans the classic formulation of the matter is in the sixth of the Thirty-nine Articles: 'Holy Scripture containeth all things necessary to salvation: so that whatsoever is not read therein, nor may be proved thereby, is not to be required of any man, that it should be believed as an article of the Faith, or be thought requisite or necessary to salvation.' For a Roman Catholic, I suppose, the appeal is to the Bible (including the Apocrypha) conceived of as verbally inerrant and supplemented by certain unwritten traditions, mostly believed to derive from apostolic times, the whole being interpreted by an infallible teaching magisterium. From the Reformed side Professor J. K. S. Reid writes[2] that 'in the Scripture of the New Testament [duly interpreted in the light of the Old] nothing is . . . lacking for the nourishment and rule of Christian life and faith'. Jackson

Case himself puts it rather differently, partly because his book was specifically concerned with Jesus and partly because at the point in question he was discussing the sort of liberal theologian whose appeal to the past is almost exclusively directed to the example and teaching of Jesus. He writes of

> a well-nigh universal belief that he [Jesus] had delivered a message and set an example valid for all time. If existing tradition failed to reveal a definite solution to any new issue that might arise, it was the business of the exegete to discover in Jesus an authorized answer to the problem. Hence quite new statements of belief were sometimes formulated, but this evolutionary process of dogma was usually supposed to consist in the mere supplementation of earlier pronouncements. Thus one recovered the correct original; the truth remained a constant quantum. It had existed historically in Jesus' thought, or indeed in the mind of God before the creation of the world, and now found its proper expression in the language of the most recent orthodox theologian (pp. 346–7).

Probably no one nowadays would use precisely that language, but *mutatis perpaucis mutandis* it would express a widespread contemporary approach; indeed I suspect we should have to do little more than substitute the words 'biblical revelation', in the quotation, for the name of Jesus. In the Lambeth Conference of 1968, for example, one constantly heard and read statements to the effect that 'the biblical revelation is normative'.

So much for the area of my concern. The question I ask within it is what such a position commits me to; though I must admit that as I ask that question I have at the back of my mind the further question how far, as a Christian, I am in fact committed to that position.

Perhaps I can most easily draw out the content of my question if you will allow me a little autobiography. As many of you will know, some four or five years ago the World Council of Churches initiated an investigation into current biblical hermeneutics with a view to finding out how far, if at all, differences between denominations and other doctrinal groups corresponded to differences in the methods and assumptions with which they approached the interpretation of the Bible. I was fairly closely identified with the project, both as a member of the organizing committee in Switzerland and as chairman of the northern European working-party. In both groups we made it our practice to begin each session with a joint attempt at the interpretation of some biblical passage and then to reflect on any differences of approach which might have revealed themselves. At one level there were few such differences. We all agreed that if the original text of a passage could be established, the discovery of its original meaning would depend on ability to contextualize it correctly both in the book to which it belonged and in its wider cultural context; and there was virtual unanimity about the detailed philological, lexicographical, historical and other procedures needed for the elucidation of this meaning.

But as the work went on, I became increasingly aware of certain assumptions on the part of many of my colleagues, assumptions which were important because they largely accounted for the zest and sense of urgency they brought to their exegetical work. They assumed, first of all, that when they had discovered the meaning of a passage, they were dealing with a word of God, part of God's self-disclosure to the situation in which the words were originally written or spoken. But more than that, they at least *started* with the assumption that that word of God would also prove to have a contemporary meaning, and that the exegete's task was not completed till he had discovered what it was. To put the distinction in a rough and ready way, the exegete has not only to answer the question: What it *meant*, but also the question: What it *means*.

A lot of this did not seem to me self-evident. Many statements in ancient texts have *no* meaning today in any normal sense of the word 'meaning'. No doubt if you reflect long enough over any ancient statement – even, let us say, an historical inaccuracy in some ancient Egyptian annals – interesting reflections of some sort will occur to you; but my colleagues seemed to mean something more positive and direct than that. When pressed, they were not prepared to assert it as a universal principle that every biblical statement has a contemporary meaning, but it clearly surprised some of them that the question should be raised as an open one; and I suppose their attitude is reflected in much contemporary preaching, in which we seek to explicate '*the* meaning' (for today) of a short biblical passage.

Subsequent reading has convinced me that I did not misunderstand my colleagues. Thus Professor Reid, for example, writes:[3] 'Biblical authority . . . gives meaning to . . . passages commonly neglected as unedifying. What, for example, are we to make of the passages which present the specification of the ark and of the temple, of the detailed legislative regulations in the Book of Exodus, and the long lists of names that occur elsewhere? The answer is that they too bear testimony to the same living and redeeming God.' They 'do not indeed possess exemplary authority to be obeyed; but they do have all the authority which God concedes to their testimony'. In these and the surrounding words Professor Reid seems to me to betray some embarrassment, and his embarrassment serves to fortify my own.

This is deepened in another way which I can best explain by means of an illustration. My first initiation into the World Council project was taking part in Switzerland in a joint investigation into the meaning of I Thessalonians 2.16, the verse which speaks (according to the RV) of the 'the wrath' having 'come upon the Jews to the uttermost'. As I did my preparation before leaving home, it struck me that this was an odd verse to have chosen; but as soon as the discussion got under way in Switzerland I understood the point – an illuminating example, incidentally, of what Bultmann means by his talk about *Vorverständnis*. Many of my continental colleagues were much exercised about the problem of the relationship between Christians and Jews, and the question they were asking was: What does it say about Jewish-Christian relations that Paul spoke of the wrath of God having come on the Jews εἰς τέλος?

I was inclined to reply that it says little or nothing – for I had been persuaded to the view of many English commentators, including such a sober scholar as E. J. Bicknell, that the words were simply what Dr William Neil calls 'an outburst of exasperation' on the part of the apostle, occasioned by treatment he had recently received from Jews in Corinth – with the corollary, presumably, that if the apostle himself had been taxed with his words a few weeks later he would not have wanted to be held to them as a fully representative expression of his own mind, still less of the mind of Christ. Once again, my colleagues were not prepared to rule out such a possibility on principle, but most of them were clearly very unhappy with it, not least on the ground that it would make it very difficult to be sure in what sense the Bible is, or even contains, the word of God. And once again, subsequent reading has convinced me that my colleagues were not by any means unrepresentative. To cite Professor Reid once more, he frequently uses such words as 'opacity' and 'distortion'[4] in connection with the human witnesses of the Old Testament, and to a lesser extent the New; but his general view seems to be that even where they distort, they distort something that was a genuine word of God to them; and that if the relevant passages are taken in conjunction with others, the genuine word of God can be descried by us despite the distorting medium.

Am I then committed, as a Christian, to the view that biblical writers can never have been simply wrong for their own times and/or irrelevant for ours?

The reluctance of many theologians to agree that they can seems to me to be related to another and broader issue. They want each passage to have a meaning because they want the Bible as a whole to have a meaning. There is a body of truth, a faith, a gospel to be found in the Bible – something which could be described as *the* meaning of the Bible. Professor Reid conceives it in such a way that he can refer to the sum of its 'cardinal and indispensable items and portions'[5]; and its existence is the fundamental presupposition of Professor Cunliffe-Jones's quest in his book on the *Authority of the Biblical Revelation*.[6]

At a time when God was thought of as in a real sense the author of every word of the Bible such a view occasioned no difficulty. It could be supposed that what he sought to do through his words was to communicate a body of truth to men. It was true that, for reasons known only to himself, he had chosen to achieve his purpose in a rather unlooked for way, πολυμερῶς καὶ πολυτρόπως, and that therefore a number of various methods, allegorical and other, were needed in order to extract the body of truth; but from New Testament times onward the attempt was continually made and the results were incorporated in creeds, conciliar definitions and the like. Since it was principally in connection with particular controversies that the attempts were made, each creed or definition was only a partial statement, relevant to the particular controverted question which called it forth; but still, so far as it went, it incapsulated *the* biblical truth on its subject and provided guidance for further biblical interpretation. And there seemed no reason to doubt that subsequent situations and uncertainties would call forth statements of further items and portions of the biblical truth which in principle, at any rate, was presumably capable of exhaustive statement in doctrinal terms.

Such a view was tenable even by those who, like Luther, did not hold a completely mechanical view of biblical inspiration. Given the circumstances of his day, Luther's hopes are readily intelligible. Granted the assumption, common to him and his opponents, that some single external and objective criterion of doctrine was necessary; and that it was not to be found in the Pope; and granted the exciting prospect that, with the invention of printing and the spread of education, the Bible would find its way into the hands of more and more readers, Luther's confidence that the scripture itself by the illumination of the Holy Spirit would say the same thing to all fair-minded readers was natural enough.

But, however natural, it was unjustified; contrary to the usual view, Melanchthon was shrewder on this point than his master. The difficulty of *his* position, however, becomes clear as one reads in a book such as Professor Owen Chadwick's *From Bossuet to Newman*[7] what bizarre logical procedures were involved in the attempts of post-reformation theologians, both Catholic and Protestant, to evoke from the Bible a coherent series of answers to the questions which troubled them, by the application of 'reason' as they understood it.

But if such a view occasioned no difficulty on an older view of the Bible, things are surely different on a modern view, which makes full allowance for the individuality of the human authors and the peculiar literary forms of what they wrote.

Modern literary critics are agreed about the impropriety of trying to isolate and state 'the meaning' of the type of writing they study. Thus Professor Helen Gardner, for example, praises Miss Mary Lascelles's book on *Measure for Measure* precisely on the ground that she makes no attempt in it to 'arrive finally at "the meaning of *Measure for Measure*". She has been content to leave the play more meaningful than it was before we read her study'. Those words are a quotation[8] and they refer, be it noted, to a single dramatic work by a single author. The Bible too contains dramatic work and it contains much poetry, parable and what I may call symbolic writing of many other kinds; it was composed over a period of a millennium or more by many writers of very different characters, beliefs and cultural backgrounds. If nevertheless we are to maintain that there is something which can be called 'the meaning' of the Bible that will surely be an act of faith; the existence in the Bible of such a coherent meaning will be due to the providential activity of God, and the guidance of the Holy Spirit will be necessary in order to discover what it is.

It is well that we should know what we are committed to, and I confess that I should have regarded this last point as self-evident had I not come across the following passage in a book by Professors R. P. C. Hanson and R. H. Fuller: 'The Bible', they write, 'contains the whole of the only tradition of doctrine which the primitive Church required its members to believe as necessary to salvation. . . . It is a stupid insult to the memory of the four evangelists and of St Paul and the other apostolic writers, to suggest that they failed in the first aim of their writings, which was to convey the meaning of the Christian gospel to their hearers. . . .'[9] Am I wrong in thinking that these words embody a serious *non sequitur*? Surely the New Testament writers did *not* have it as their explicit aim to 'convey the meaning of the Christian gospel' in the sense suggested in this quotation, namely to communicate the whole tradition of doctrine necessary to salvation. Indeed, if we stop to think about it, the whole notion is absurd. Are we to think of St Paul saying to himself: 'I am sure the evangelists and my other New Testament successors are going to omit such and such a vital element in the tradition; therefore I must take care to include it in one of my epistles which I am sure will be preserved to posterity'? Or are we to think of the author of II Peter carefully examining the work of his New Testament predecessors for vital omissions, conscious that the biblical canon was fast approaching its final form?

No, the fact is that to outward, human seeming the Bible, and even the New Testament, does not look like a book which conveys a single coherent body of truth; and if we are to think along such lines, we should surely have to regard Monsignor Ronald Knox as nearer the truth when he writes of 'the scarce literary relics that have come down to us from the first two centuries', and says, 'you cannot expect every single element of that tradition to appear in written form.'[10]

At this point I think I know what I shall be told, namely that I am involved in unnecessary difficulties because I am looking at the matter in a way that is too purely verbal and literary. 'The revelation', you will say, 'was not *about* God, it was a revelation *of*

God, and it was given not in propositions but in events, or maybe in a person. The unity or coherence of the biblical literature lies in the fact that it all, in one way or another, witnesses to the events in which God's self-disclosure took place.'

Obviously such a view affords a good deal of relief and I am sure it contains much truth. To begin with, it works with a model readily intelligible from everyday life. A man, let us say, has an accident and injures his knee. The doctors operate and carry out post-operational treatment. They then tell the man that there are certain things he must do, for example certain exercises, and other things he must not do, for example climb mountains. In short, he must live in a way appropriate to the situation created by their healing activities; and if he does not, painful consequences will follow. Somewhat analogously, God has performed a unified series of saving acts in history in order to reveal himself to us, the God with whom we have to deal, and to create the situation in which free and healthy dealings with him are possible. To be a Christian is to live before the God thus revealed in the way appropriate to the situation he has created.

If we look at it like that, there is no obvious reason why God should have infringed the liberty of the human witnesses to the degree necessary to achieve absolute economy and accuracy in the biblical testimony; and such a view can thus easily allow for erroneous, irrelevant and even downright irresponsible statements in the Bible. Its champions will add that it has the further advantage of being broadly the way in which the Bible understands itself.

Over this last statement certain difficulties begin to arise for me. I feel that only by something of a *tour de force* can all the biblical literature be brought under this viewpoint, and I am not sure that the biblical writers themselves saw things in terms of a series of 'mighty acts of God in history' to anything like the extent that is often suggested nowadays; I am not even sure that the words μεγαλεια του θεου (Acts 2.11) are correctly translated 'mighty works of God'. Even so far as New Testament writers did think in that way, modern exponents of this view seem to me to be involved in a 'scandal of particularity' quite other and greater than they were. For the New Testament writers, God had been active in a *heilsgeschichtlich* way throughout the world's history from creation day to Doomsday; for remember that, to a man, they believed that, whatever else God had done in Christ, he had brought very close the end of this world and of history as we know it. For modern exponents of this view, on the other hand, *Heilsgeschichte* did not begin until millions of years after the original creative act, and it finished, in the full sense, at least 2,000, and possibly many million, years before the close of human history. This is a 'scandal of particularity' indeed, and it seems to give to long periods of history what I might perhaps call a certain vacuous character.

To this I shall return later, but meanwhile I have certain other questions about this position. As the analogy of the knee operation was intended to suggest, the plausibility of the view we are discussing depends on our ability to pinpoint what it was that God was doing through his mighty acts, and so to define what is the appropriate response to it. Doctors can describe to a patient exactly what they have done to his knee, they can prescribe the precise regimen he is to follow and, if need be, they can show why the one necessitates the other. It is, I suppose, some such model as this that theologians like Anselm sought to follow in their attempts to construct a theology of atonement on the basis of the biblical revelation. But in more modern times it has been increasingly realized that language about the mighty acts of God in history is nothing like as simple and objective as might at first appear. To speak in this way is not to speak objectively in the sense in which we can speak objectively about doctors operating on someone's knee, or even, say, about certain historical events having great significance for Russian economic history. To speak of mighty acts of God is to offer a theological – and in an important sense, a subjective – interpretation of certain historical events. It is, as one writer has put it, to 'throw out human ideas toward the ineffable revelation of God'[11] in certain historical events. You may say that the events in question were such as to demand – or at least legitimate – interpretation in such terms; and you may also say that the terms – or images – in question were selected under the guidance of the spirit. But in either case the fact will remain that they were human terms and images and as such inevitably inadequate to their task and, if they were to be intelligible, rooted – or must I say 'contextualized'? – in the culture peculiar to a particular time and place. We are told, quite justifiably, that we have no right to deny *a priori* that God may have intervened in history in special ways, and even signalized his interventions by breaches of the natural law; but we are still bound in integrity to ask whether if we, with our twentieth-century background, had been there, we should have felt the historical events in question to demand any explanation in supernatural terms; and we can be sure that if so, the terms we should have used would not have been the ones used by the biblical writers. This type of approach is thus faced fairly and squarely with the whole complex of basic problems that lie behind Bultmann's suggestions about demythologization. I know of course that these problems are much older than Bultmann and that not only Bultmann, but Leonard Hodgson, John Knox, Austin Farrer and many others have made suggestions for dealing with them. I am not concerned now to describe or assess these suggestions; my point is only that on the basis of any of them – or at least any known to me – you can only extract revelation from the Bible when you have decided on the terms in which you are going to 'translate', or 'demythologize', or understand, the biblical terms and images; and that means allowing your contemporary statement of the faith to be determined by facts and considerations not directly derived from the Bible at all. The gospel we preach today may be 'out' of the Bible, but if so it is 'by' *some Vorverständnis*. The Bible is thus normative for preaching in a rather special and indeterminate sense, and it is this to which Barth objects as being incompatible with the *sola scriptura*. Certainly there is here, I think, an important break with the traditional approach to the Bible, but before I come to Barth I should like to make two further points.

First, the direct practical relevance of the issues involved. The aim of the preacher is to make clear to men the nature of the God with whom they have to deal and the appropriate way of dealing with him, or opening themselves to be dealt with by him. In the light of the above considerations, what are they to say on these topics? Clearly the God in question is not one who plans to closure history in the next thirty or forty years, as the New Testament writers say; nor, *pace* Professor Cullmann, is he a God who has won a decisive encounter with personal demonic forces and is now engaged in mopping-up operations, as the New Testament writers say. Is he then, as they say, a God who is interested in sacrifice of some sort as a necessary precondition of forgiveness? Does he reject all who do not believe, and if so, in what sense of 'believe'? Is he in fact a God who rejects anyone? Competent and believing theologians would answer all these questions in very different ways. What does that suggest about the nature of the biblical revelation as an objective norm?

Secondly, I should like to suggest that what may seem a different way of dealing with our question is not as different as it seems. I am thinking of the work of scholars who do not profess to take the biblical account and interpretation of God's acts at their face value, but seek, as it were, to read between the lines of the Bible. Using modern scholarly methods to set the various authors and documents in their original contexts, they try to discern for themselves what God was seeking to do in the events as they reconstruct and understand them. Such attempts have been frequent in modern times and if I single out as an example Professor Dodd's book *The Authority of the Bible*[12] that is because it seems to me supereminent of its kind. It is indeed a magisterial work, to which I owe much; yet even in its revised form, it is by now unmistakably dated. And if one asks why, is not the answer that in the last resort Dodd's procedure is the same as that of Bultmann or Hodgson, though he has carried it through in a different manner? He is more generous than Bultmann in his estimate of what the man on the Clapham omnibus can accept with integrity, and he wisely refrains from any attempt such as Bultmann makes to list summarily what such a man does, and cannot, believe. But a close study of his book shows that his argument rests on certain assumptions about these matters, and the overall validity of his conclusions stands or falls with the correctness or incorrectness of these assumptions. So we may yet awake one morning to discover from the bookseller's catalogue that Barth left a draft entitled: *Charles Dodd: Ein Versuch ihn zu verstehen*!

It is of course precisely with the sort of questions I am raising that Barth himself wrestled for so many years. His view, as I understand it, could be put briefly, if frivolously, like this: The serious Bible reader seeks to learn by listening-in on saving dialogues which took place between God and certain groups and individuals in the past. The exegete is like a fly on the wall of a room in which a wise spiritual director wrestles with the problems of a series of tormented souls. As he listens, the fly learns more and more both of the character and dimensions of the human problem and also about the mind and policy of the director towards them. Gradually but surely, the problems of the fly himself and the mind of the director towards him and his situation are established and revealed. Of course such language does the greatest injustice to Barth, not least to the vital part he assigns to the working of the Spirit and the authority of the community in making the biblical revelation contemporary; but perhaps it may serve as the basis of a brief critique.

The strength of this position is supposed to be that according to it purely human assumptions are in no way normative; no 'pre-understandings', conditioned by the cultures of a fallen world, enter in as distorting media, and so the revelation is the pure word of God. My difficulties about this are the well known ones and so can be stated summarily. In the first place the ideal seems unattainable, and in his later lectures I understand that Barth admitted in effect that he had not attained it. The *Dogmatics* is unmistakably a mid-twentieth century, West-European, Protestant production; the illuminating section on *Das Nichtige*, for instance, may owe its initiation to Genesis 1.2, but it could never have been what it is but for certain strands in twentieth-century continental philosophy. I cannot forbear to quote the revealing comment of Professor A. B. Come, a definite, if discriminating Barthian:[13] 'In Barth's concept of *Nichtige* . . . we have one of those theological insights which *is nowhere explicitly spelled out in Scripture* (italics mine) but . . . is arrived at by our intuition of the whole'. My difficulty is to see that so far as this matter goes there is any basic issue at stake in the controversy between Barth and Bultmann. It is true that Barth is more eclectic in his approach towards modern attitudes and philosophies than is Bultmann – at any rate the Bultmann Barth sees; he may change his spectacles more often, but it surely remains true that the gospel he, or any other, derives from the Bible depends on the spectacles through which they read the text. It could, of course, be argued that in the particular case of Barth the eclectic choice of interpretative categories is more or less completely appropriate as a result of guidance by the Holy Spirit. But such a claim would be arbitrary, and for us outside the charmed circle the stubborn fact would remain that when Barth listened in, for example, to that part of God's dialogue with men represented by Matthew 16.18ff. one thing was revealed to him, whereas when Cardinal Heenan listens with equal seriousness – well, nowadays I am not quite sure what is revealed; but even now I think something different from Barth's understanding!

One subsidiary point before I turn to another aspect of the matter. It would appear that on all the modern views I have been discussing (including Barth's, if he means what he says) the discovery of the supposed normative revelation depends on a knowledge of the detailed circumstances of the biblical peoples and writers such as only a professional, or at any rate semi-professional, could hope to possess. I am not quite sure what that says for the traditional doctrine of normativeness. Does it perhaps mean that the Bible is not, after all, a book who runs may read, but that the elucidation of the normative revelation is a special vocation of Christians with a bent and leisure for it?

May I now turn abruptly and briefly to look at the matter from another angle? What are the questions currently agitating the church to which, on the traditional view, a normative answer could reasonably have been looked for? To anyone who attended the Lambeth Conference of 1968 one obvious example is the question whether women can or should be ordained to the priesthood. It is perhaps significant that after the most careful study of the question by competent theologians, and discussion by the bishops at the conference, the conclusion was reached that 'theological considerations are inconclusive'; that is to say, whatever else it says, that on this matter the biblical revelation is not normative. Such a question may perhaps be dismissed – though if so, wrongly – as a thing indifferent, as if the man who had the operation on his knee should write to the doctors to ask if he might waggle his little finger, and receive no reply. But suppose the questions were to be widened into the question whether we need priests at all – at any rate in the sense of people who have received the imposition of episcopal hands and thereby indelible 'character'? Is it not possible that here too, not perhaps 'theological considerations', but biblical evidence would prove inconclusive? And what about the questions increasingly being raised in some quarters about the permanent adequacy and validity of traditional statements about the Trinity and their relation to christology? Or, to go still nearer the heart of the matter, what about the questions raised by Dr John Robinson and others about the right way of understanding the transcendent, or by Professors Braithwaite, van Buren *et hoc genus omne* about the meaningfulness or propriety of any talk about the supernatural? It is, I hope, clear that I am not agreeing with, or even assessing, anyone's views in these areas; my question is simply whether 'the biblical revelation' could possibly be normative in these fields, since in each case the question at issue is precisely the possibility or propriety of understanding things in the twentieth century in the way the biblical writers understood them in the second and first and earlier centuries.

The question of course is no new one and a way of answering it that seems increasingly popular is to say that the church must learn to travel lighter and to jettison a lot of the doctrinal baggage it has carried in the past. Many tenets – so the argument runs – which seemed in the past to be guaranteed by the biblical revelation are now seen to have been largely the result of 'nontheological factors'; and we must learn to be less dogmatic, not only about the number of angels who can dance on the point of a needle, but about the inner structure of the divine existence, the mode of operation of the atonement and a lot else besides. This type of answer may well be the right one, but, at any rate in the forms in which I have met it, it usually seems to go with a conviction that there are still some areas in which a normative revelation can be expected, and should be sought, in something like the traditional manner. It is sometimes suggested, e.g. that belief that divinity once became incarnate is still an *articulus stantis aut cadentis ecclesiae*. I want to ask – and I do it very tentatively – whether this may not involve something like the fallacy of the 'god of the gaps' and whether we should not do better to explore the possibility of giving up the dogma of normativeness in its traditional form altogether, as Jackson Case suggested.

Would this mean the end of Christianity as we know it – Christianity as a revealed religion? Should I as a preacher be simply a particular type of adult education lecturer, distinguished from my hearers only by the fact that I have had more time and leisure than most of them for reflection on religious questions?

Certainly I had to admit to my colleagues in the World Council project that I often preach without a text or on a text from a non-biblical writer, Kierkegaard, for example, or even, on occasions Katherine Whitehorn! And I have to admit to myself that the spirit of my sermons is very much that expressed in Leonard Hodgson's formula: 'This is how *I* see it; can *you* not see it like that as well?'

But still, I have to ask myself *why* 'this is how I see it' rather than some other way. I was myself brought up as a Christian, though I think that affects only the form, and not the substance, of what I want to say. It means that from the earliest age I was brought to adopt a stance, a stance towards God, the world, history, the neighbour, the church – and I should like to be able to say everything else; in fact, of course, not all areas of my personality were integrated into this stance and I have suffered much as a result. But much more was involved than just the intellect; to do justice to the matter I should have to use language about the emotions, commitment, and much else besides consciously held intellectual convictions. My original formation was in an extreme evangelical Anglican tradition, crossed with a strong streak of Pelagianism, and over the years I have, partly consciously and partly unconsciously, modified my stance, moving, as I believe, towards a more centrally and characteristically Christian position, which is yet unmistakably only a variant of the one basic stance.

I realize, needless to say, that at any time my whole understanding of myself and my stance may be called in question by the disciples of Karl Marx or Professor Ayer or anybody else. So far as this has happened, or happens, I think I know what I must do – try to understand the objections, consider the possibility of their validity and, if honestly moved to do so, try to meet them on their own (philosophical) grounds – which is not necessarily the same thing as their own terms. It is partly the attempt to do that which has led to some modification of my stance.

Yet this does not seem to me the central issue, which is how I came to adopt my original stance and to alter it to my present one. Obviously I did not argue myself into it, and argument has been only one factor in the modification of it. Equally it is only to a minimal degree the fruit of unmediated private experience, whether 'religious' or of any other kind. Nor does it come directly from the Bible; even those very rare people (the Susie Youngers of this world) who, coming out of a non-religious background, are apparently converted simply by private reading of the Bible, do not in fact start their reading 'from cold'. Their understanding of the Bible is mediated through the countless ways in which our culture is still moulded by the Christian community and tradition.

Which surely brings us to the crux of the matter. My stance was derived – partly through my family – from the Christian community and it is basically under influence of various sorts within the community that it has been modified.

Where then did the community get the stance it gave me? Which in turn involves the question where did the community get its origin – a question with endless ramifications. One obvious answer is from Jesus, or, as I should prefer to say, from the Christ-event. As you will know, I am by no means sure where precisely in the New Testament story the balance lies between Jesus himself and the beliefs of his earliest followers. But I could not be a Christian unless I believed that the balance could be struck, in *some* such way that it is plausible to see the New Testament story as a cardinal item in God's self-disclosure to men.

Yet on any showing we cannot stop our search at the Christ-event. It could not have been what it was except in the already existing Jewish community; indeed, looked at from one point of view, it was precisely a reformation of that community.

Yet again, we cannot stop with the Old Testament community, for modern scholarship shows us how much it in turn owed to the Babylonians, and to other communities and beliefs earlier than its distinctive emergence. And all down its history, before, at, and after its reformation, this community has owed much to elements derived from other communities and beliefs.

Can we then say anything else than that the community owes its existence to God? And does that allow us to say that the community is the revelation – or at least the locus or source of revelation?

Can we, or should we, try to pin-point some special locus of divine action and self-disclosure within its history? That is clearly a question with extremely wide ramifications, christological, soteriological and of many other kinds; a great deal depends on how it is understood. According to the letter of the New Testament, in 'the things concerning Jesus' God was active, as it

were, behind the natural scenes carrying through certain trans-
actions between the natural and the supernatural which permanently and once and for all set their relationship upon a new
basis. Without going all the way with Charles Clayton Morrison[14]
and saying that all such pictures are in the last resort gnostic and
docetic and belie the truly historical character of Christianity, I am
not quite sure that even the most faithful Christian in the twentieth century is committed to them.

But someone will object: surely the Lord's resurrection was
something as objective, decisive and once-and-for-all as could
well be conceived. Once again, much depends on how the matter
is looked at; on what you think happened and how you understand it. I would venture to suggest that essentially the resurrection *can* be understood as the initiating by God of a new
relationship with himself which we still call life 'in Christ', however precisely we should 'unpack' that phrase if asked to do so. I
suggest it could be unpacked in a way that would not commit us
to the particular dynamics suggested in the New Testament, or to
Jackson Case's 'constant quantum of truth' which can subsequently only be clarified and explicated. We who are no longer
tied to the eschatological perspective of the fourth evangelist can
perhaps assign to the Holy Spirit a broader role in this connection
than simply that of taking the things of the incarnate Christ and
declaring them unto us (John 16.14).

Can we not maintain the possibility and reality of a relationship
with God which would have been impossible without the Old
Testament community and the Christ-event; which is the true
descendant of that relationship which St Paul categorized as life
'in Christ', though in the course of the church's life since, and
under the influence of the Holy Spirit, it has come, and is coming,
to be differently conceived and differently – and even perhaps
more profoundly – lived?

It is, I think, worth noting that Karl Barth, of all people, at least
twice in his *Dogmatics* discusses the theoretical possibility that
God might have adopted modes of revelation different from the
one to which, on Barth's own view, he has in fact exclusively
confined himself.

In one place he envisages the possibility that revelation might
have been laid up for us, as it were, within human nature itself,
and so taken the form of a 'timeless essential state of man himself,

namely his relationship to the eternal and absolute', in which case proclamation would have been a process of *anamnesis* – a 'heart searching', by which a neglected or hidden part of human nature would be rediscovered and unfolded.[15]

More apposite for us is the following statement:[16]

> . . . it might also have pleased God to give His Church the canon in the form of an unwritten prophetic and apostolic tradition, propagating itself from spirit to spirit and from mouth to mouth. It will not be disputed that there is something of this kind in the Church apart from the real canon. But it would have to be said that, so far as it had pleased God to make this unwritten spiritual-oral tradition the canon of His Church, the canon would be as faintly distinguishable from the life of the Church, as we can distinguish the blood of our fathers which flows in our veins from our own blood; in other words, the Church is . . . left to her solitary self and concentrated upon herself, upon her own aliveness.

Precisely. But in the former quotation Barth simply concludes with the bald statement: 'in fact the matter has been contrived differently' (he does not say how he knows), and after the second passage he writes: 'Whatever of such spiritual-oral tradition there may be in the Church, obviously it cannot possess the character of an authority irremovably confronting the Church. In the unwritten tradition the Church is not addressed, but is engaged in a dialogue with herself.' With all due respect, do not these quotations beg the question? Barth nowhere, so far as I know, considers the possibility that God may have chosen to work through a combination of all three of these modes; and that is because he does not consider the possibility – which is precisely the question at issue – that God does not *wish* his self-revelation to 'possess the character of an authority irremovably confronting the Church'. What if God, taking history really seriously, actually *wants* the church to be 'engaged in a dialogue with herself'?

Needless to say, I can see that such a position bristles with difficulties. For brevity's sake I conclude with a brief reference to just two of these.

First, the Bible: it is simply a historical fact that at all periods of the community's history – before and after its reformation – some members of it have been moved to give written expression to some aspects of its life and experience, setting down accounts of certain events and their meditations upon their meaning, in prophetic, poetic, parabolic and many other forms. Certain of these writings have won such esteem with the community as to become authoritative in a special sense, though different writers have approved themselves in this way at different times and in different sections of the community.

We habitually think of all this as providential – on the whole, I believe rightly; though at the same time I can well understand why the question of the canon is becoming increasingly problematic in some quarters, why an eminent, and by no means extreme, English theologian was moved to speak recently of 'the curse of the canon' or why Robert Henry Lightfoot in an uncharacteristic moment of self-revelation once shared with me his uncertainty whether the production of the first gospel may not have been 'the first serious failure of nerve on the part of the infant church'.

Still, it is easy to see why, at least by the permissive will of God, the scriptures have come to enjoy the esteem they have, and will continue to do so. You will all have had again and again the experience the church has had – and I certainly have constantly – of finding that it is only as you go back to the Bible that you regain your balance, as Sir Edwyn Hoskyns put it[17] – your unfaith is rebuked, your fears and frettings removed, your path made clear. Yet does all this require more than a basically Coleridgean explanation – provided it be in community, as well as individual terms? Does it necessitate any dogma of normativeness in the sense in which I have been understanding the phrase?[18]

Then finally the problem of a criterion. 'In effect', it will be said, 'the line you are following is that of Newman and Karl Adams, if not indeed of Loisy and Tyrrell; this is a theology of the acorn growing into the oak, a theology of development, and the fatal difficulty of all such theologies is that of distinguishing true development from false'. 'You speak of "the community"', it will be asked, 'but where, amid all the variety of denominations, is this community to be found?' My answer to all that has been hinted at in my remarks about Barth. I confess that I have never been much moved by this type of objection, even when forcibly and plausibly expressed, as it was, for example, by Oliver Quick. And so far as I can tell, the reason is this: whatever may be said in theory, I do not believe the church ever does, or ever can, settle its questions by reference to some allegedly external and objective norm. I simply do not believe, for example, that by reference to any such norm, knock-down arguments can be produced to prove the Methodists right against the Congregationalists, or both of them right or wrong against the Orthodox. That is just not the way it works; we are dealing with something which is essentially *solvendum ambulando*, which means, according to the good old Hebrew understanding of *ambulare, credendo, precando et vivendo* at least as much as *biblia sacra legendo*.

On the principle that 'he that is not against us is for us' (Mark 9.40) I am more than content to live in communion with Professors Braithwaite, van Buren, Altizer and the rest – from whom indeed I am sure I have much to learn – convinced as I live and worship with them and my other fellow Christians, in the community, under the power of the Spirit, that most of us have meat to eat that these thinkers wot not of, and that together we shall all come to recognize dimensions of our common life and worship to which the views they hold – or think they hold – fail to do justice. Is it not in some such way that we must deal with their views, and the views of the countless other 'way out' Christians who will no doubt follow them as the years go by; and not by attempted reference to alleged objective norms from which logically irrefragable positions can be derived? *As such a norm* – though not necessarily in any other way – the Christ of 2,000 years ago is already problematic. What will be the case with the Christ of 2,000,000,000 years ago? That is a question theologians should not ignore, for we are quite credibly informed that the human race may yet have 2,000,000,000 years to go. When the Lord then comes will he find '*the* faith' on the earth? Do we really expect him to?

8

Schweitzer Revisited

The successive editions of *The Quest of the Historical Jesus*,[1] the English version of Albert Schweitzer's big book on the history of the study of the life of Jesus, have all been based on the first German edition of 1906. In 1913, however, Schweitzer introduced modifications and additions (particularly the latter) so extensive as to make the second edition virtually a new book. He gave it the title: *An Account of the Scholarly Study of the Life of Jesus* and under that title it has several times been reprinted in Germany with only slight further modifications. The changes added considerably to the value of the work and as long ago as 1931 Schweitzer himself expressed his regret that the later English editions continued to be based on the first German one.[2]

Some years ago the question arose whether the book deserved translation into English in its full and final form. I was inclined to feel that it did, and to test my feeling I sketched out an essay on the abiding importance of the work such as might accompany and commend a full English edition. My reasoning convinced a publisher, and a translation of the additional material was commissioned and completed; but then rising costs and other publishing difficulties led to the abandonment of the project. The work involved in preparing my 'preface' convinced me that Schweitzer's work still has many pertinent things to say, and certainly many pertinent questions to raise, so I have ventured to include a suitably modified version of the essay in this volume.

At a time of unprecedented change in religious thought it may well be asked what useful contribution can be expected from a book published over sixty years ago, especially as many of the views and theories with which it deals were already very much past history at the time of its publication.

Schweitzer himself provides a partial answer when he remarks, as he does several times, how slow New Testament scholars are to learn from the experience of the past. If, as he rightly says, 'No one can justly criticise, or appraise the value of, new contributions to the study of this subject unless he knows in what forms they have been presented before', this book might be expected to have been a godsend to all those who wanted to engage in serious study of gospel problems and the life of Jesus. In fact, however, what Schweitzer says about a book by David Friedrich Strauss can be applied all too exactly to his own work:

> It is far from having lost its significance at the present day. It marked out the ground which is now occupied by modern critical study and it filled in the death-certificates of a whole series of explanations which at first sight have all the air of being alive, but are not really so. If these continue to haunt present-day theology, it is only as ghosts, which can be put to flight by simply pronouncing the name of David Friedrich Strauss, and which would long ago have ceased to 'walk', if the thologians who regard Strauss' book as obsolete would only take the trouble to read it.[3]

Any reader of Schweitzer's book who has some acquaintance with the present situation in New Testament scholarship is bound to notice how often theories put forward in recent years as if for the first time, and currently discussed as if they were new, were in fact canvassed in very much the same form in the nineteenth century and subjected at that time to careful and illuminating scrutiny which often uncovered fatal flaws in them.[4]

Schweitzer's book, however, is far from being just a catalogue – even a *catalogue raisonné* – of nineteenth-century views about Jesus and their subsequent fortunes. Schweitzer himself describes how, after reading Aristotle's *Metaphysics*, he always felt the need 'to try to grasp the nature of a problem not only as it is in itself, but also by the way in which it unfolds itself in the course of history'.[5] His unfolding of the story of gospel criticism – and this largely explains the scope and format of his book – is thus an attempt to grasp and communicate *the nature of a problem*; and no one will read the book with full profit unless he has an inkling at least of what the problem is. It is, as the book itself repeatedly emphasizes, a problem of the greatest complexity; so complex in fact that its nature cannot easily be stated concisely. We may perhaps get some initial help from the title of the English translation: *The Quest of the Historical Jesus*.[6] That is a deceptively simple title, and the source of the complexity in it lies in the word 'historical'. The church had, of course, had a perfectly clear picture of Jesus for centuries before the time at which Schweitzer takes up his story. It was a picture derived from many sources; for example, since it originated at a time when the complete inerrancy of the Bible was taken for granted, it was able, by various harmonizing devices, to comprehend every statement about Jesus in all four gospels and every other part of the Bible thought to refer to him. Then, since there was no suspicion of any incompatibility between that composite account and the doctrinal statements of the creeds and other classical Christian writings, this picture also embodied traits derived from these latter; it depicted Jesus as the incarnation of the Second Person of the Trinity who, as such, was omniscient, for example – the questions he was said to have asked in the days of his flesh being taken as deriving not from genuine ignorance but from the need to sustain his role as man among men. The picture was in fact a traditional, and not a critical or historical, picture.

Therein lies much of the significance of the story Schweitzer has to tell. For it was precisely in the latter part of the eighteenth century when his story begins, that traditional accounts of the past of every kind, both secular and religious, began to come under suspicion. More and more reasons were discovered for thinking that if the available evidence was subjected to the sort of scrutiny and rigorous cross-questioning to which witnesses in a law court are subjected, a picture of the past would emerge widely different from that which had been handed down unquestioned for generations. Whatever the original motives and context of this new approach, it was bound to be applied to the accounts of the past contained in the Bible, if only through the exertions of opponents of Christianity, men like Hermann Samuel Reimarus (1694–1768), who would have been glad to see the traditional picture of Jesus discredited. Schweitzer himself notes that 'Hate as well as love can write a life of Jesus', and acknowledges that some of the most valuable work on the subject, especially in the early days, was inspired by hatred of the figure of Jesus, or rather of what he calls 'the supernatural nimbus with which it had been surrounded' in the traditional picture.[7]

Inevitably apologists for Christianity felt obliged to meet such opponents on their own ground, and so students of very different persuasions had compelling reasons for starting a full-scale quest of the *historical* Jesus. There may have been doubts in some quarters about the *propriety* of such a quest, but it is not surprising if at first sight there seemed no great *difficulty* about it, at any rate in principle. All that was needed, it seemed, was to subject the gospel records to exactly the same sort of criticism as any other historical records and then to ask what picture would have been deduced from them had they concerned any ordinary figure of the past.

In practice, such a programme soon revealed itself as involving a whole nest of difficulties. To begin with, it seemed to traditionalists to beg the essential question. The claim of orthodoxy was precisely that the gospels were *not* ordinary books and that Jesus was *not* an ordinary man; any investigation which started out with the contrary assumptions was therefore bound to be misleading both in its conclusions and its handling of evidence. For example, evidence that would not have been adequate to justify belief in miraculous powers on the part of an ordinary man would have to be very differently evaluated in the case of one admitted to possess a unique status.

Such contentions were obviously not without force; on the other hand, they placed even the most fair-minded quester in an impossible position. He sought to apply the historical method to the accounts of Jesus, but it was – and surely is likely to remain – a cardinal presupposition of the historical method that people and things in the past exhibited broadly the same character and modes of behaviour as do the people and things of the present.[8] It was felt that if any exception was claimed to that rule, while the historian could not of course disprove the claim, it removed the events in connexion with which it was made out of the class which could be submitted to testing and so affirmed or denied to be historical in any normal sense of the word. The conviction that supernatural, or miraculous, events had occurred, even if it could not be dismissed as simply due to an act of faith, involved a subjective element quite beyond that involved in normal historical judgments.

Schweitzer poses the point in the form of a clear either–or: '*Either* purely historical *or* purely supernatural' (p. 237). Admittedly, recognizing this question is by no means the same thing as resolving it – it has perhaps never been satisfactorily resolved –

but to recognize it does add greatly to the clarity of our thinking, and it may perhaps be suggested that greater clarity on this question has been one of the points at which German theology has been at an advantage over English theology.

Be that as it may, those, both Christian and non-Christian, who could not accept the idea of a radical discontinuity in the course of history outfaced the opposition of the orthodox and continued to apply the historical method to the story of Jesus. Their earliest attempts were largely conditioned by a belief, which they shared with the orthodox, in the factual character of the various gospel narratives. Although they did not share the orthodox belief that the facts in question had happened more or less exactly as related, it did not occur to them, any more than it did to historical pioneers working in other fields,[9] to 'rid themselves', as Schweitzer puts it, 'of the prejudice that an actual, even if not a miraculous fact must underlie all the recorded miracles'. Accordingly, their approach was essentially rationalizing. Assuming that behind every gospel story, however miraculous, there lay some historical incident, they attempted in each case to penetrate to the original incident, which they took to be fully capable of explanation in natural terms, but to have been blown up into a supernatural event as the result of credulity, illusion or misunderstanding. One of the difficulties was that the various incidents in the career of Jesus, as thus reconstructed, often seemed so banal, and sometimes even faintly ludicrous, that it became difficult to understand why they should ever have given rise to the process of supernaturalizing transformation which on this view they had.[10]

A quite different way of approaching the whole matter, alternative both to the supernaturalist and to the rationalist approach, was suggested by David Friedrich Strauss and underlay his epoch-making *Life of Jesus*, first published in 1835. Strauss suggested that many of the supernatural traits in the gospels were neither to be accepted *au pied de la lettre* as the orthodox supposed, nor yet regarded with the rationalists as misinterpretations of quite ordinary occurrences, but seen as entirely legendary constructions; constructions, that is, not deliberately contrived with any intention of deceiving, but arising spontaneously as the appropriate means, at a relatively primitive stage of cultural development, for communicating the reverence and high estimation in which Jesus had come to be held. As Strauss himself put it: 'Orthodox and rationalists alike proceed from the false assumption that we have always in the gospels testimony, sometimes even that of eye-witnesses, to fact'. In reality,

> The narrators testify sometimes, not to outward facts, but to ideas, often most practical and beautiful ideas, constructions which even eye-witnesses had unconsciously put upon facts, imagination concerning them, reflections upon them, reflections such as were natural to the time and at the author's level of culture. What we have here is . . . a plastic, naive and, at the same time, often most profound apprehension of truth within the area of religious feeling and poetic truth. It results in narrative, legendary, mythical in nature, illustrative often of spiritual truth in a manner more perfect than any hard, prosaic statement could achieve.

Strauss ascribed the production of such material to what he called the 'mythopoeic faculty', and he classified his approach as mythological, in distinction from the supernaturalist and the rationalist approaches. Strauss's approach has been very influential and an understanding of it is indispensable to an understanding of subsequent New Testament study, especially in Germany. What is more, it is indispensable to an understanding of the gospels themselves; for though Strauss may no doubt have fallen victim to the common temptation of discoverers to overvalue their discovery and see in it the key to every lock, the phenomenon to which he pointed is a very real one, and it played an important part of making the gospels what they are. Indeed, it may be suggested that the study of the gospels in the British Isles has suffered considerably as the result of a general ignoring or underestimation of the phenomenon to which Strauss pointed.

The work of Strauss, Ferdinand Christian Baur and others provoked dissent from a number of writers in the nineteenth century who sought to occupy a middle position. Unconvinced by Strauss's very negative conclusions with regard to the historical trustworthiness of the gospels, they were none the less convinced, as against the thorough-going supernaturalists, that the historical method must be applied to the gospels; and they fully accepted that its application might lead to significant modifications in the traditional picture of Jesus. Among these men were some very considerable scholars such as H. J. Holtzmann, whose work, like that of a number of the others, was admired and widely influential in England. Indeed, their 'mediating stance'[11] has been so widely approved and taken up in England that it may come as a shock to English-speaking readers to discover that for Schweitzer, despite his recognition of the outstanding work done by these scholars, the word 'mediating' is by no means a term of approval. Indeed, he roundly asserts that,

> Progress always consists in taking one or other of two alternatives, in abandoning the attempt to combine them. . . . The pioneers of progress have therefore always to reckon with the law of mental inertia which manifests itself in the majority – who always go on believing that it is possible to combine that which can no longer be combined, and in fact claim it as a special merit that they in contrast to 'one-sided' writers, can do justice to the other side of the question. One must just let them be, till their time is over. . . .'

What is the meaning of such a forthright declaration?

Of course on occasion it is perfectly proper that an account of Jesus which is unacceptable as it stands for historical reasons, because it fails to 'save all the phenomena', should be supplemented with insights derived from one or more alternative accounts, provided that the resulting combination adds up to a coherent account more plausible, overall, than any of the accounts it is designed to replace. What Schweitzer has in mind is something different. He suspects that very often, when mediating theologians are considering a scientific account of Jesus, 'the other side of the picture' to which they seek to 'do justice' is not so much the existence of alternative scientific accounts in some respects superior to the one they are considering, as the features of the *orthodox* picture. So far as he is right in this suspicion about 'mediating theology', he is surely right in rejecting it on the grounds that its method is essentially 'arbitrary'. Once the historical method has begun to be used, only considerations which have validity within its terms may be taken into account: 'the historian simply must not be an apologist'. The mediating theologian, however, by the very nature of his enterprise, is bound sooner or later to have to say in effect: Although purely historical considerations might seem to point in a certain direction, we cannot go further in that direction because it would take us unacceptably far from the traditional, orthodox, picture of Christ. As Schweitzer puts it, 'in the end religious considerations get in the way of a scientific judgment'.

Mediating theologians will not represent their procedure in such terms, even to themselves. They will say, and no doubt believe, that they have simply followed the historical argument to the end, uninfluenced by any extrinsic considerations, and only then discovered, to their great satisfaction, that the picture of Jesus to which they have been led is, at least in essential features, quite similar to the Christ of orthodox faith. Can they be mistaken about their own procedure? We must remember how many and intricate are all the steps in every argument in this field. For example, everything will often turn on the version of the original Greek from which a scholar starts. How easy to opt for a reading which is *reasonably* well attested and would support the conclusion at which the scholar would like to arrive, without stopping to make sure that that reading is in fact the most likely on strictly text-critical grounds.[12]

Professor John Knox discusses another way in which arguments in this field may be unintentionally 'weighted'.[13] He shows how certain English and American scholars unconsciously demand a much higher density of proof from arguments which tell against the New Testament account than they do from arguments which tell in its favour. The late Professor C. H. Dodd's choice of words, for example, suggests a bias in favour of the New Testament account which leads him to stick to it unless 'compelled to reject it'; even when the evidence against it is, on his own submission, very weighty, he will do no more than 'hesitate to believe' it. To compare such an attitude with the account given by R. G. Collingwood, for example, of the genuine historian's attitude, which starts out with an initial scepticism and will arrive at no verdict till it has thoroughly sifted and 'tortured' the *prima facie* evidence, is at least to understand Schweitzer's distrust of all 'mediating' approaches and his rather depressed conclusion that 'apologists . . . can get the better of any historical result whatever'.[14]

It should in fairness be added that bias, conscious or unconscious, is no monopoly of mediating theologians. Readers of existentialist works on the gospels, for example, are likely to have noticed their reluctance to admit the authenticity of passages in which Jesus is represented as defining his status or giving grounds for his claims. It is also true that the study of historiography since Schweitzer's book appeared has relentlessly

exposed the unconscious assumptions with which even the most
'impartial' historians go to work. If this calls in question, to some
extent, Schweitzer's very sharp distinction between 'scientific'
scholarship and that which has an axe of some sort to grind, it
makes all the more pertinent his penetrating analysis of the
assumptions which lie behind various types of approach to the
problem of Jesus. No one who has read his account of
nineteenth-century gospel study can fail to have a sharpened eye
for the assumptions and biases – so often still the same – behind
contemporary work, no doubt including his own.

The second great alternative Schweitzer picks out in his story is:
'*either* Synoptic *or* Johannine', and it illustrates admirably what
has just been said. Until the publication of Strauss's book
scholars generally had used the Fourth Gospel at least as much as
the other three in their attempts to reconstruct the historical and
geographical facts about the life of Jesus; Strauss was effectively
the first[15] to question this procedure; after full discussion he
concluded that John is altogether inferior to the Synoptists as a
historical source, basing his argument mainly on the different
theological character of the Johannine and synoptic traditions. As
he saw it, John represents a more advanced and self-conscious
stage of the mythopoeic process, substituting as he did, according to Strauss, Greek metaphysical conceptions (Logos, Sonship)
for the Jewish, Messianic, eschatological conceptions of the
Synoptists, and portraying Jesus as applying Greek speculative
categories to himself. As C. H. Weisse was to put it, following
Strauss,

> It is not so much a picture of Christ that John sets forth as a conception
> of Christ; his Christ does not speak *in* His own person, but *of* His own
> person.[16]

In view of the fact that, as Martin Werner points out, the
traditional picture of Christ depends on reading the synoptic
gospels through Johannine spectacles, it is particularly interesting that 'apologetic' scholars, such as Tholuck and Ewald,
continued to use John in the old way, ignoring rather than coun-
tering Strauss's careful arguments. Eventually, thanks largely to
the work of the Tübingen school, and of Holtzmann, who on this
matter took a 'one-sided position', Strauss's view came to be
generally accepted, and Schweitzer could say in 1906, and repeat

in subsequent editions, 'the question is decided . . . Johannine study has added in principle nothing new to what was said by Strauss'. If that is true – and there is much to suggest that it is – what is to be made of the fact that the sort of conclusions which seemed to Schweitzer so definitive have never been accepted by a considerable number of scholars? B. F. Westcott, for example, to the end of his life[17] continued to maintain the Johannine authorship and substantial historical accuracy of the Fourth Gospel. No doubt he would have been as ready as J. B. Lightfoot and William Sanday were to admit the 'apologetic' and 'defensive' nature of his work on John,[18] but more recent writers who rate the historical value of the gospel more highly than Strauss – for example, C. H. Dodd, J. A. T. Robinson or A. M. Hunter – can point to archaeological discoveries, the finds at Qumran, the rise of form-criticism and other relevant evidence not known to Strauss, or to Schweitzer when he first wrote. Nevertheless, it will be an interesting question for readers of Schweitzer's book how far he would have regarded these new and more conservative positions with regard to the Fourth Gospel as the legitimate or inescapable upshot of these new discoveries, or how far he would have felt that the discoveries were being used in an essentially apologetic interest.

The third great alternative highlighted by Schweitzer, '*either* eschatological *or* non-eschatological', involves at least two vitally important points. As we have seen, the aim of critical scholarship was to give an 'historical' account of Jesus and, as things were understood in the nineteenth century, an adequate biographical account involved not only a knowledge of the outward course of events, but also of the internal connections between them in the mind of the subject; it involved, to borrow Collingwood's terminology, nothing less than the ability to 'think the person's thoughts after him'; and in order to be able to do that, you need to know not only what he believed, but what things he assumed, took for granted, or regarded as important; what authorities he accepted, what passed with him for a valid argument, and so on. That might seem a lot to ask in this case, yet with surprising unanimity the critical scholars of whom Schweitzer writes believed themselves to have enough material to produce an historical account in their sense of the term.

As far as the external course of events was concerned, Mark's gospel with its two clearly distinct sections (1.14-8.26 and 8.27-10.52) seemed to suggest a corresponding twofold ministry, first to the crowds publicly and then to the disciples privately. As for Jesus' thought and personality, here nineteenth-century liberal scholars made an interesting bow in the direction of orthodoxy. Although they envisaged Jesus as basically a human being, they took it for granted that he was a *perfect* human being with the highest imaginable standards and values.[19] In practice that was bound to mean the highest imaginable by nineteenth-century culture, or at any rate the particular representative of it who happened to be writing. Armed with this assumption, scholars were able to divine Jesus' thoughts and reactions at all sorts of points not explicitly dealt with in the gospels. It is one of Schweitzer's most constant, and most fully justified, complaints that nineteenth-century scholars knew far more about Jesus than the gospels themselves.[20] As a result, the Jesus who emerged from these studies was, if not a characteristic nineteenth-century figure,[21] a figure calculated to attract cultured people of the nineteenth century.

This situation could arise the more easily because comparatively little was known at the time about first-century Judaism, the real context and basis of Jesus' thinking and values.[22] Once the historical superiority of the synoptic gospels had been established, however, their very contents might have been expected to suggest that eschatological and apocalyptic ideas loomed large in the mind of Jesus. That nineteenth-century scholars failed to take the point is, as Schweitzer says, an index of the extent to which the liberals of the period were the prisoners of their own presuppositions, especially since already in the eighteenth century Reimarus had put forward an acute and in some ways plausible account of Christian origins, according to which imminent eschatological expectations were the key feature both of Jesus' teaching and of the beliefs of the early church.

It was not till the publication of Johannes Weiss's book *The Preaching of Jesus about the Kingdom of God* in 1892 that a claim was again seriously advanced for eschatology as the key to the whole matter, and even then, Schweitzer asserts (perhaps a little unfairly), the claim was substantially modified by the author in his second edition (1900). Schweitzer, however, never wavered in his conviction that eschatology was the fundamental clue, from the time when, as a student, he embarked on the line of thought that led to his first two books. He took the same line when he wrote *The Quest of the Historical Jesus* in 1906; his continued adherence to it is shown by his preface to the sixth edition of 1950 and by his posthumously published *Kingdom of God and Primitive Christianity*.[23] He argued that almost all the material in the synoptic gospels – or at any rate the first two – could be accepted more or less as it stood, once it was recognized that the categories in which Jesus understood his person and role were not categories familiar to the nineteenth century but ones derived, with little or no change, from Jewish eschatological beliefs of the first and second centuries. Jesus believed that his ministry would mean the end of history and be the occasion for the appearance of God's kingdom conceived very much along the lines of contemporary apocalyptic; and he expected that when it arrived, he would be manifested as its head.

Schweitzer even claimed to be able to trace the stages by which circumstance forced Jesus to modify and restate his expectations until he was finally led to challenge the Jewish authorities in Jerusalem in the conviction that the sufferings he was bringing on himself would be allowed to count as the dreaded 'pangs of the Messiah' foretold in apocalyptic, and would thus remove the last obstacle to the 'coming of the kingdom in power'.[24]

Schweitzer's position thus stood in sharp contrast to that taken in another justly influential book, published five years earlier, *The Messianic Secret in the Gospels* by William [*sic*] Wrede of Breslau. Wrede carried the liberal point of view to its logical conclusion by denying that Jesus made messianic claims of any sort; he attributed those ascribed to him in the gospels to the theological activity of the early church. On Wrede's showing, Mark's gospel already had in no small measure the character assigned to the Fourth Gospel by scholars such as Strauss and Weiss.

In its original form Schweitzer's book ended with Wrede, as it had begun with Reimarus, and to emphasize the point that it was essentially polemical, the vehicle of a thesis directed against Wrede and his liberal predecessors, it was entitled *Von Reimarus zu Wrede*. It is clear what the thesis was: that the eighteenth century, in the person of Reimarus, had already provided the essential answer to the problem of Jesus, but that nineteenth-century preoccupations had led to its being ignored and finally, in Wrede's work, repudiated. The quest for Jesus would make no real progress until it changed course drastically and followed Johannes Weiss and Schweitzer in taking up and developing the essential core of truth in Reimarus's position. Schweitzer's thesis dictated not only the limits and title of his book, but also to some extent his selection and treatment of material. Here lies the explanation of the 'one-sidedness' which J. M. Robinson, not altogether unjustly, finds in the book.[25]

It is of great importance to understand the essentials of the debate between Schweitzer and Wrede, because virtually all the theories put forward in this century have been reactions of one sort or another to it.

Wrede's denial of any messianic consciousness or claims on the part of Jesus was naturally not very popular with the orthodox and has led to long-drawn-out discussions; so far these have proved quite inconclusive, and from an historical point of view the only possible verdict is 'non-proven', one way or the other. Whether or not the problem is ever solved with anything approaching finality, it is now generally agreed that Johannes Weiss and Schweitzer were right in emphasizing the importance of eschatology both for Jesus and the early church.

Two questions, however, have been raised: how much importance? and what sort of eschatology? Schweitzer's view is generally described in German as *konsequent-eschatologisch*, an untranslatable expression which means that according to Schweitzer, Jesus' outlook and activity were so largely shaped by his expectation of an imminent *parousia*, and of the part he was destined to play in connexion with it, that no other aspect of his ministry can be properly understood except in relation to that. In one sense, therefore, Harnack was justified in saying that on this view 'the eschatological element dominated the purely religious and moral content'. It is a misleading way of putting the matter, however, because Schweitzer had no intention whatever of playing down the religious and moral sides of the matter, but only of emphasizing that they were 'contextualized' by Jesus' eschatological expectations, and can only be appreciated at their true value in relation to that context.

Schweitzer himself pointed out that 'an important test of the adequacy of any account of Jesus is the degree to which the development of early Christian thought becomes intelligible in the light of it'. The test is one which can readily be applied to his own account of Christianity because he wrote two important books in addition to his work on the gospels – *Paul and his Interpreters* and *The Mysticism of Paul the Apostle* – in which he sought to explain the development of later New Testament thought in the light of his account of Jesus. In 1941, in a book which won Schweitzer's approval, Martin Werner of Bern sought to show how the whole development of Christian doctrine in the first four or five centuries can be made more intelligible on the basis of Schweitzer's account of Christian origins.[26] The thesis that early Christian faith and doctrine were profoundly affected by the ever-increasing delay in the appearance of the expected *parousia* deserves far more attention than it has generally received, despite the views of J. A. T. Robinson and others; Fritz Buri's words are almost as true today as they were when they were first written in 1935:

> When all is said and done, the thesis put forward for discussion by Albert Schweitzer years ago concerning the delay of the *parousia* and the process of de-eschatologization it made necessary, has provoked remarkably little reaction – I might almost say uncannily little reaction – from subsequent theology.[27]

To many scholars, Schweitzer's eschatological interpretation of Jesus seems to involve an underestimation of other independent concerns which, they think, also weighed heavily with Jesus. Their arguments are often linked with the contention that when Jesus took over the eschatological terms with which he worked – Son of Man, Kingdom of God and the like – he radically and creatively reinterpreted them. In particular, according to the theory of 'realized eschatology',[28] Jesus' message was, not that the kingdom of God was near, but that with and in his ministry it had already broken in. If so, the point would be of far-reaching significance; for if Jesus could regard the relatively normal conditions of his earthly lifetime as constituting even a partial presence of the kingdom, then his understanding of eschatology was indeed widely different from any of those current in contemporary Judaism; and the importance of such apocalyptic expectations as he may have retained will have been very greatly reduced.

In the·course of his criticism of various nineteenth-century theories, Schweitzer had much to say which is pertinent also to these more modern arguments. Since our sources contain no hint of Jesus' having explicitly redefined the eschatological terms he used, the assumption must be that he expected and meant them to be understood in the sense generally attached to them at the time. Any contention to the contrary must bear the full *onus probandi*, and in the absence of incontrovertible evidence, is probably to be ascribed largely to the natural desire for a Jesus less culturally conditioned, and more immediately acceptable by modern standards, than the figure who emerges from the most natural interpretation of the data. Moreover, if the realized eschatology theory were correct, we should have to suppose that Jesus was grossly and disastrously misunderstood by his earliest followers, including Paul; the postulation of such an initial 'Fall' on the part of New Testament Christians is as unacceptable in this context as it was in the positions of Harnack and Wernle, in connection with which Schweitzer strongly criticized it. He agreed with Kalthoff that to presuppose 'an immediate declension from, and falsification of, a pure original principle . . . is deserting the recognized methods of historical science'.

For these and other more technical reasons, realized eschatology is now generally, and rightly, recognized to have been a blind alley. So far as the gospels enable us to judge, Schweitzer was right in his contention that Jesus expected the more or less immediate future to bring the kingdom of God in roughly the form in which it was pictured in contemporary expectations. He is not likely to have reinterpreted the eschatological terms he used, at any rate on anything approaching the scale often claimed by the modern scholars just referred to.

Before discussing the implications of that, we must notice one aspect of Schweitzer's work which has not found general acceptance, namely his detailed reconstruction of the development of Jesus' outlook and expectations. This, it is generally agreed, goes far beyond the evidence, and it is ironic that the very scholar who repeatedly pricked the bubble of the allegedly 'assured results' claimed by his predecessors, and whose survey showed the impossibility of writing a life of Jesus or tracing his 'development', should have thought himself able to trace that development in some detail; and should have claimed that the view he championed rested on a 'scientifically unassailable basis' (p. 240).

His thesis was, as we have seen, that,

> The progressive recognition of the eschatological character of the teaching and action of Jesus carries with it a progressive justification of the Gospel tradition . . . thoroughgoing eschatology . . . is able to accept and explain as historical on the whole everything which is contained in the two earliest Gospels about Jesus' activity.

This rested on at least two serious misjudgments: Wrede had much stronger grounds than Schweitzer appreciated for his contention that even the earliest evangelists – and indeed the pre-gospel tradition – were as much interested in theological interpretation as in accurate chronicling, and that neither their material nor their purpose was conducive to the sort of circumstantial and chronologically-arranged narrative Schweitzer's reconstruction would require. The work of subsequent scholars, especially that of various form-critics, has vindicated Wrede, and it must be admitted that over this matter Schweitzer had something of a blind spot. He repeatedly poses the false dilemma: either the earliest gospels were essentially dogmatic treatises, which just happened to be cast in an ostensibly historical form, or they 'could be accepted *en bloc*'.[29] It is noteworthy that one of the few nineteenth-century scholars to whom Schweitzer failed to do justice in his book is Ferdinand Christian Bauer of Tübingen, who emphasized precisely the element of *Tendenz* in the New Testament writings and justly criticized Strauss for his failure to allow sufficiently for it. Schweitzer in his turn failed to appreciate the justice of this criticism of Strauss.

Secondly, if form-criticism was to underline Schweitzer's failure to appreciate the extent to which interpretative and edificatory motifs moulded the development of the gospel tradition, synoptic criticism has done little to support his view about the individual gospels. He sharply distinguished Matthew and Mark from the other two and assigned to them both an origin in Palestine about AD 70. They rest, he claimed, on a common source, which is more accurately reproduced now by the one and now by the other. This source, 'as well as the special material of Matthew, go back to men who were present during the ministry of Jesus. They have . . . a clear conception of the order of events and give a reliable report of the speeches of Jesus'.[30] The very different outlook of subsequent scholarship is shown by the fact that even the extremely modest claims made by C. H. Dodd for a historical basis to *some* of the Marcan framework has received relatively little support (cp. p. 6ff. above).

It is true that many modern scholars date Luke later than used to be customary, and see in it a consistent attempt to 'de-eschatologize' the tradition; and that the priority of Mark has recently been called in question once again; but even if these views were eventually to be generally accepted, neither of them would do anything to justify the implicit and detailed trust in the contents of both Matthew and Mark which Schweitzer's position requires.[31] In particular Schweitzer's position is heavily dependent on the authenticity of Matthew's accounts of the sending out of the disciples (Matt. 10.5ff.) and of the visit of the disciples of John the Baptist (11.2ff.).

His misjudgments have cost Schweitzer dear. They have meant that in an important area of New Testament study – and one which has proved the chief focus of interest in the period since he wrote – his views have run directly counter to the almost universal current of opinion. As a result, the speculative and theoretical, as distinct from the strictly historical, side of his work has tended to be eclipsed and ignored.[32]

That is understandable, and up to a point justifiable; but Schweitzer is not so easily written off. It stands to his credit to have insisted on the essential importance of eschatology for the New Testament as a whole, and to have recognized, perhaps more clearly than Johannes Weiss himself, the significance of the latter's demonstration that eschatology formed the essential context of the mind and ministry of Jesus. Also, as we have seen, Schweitzer's contention that the eschatology in question was broadly that of contemporary Jewish expectations has, on the whole, withstood subsequent attempts to play up the originality of Jesus and show that eschatological ideas were radically transformed as they passed through his mind.

While it is true that a small number of distinguished scholars have doubted whether eschatology was as central to Jesus' outlook as Schweitzer and most scholars since have supposed – I think especially of H. J. Cadbury and Amos Wilder – even they would not dispute the general conclusion Schweitzer drew from his studies, that, whatever else Jesus may have been, he was essentially a figure of his time, whose thinking and teaching were carried on in first-century Jewish categories and was therefore in at least one important respect a culturally conditioned figure.

We are thus brought to the heart of the issue raised by Schweitzer's book. What Schweitzer has done is to show that when the historical method is applied to the New Testament, the result is not just to necessitate minor modifications in the picture it gives of Jesus, but to confront the timeless Christ of orthodoxy with a historical Jesus who, as such, inevitably belongs to a particular cultural and religious context and cannot belong to any other in the same immediate way that he belonged to his own. As Schweitzer himself puts it, 'Jesus of Nazareth will not suffer himself to be modernized as an historical figure. He refuses to be detached from his own time'.

There may well be mistakes in Schweitzer's (or anyone else's) analysis of the precise traits which make 'the historical Jesus a stranger and an enigma to our time' as to all future times; but about the fact itself there can be no dispute, especially in view of the later work of scholars such as Ernst Troeltsch and Max Webber. Jesus will never again 'be a Jesus Christ to whom the religion of the present can ascribe . . . its own thought and ideas. Nor will he be a figure which can be made by a popular historical treatment so sympathetic and universally intelligible to the multitude.'

Here lies one of the central problems of contemporary Christianity. If, in England especially, we have been slow to recognize or tackle it, that is perhaps because the full scope of the question has hardly been appreciated.[33] In particular it has not been sufficiently realized that the emergence of the historical question separates our period sharply from the periods which produced the classical statements of the Christian faith, so that nothing in this connexion can be settled by appeal to orthodoxy. For almost by definition, orthodox Christianity, whether the expression is used by Roman Catholics or Protestants, means an understanding of the Christian faith arrived at at a time when the Christ of faith and the Jesus of history were not even notionally distinguished, because nothing had occurred to raise any suspicion that they did not tally completely. It was a time, moreover, of such cultural stability that the notion of the 'culturally conditioned' had hardly been formulated and was certainly not seen as raising any problems in connection with Christ.[34]

What is the nature of Christianity's relation to its founder? Nothing less than that is the question with which this book confronts us.

As Schweitzer himself says in his autobiography, 'the question was . . . what the eschatological Jesus who lives expecting the end of the world and a supernatural Kingdom of God, can be to us'. Although he discusses the matter in *The Quest of the Historical Jesus*, he does so, as might be expected in a work devoted primarily to the history of critical scholarship, rather allusively; so it may be useful if attention is directed to other books in which he confronts it more directly.

Schweitzer saw clearly where the nub of the problem lay, in the fact that the Jesus of history proves to have been a culturally conditioned figure and one who was mistaken in his unquestioning conviction that the kingdom of God and the end of the world would come within a few years of the time when he was speaking. He writes:

> The ideal would be that Jesus should have preached religious truth in a form independent of any connexion with any particular period and such that it could be taken over simply and easily by each succeeding generation of men. That, however, He did not do, and there is no doubt a reason for it. We have, therefore, to reconcile ourselves to the fact that His religion of love appeared as part of a world-view which expected a speedy end of the world. Clothed in the ideas in which He announced it, we cannot make it our own; we must re-clothe it in those of our modern world-view.[35]

His solution to the problem depended on his conviction that the real subject of Jesus' teaching was love. Although the structural framework of Jesus' preaching was provided by first-century eschatology,

> the mighty thought . . . Jesus introduces into the late-Jewish, messianic expectation, without being in any way concerned to spiritualize those realistic ideas of the Kingdom (is) that we come to know God and belong to Him through love . . . His concern is, not how believers ought to picture things but that love, without which no one can belong to God, and attain to membership of the kingdom, shall be powerful within it.

Even the fact that the message comes to us in the context of an alien world-view has its advantages, for,

In our own world- and life-affirming world-view Christianity is in constant danger of being externalized. The gospel of Jesus which speaks to us out of an expectation of the end of the world leads us off the highway of busy service for the kingdom of God on to the footpath of inwardness, and urges us, in spiritual freedom from the world, to seek the true strength for working in the spirit of the Kingdom of God. The essence of Christianity is world-affirmation which has gone through a period of world negation. In the eschatological world-view of world-negation Jesus proclaims the ethic of active love!

When once the essential content of Jesus' message is thus understood we can see that,

The true understanding of Jesus is the understanding of will acting on will. The true relation to Him is to be taken possession of by Him. Christian piety of any and every sort is valuable only so far as it means the surrender of our will to His.

Schweitzer frequently insists that the Christianity of the future will not be defined by reference to any particular speculative understanding of Jesus' person and status. Just as, on Schweitzer's analysis, Jesus did not admit his contemporaries to the secret of his status as Son of David and Messiah designate, so he 'does not require of men today that they should be able to grasp either in speech or in thought Who is . . . . The one thing he does require of them is that they should actively and passively prove themselves men who have been compelled by Him to rise from being as the world to being other than the world, and thereby partakers of his peace'.[36]

It is in the light of all this that readers will grasp the full significance of the famous paragraph with which Schweitzer concluded his book in the first and all subsequent editions:

He comes to us as One unknown, without a name, as of old, by the lake-side, He came to those men who knew Him not. He speaks to us the same word: 'Follow thou me!' and sets us to the tasks which He has to fulfil for our time. He commands. And to those who obey Him, whether they be wise or simple, He will reveal Himself in the toils, the conflicts, the sufferings which they shall pass through in His fellowship, and, as an ineffable mystery, they shall learn in their own experience Who He is.[37]

Whatever the merits of such a view may be, it clearly finds little or no lasting validity in the eschatological elements of the New Testament; they are more or less written off as the outer covering which obscured, even while it preserved, the ageless kernel of the gospel of love.

So far as Schweitzer's view is of this 'kernel and husk' variety, it seems to fall short of his own demand as expressed in the following words:

> In fact it is not a matter of separating the transitory from the permanent elements, but only of translating the basic thinking of that world-view into our own terms. How can the will of Jesus, in its immediacy and precise orientation, and grasped in its entirety, attain complete expression in the thought-forms available in our own age, and there create a world-view of such a moral and powerful kind that it holds the same place today as it did in late-Jewish metaphysics and eschatology?

It has been the attempt of Bultmann and his school to solve precisely that problem, and in the process Schweitzer's de-eschatologization has become de-mythologization. Working with the postulate of what Hans Jonas called 'an unchangeable fundamental structure of the human spirit as such'[38] – incidentally a highly dubious postulate – thinkers of this school maintained that in the eschatological 'mythology' of Jesus and his early followers there was expressed a self-understanding which is still a live option for twentieth-century man, if only it is de-mythologized, that is, understood and expressed in a form which is all of a piece with the rest of our understanding of ourselves and our existence.

On this view, the eschatology of the New Testament, so far from being expendable, is the very core of the Christian gospel. In the light of Wrede's work and the form-critical method, these scholars regard it as impossible to determine how much of New Testament eschatology is attributable to the historical Jesus; but that is not important, because the figure which matters is not the Jesus of history but the Christ proclaimed by the early church. To be a Christian is to be challenged and freed by the Christ of faith to live eschatologically, that is, to live no longer on the basis of the world's wisdom and resources ('the flesh') but out of God's resources, a process which emphatically brings to an end the little worlds each of us constructs to further his own immanent purpose.[39]

This is not the place to discuss the merits of Bultmann's or any other, solution of the problem. In fact not many other solutions could be found to discuss. In England especially, theological attention has been directed not so much towards the solution of the problem Schweitzer raises as to the attempt to show that, if a more 'moderate' and 'less one-sided' critical approach is employed, the problem does not arise, at any rate in the radical form in which Schweitzer posed it. Christ, we are told, is not after all a complete 'stranger and enigma to our time'. The reader must decide for himself – preferably on the basis of familiarity with Schweitzer's *full* text – to what extent such a response is well-founded or how far it is a further essay in 'mediating theology' in the bad sense. Anyone who attempts to arrive at such a decision should bear in mind Schweitzer's important insistence, already referred to, that an account of Jesus is only really plausible if it makes readily intelligible his followers' understanding of him as witnessed in the pages of the New Testament, and the subsequent development of Christian doctrine. A fair judgment will therefore demand a knowledge, not only of *The Quest of the Historical Jesus* but of Schweitzer's work on the early church and of the discussions by Werner and others of the formation of Christian dogma.

The importance of the matter can hardly be exaggerated. Whatever may be thought of Schweitzer's solution to the problem, or even of his way of posing it, we should at least be grateful to him for having faced us squarely and clearly with the question which is now with us for good. What must be our relation to our founder now that our knowledge of him as he was in the days of his flesh is derived not only from a static traditional picture but from the researches of historians? The results of such researches, we now know, must always be tentative and are bound in some measure to change from age to age; and the figure they reveal, to the extent that it belonged to a cultural and religious situation very different from our own, will always be, 'a stranger and an enigma to our time', whatever that time may be.

9

A Partner for Cinderella?

In his inaugural lecture at Durham[1] Professor Evans made the important point that Christian theology is not a discipline which can profitably be carried on by itself in isolation from other disciplines. To use his own analogy, 'theology . . . is always driven to look for a partner before she can dance to full effect'.[2] Doing theology, like dancing, is an activity for which the co-operation of at least one other person is needed. After dancing with philosophy more or less continuously for many hundreds of years, theology took on a new partner at the time when the critical study of the Bible arose, and has danced pretty consistently since then with history. The lecture suggested reasons for thinking that the time has now come when 'the historical method no longer suffices, and the theologian has to look around for assistance from another quarter',[3] but it left open the question who the new partner, or partners, should be. It did make the point, however, that the character and preoccupations of philosophy have changed radically since the days when theology used to dance with him; and that, at any rate as he exists in England, almost entirely preoccupied with linguistic and logical analysis, he is so earthbound, and his interests are so humdrum, that a return to an exclusive partnership with him would not be a good idea, even if he were willing.[4] Where then may other partners be found?

This essay is intended to advance a tentative plea for sociology, and more specifically for the sociology of knowledge, as a possible candidate. Perhaps if theology were to seek a partnership in that quarter, she might discover that there are new steps, and even whole new dances, to be learned of which she has previously known nothing; and she might also get an introduction to other partners with whom it would be well worthwhile to take the floor.

We must now drop the metaphor and even at the risk of some over-simplification[5] give a brief account of the present position with regard to theological method and how it came to be what it is. No one will dispute that the theological enterprise of the Christian church, as traditionally carried on, has taken as its basic datum the Bible, or rather the events and teaching reported and interpreted in the Bible. As it stands, this material displays a bewildering variety and lack of organization; but the theologians of the early Christian centuries, including some writers whose works are included in the canon, are generally credited with having discovered a way of interpreting it which revealed an underlying unity, in the light of which it could be reduced to systematic form.

The work of systematization was carried out not only by individuals – usually in the course of some controversy – but by councils and synods; and the creeds and definitions resulting from their work have usually been seen, if not as embodying *the* meaning of the Bible, at any rate as defining its meaning so far as the areas they cover are concerned. In practice, the construction of a Christian system on the basis of the Bible was the result of bringing to bear on the biblical material questions, categories and insights derived from a widespread but fairly specific single philosophical position.[6] The period, however, was one of relative cultural stability and also relative cultural homogeneity. In the Western world to which Christianity spread, no philosophical tradition, or at any rate no philosophical tradition serviceable to a theist, was available except the one actually employed. Consequently the Christian system as it emerged came to be regarded as a constant quantum of truth and also as embodying the only possible reasonable interpretation of the Bible.

A coherent system is easier to handle than a mass of heterogeneous material, and for this reason if no other, a tendency naturally arose to treat the system, rather than the Bible itself, as the basis for further theological activity; or at any rate to use the Bible only as filtered through the system. To make such a statement is not for a moment to ignore the fact that the system itself has consistently been subject to revision in the light of the Bible. The reformation alone suffices to prevent our ignoring that; and in fact a critique of the creeds on the basis of the biblical material has almost always been the ostensible – and very often the real – origin of other denominational and confessional divisions, and of differences of opinion within the denominations.

Eyebrows may therefore be raised, especially in Protestant circles, at our suggestion that it is very largely the creed, as understood in his denomination, which has effectively guided the thinking of almost every Christian theologian and exegete. A little reflection, however, will show what a large amount of truth this statement contains. For since the doctrines of the Trinity, the incarnation and the rest, once they had been formulated, were thought to enshrine *the* meaning of the Bible, they inevitably provided both a framework of reference and also an ultimate criterion for all subsequent exegesis and theological investigation. Anyone, for example, working on a New Testament passage which referred to 'the Son' or 'the Spirit' now started from the conviction that the reference was to the Second or the Third Person of the Trinity as defined in the creeds and conciliar definitions. Thus, for example, John 14.28b ('the Father is greater than I') and John 7.39 ('as yet there was no spirit') now became *cruces interpretum* because they seemed *prima facie* to conflict with the Nicene and Chalcedonian doctrine. The orthodox doctrine of the Trinity indicated the area in which the correct interpretation of any such biblical text must lie, whatever the interpretation eventually turned out to be.

Examples could equally easily be cited in connexion with other doctrines, so we may say that the work of the Fathers, based as it was on a partnership with the philosophy of the period, controlled subsequent exegesis in at least two ways. It controlled its general character because exegesis came to be understood essentially as the translation of biblical statements into the categories of the dominant philosophical tradition;[7] and secondly, as our examples have shown, it often went a long way towards defining the exegete's detailed conclusions.

In principle what has been said about the creeds of the 'undivided' church could be said about the detailed contents of the formularies of each denomination. In the Roman tradition, for example, the doctrine of the perpetual virginity of Mary has defined exegesis of gospel passages about 'the brethen of the Lord' which are *prima facie* incompatible with it. For the purposes of our argument, however, it will suffice to confine ourselves to the contents of the classical formularies accepted by the great majority of Christian groups – the doctrines of creation and of the Trinity and the incarnation, the need for atonement, the divine foundation of the church and of the two main sacraments within it, and so on. In order to recognize how largely these have dominated subsequent theological thinking, even about the Bible, we have only to remind ourselves how far individual theologians have been from even the remotest suspicion that any work they might do on the Bible could conceivably call in question any fundamental doctrines of the creed.

In view of its character as a supposedly constant quantum of truth, we may perhaps symbolize the doctrinal system of the church as Q. If we then symbolize the Bible as B, we may represent what has been said so far, in diagrammatic form, somewhat as follows:

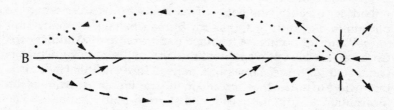

B originally gave rise to Q in co-operation with various philosophical influences ( ) and continues to exercise at least a negative critique of it ( ); but once Q has been established, it exercises its own retro-active influence on the interpretation, and thus the meaning, of B ( ). It also stands in a reciprocal relationship to each culture in which it exists, exerting pressure on its surroundings through the work of its evangelists and other Christian spokesmen, but at the same time having its meaning significantly, if subtly, altered as a result of pressures from the environment, pressures which at the time were seldom recognized, still less exerted consciously.

If that is agreed, we may broadly differentiate the theological activities which have been proceeding on the basis of Q into two types. There is first what might be called 'theoretical theology', theological activity which takes Q, or some element of it, as an unquestioned datum and treats it rather as a physicist treats his experimental data, seeking to explain how it works and to understand what we might almost call the 'mechanics' of it – usually, as in the case of the physicist, with a view to taking more effective advantage of it. This is theology in its character of *fides quaerens intellectum*, and Anselm's *Cur Deus-Homo* is a typical example of it. Anselm accepts the traditional doctrine of the incarnation of the Second Person of the Trinity (not, be it noted, the Johannine doctrine of the *logos sarx genomenos*) as an unquestioned truth and seeks to discover how the incarnation worked, by what means it produced the desired result, why just that phenomenon, a God-man,[8] was necessary for the achievement of salvation. A little reflection will show how much traditional Christian theology has been of that type.

The other main type of Christian theologizing may be described as 'practical theology'. This seeks to discover what implications the truth of Q has for human behaviour, both individual and corporate. A characteristic example would be the Christian socialist movement of the turn of the century, which is connected with the names of Charles Gore and his circle. It is instructive to notice that here again the traditional[9] doctrine of the incarnation was the unquestioned starting-point and basis. The constantly repeated thesis of this group was that God cannot be thought hostile or indifferent to material things and conditions because when men's salvation demanded it, he was willing to enter personally into the material world and immerse himself fully in it. God became man and in his human form busied himself about the physical, as well as the spiritual, needs of his fellow men. Any attitude which treats the material world or men's material needs with indifference or distaste is thus totally inconsistent with Q. The very nerve of the argument is the doctrine of the incarnation of the godhead *as defined in Q*; yet the historical-critical method makes it difficult to find the doctrine in anything like that form in any New Testament passage, that is, in B. The incarnation of Yahweh would have been an unthinkable thought for any Jew and it is doubtful, to say the least, if any New Testament writer was sufficiently removed from Jewish categories of thought to have been able to entertain it. The appearance of the Messiah, or even of the *logos* of God, belonged to a very different universe of discourse from any involved in patristic theology.

If the steps to which theology has been accustomed are of that sort, a very short period dancing with the sociology of knowledge is likely to convince her that she must learn to cut some new capers. For almost the first advice her new partner will whisper in her ear is that if she wishes to dance with him, she must learn to contextualize any statement on any subject whatsoever with the question: 'Says who?'[10] He will explain that the meaning of any set of words is relative to the historical situation and cultural context of the person who speaks or writes them. Thus any interpretation or exposition must always be in terms of some specific set of presuppositions. To give a ludicrously crude example of the general principle, the word 'fire' will produce one understanding and response when shouted by an usherette in a crowded cinema, and quite another when shouted by an officer in charge of a firing-squad. Since almost all our presuppositions are so widely different from those of the people who laid down the main lines of Q,[11] any response their words evoke from us is likely to be quite appreciably different from the response they were originally intended to evoke. Phrases and images appropriate for expressing the meaning of the Bible in their cultural situations will be likely, to say the least, to convey a very different meaning in a situation divided from theirs by as wide a gulf as ours is. Consequently we cannot expect to be able to take over Q as the meaning of the Bible for us. If we are to express what the Bible means for us it will have to be in our own terms. In order to appreciate how different those are likely to be from the terms of Q, we have only to indulge for a moment in the fancy that immediately after its completion, the sole text of the Bible was lost until its discovery in a cave near the Dead Sea some few years ago. In that case, however deeply impressed modern readers might have been by the newly discovered text and however much they might have pondered over it, they would never have constructed on the basis of it anything like those essentially late-Hellenistic constructions, the doctrines of the Trinity and the incarnation.

So we may repeat: what the Bible means for us must be expressed in our own way. If that seems a truism which has been recognized for a considerable time, it may be suggested that the problems involved have for the most part been sensed rather than carefully analysed, and the recognition of them has led to a rather hasty 'back to the Bible' movement on the part of many scholars. The aim – seldom clearly articulated – has been to bypass Q as far as possible and bring about a direct, and it is hoped creative, confrontation between the Bible and the modern world, as if for the first time.[12] Consciously or unconsciously, for example, some such intention seems to lie behind Bultmann's programme for demythologizing the Bible, where the idea is to confront the New Testament *kerygma* directly with the categories of Heideggerian existentialism.

Whether it is along Bultmann's lines or those of older liberal scholars that such an approach is made, one of the first results of it is to bring about the existence of two contemporary versions of Christianity. There is first the Christianity of the scholars, purportedly arrived at by the direct confrontation of the Bible with modern ideas,[13] and then there is the Christianity of more traditional clergy and laity who seek either to preserve Q, even if in a somewhat modified form, or at least to allow full weight to it in the formulation of a contemporary faith. If the present theological outlook is symbolized by the letter P, the two approaches might be represented as follows:

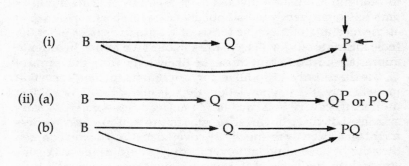

In both its forms (ii) seeks, in the language of the studbook, to produce P out of B by Q.

There is, however, a further difficulty about (i): it writes off the contents of Q altogether too precipitately. Although the contents of Q are not what *we* should have produced on the basis of B, and we may even on occasions have doubts whether they were primarily derived from B at all, they may still contain, couched in their own terms, truths which are deeply significant for us. For in many cases they were their authors' way of dealing with what are still real problems. If, as Leonard Hodgson used to insist, the Bible should always be approached with the question: What must the truth be now if people who thought as they did put it like that? there seems no reason to suppose that the posing of the same question with regard to Q would be any less fruitful, or at any rate that it would be entirely fruitless. Certainly failure to ask it will in practice doom any proposed solution of our problem. For some of the contents of Q have become so much part of the Christian consciousness, and are, quite justifiably, so deeply prized by most Christians, that any position which simply writes them off will prove unacceptable. The more enlightened among contemporary Christians may well be prepared to have Q confronted with some such question as Hodgson's in the sort of way that C. C. Richardson, Norman Pittenger, or, more radically, Erich Fromm, have confronted it;[14] they are not prepared to see it simply ignored. Indeed even to suggest the ignoring of it is to betray a basic failure to understand how things work either sociologically or psychologically; it is a symptom of the excessive individualism and the failure to apprehend the community dimension of the Christian religion which characterize much existentialist theology – another indication, incidentally, that the time is ripe for theology to dance with sociology. Whatever else it is, the communion of saints is an important sociological reality.[15]

When the sociology of knowledge has provoked such reflections as these, it will by no means have finished; indeed in a sense it will barely have begun. For it will want to question not only whether Q, as traditionally formulated, can constitute the meaning of the Bible for our generation, but whether for us *any* form of words could constitute *the* meaning of the Bible. It will in fact want to raise the whole question whether it any longer makes sense for us to talk of 'the meaning' or 'the message' of the Bible as something which can be formulated in set terms and used as an authoritative touchstone of what Christians are, and are not, committed to believing.

The argument is likely to go something like this. Sociology will insist that if every statement is to be submitted to the question 'Says who?', that must apply to the statements of the Bible, even the most central of them. Sooner or later, perhaps in relation to one of those luminous biblical passages Gadamer calls 'immanent texts',[16] theology will naturally want to reply 'Says God'. The sociologist, if he knows his business, will not dream of denying the propriety of such an answer in principle; but he will want to point out that the statement is one which needs very careful handling if the logic of it is not to be open to grave objections. He will point out that even insights derived from God must be conceived in the terms and categories of some particular culture if they are to find any recipients who can entertain them and so make them available to subsequent generations. The inspired status of B, if such it has, does not therefore exempt it from any of the relativist problems which arise in connexion with Q.

So far as the biblical insights are concerned, they were conceived – or received – and expressed in the cultural terms of a single, evolving but recognizably continuous, religious tradition, the Judaeo-Christian tradition. It was characteristic of the Jews and the early Christians that they normally gave expression to the supernatural dimension of human affairs by incorporating the history of human life into a story – a story of God's actions upon, and interventions in, the world from creation day to doomsday. 'Story' is the word a twentieth-century Westerner is more or less bound to use in this connection because the account of the past in the Bible, while it contains a fair amount of more or less accurate history, also contains many narratives – and those some of the most important – which from our point of view are wholly or partly mythical. The biblical writers have in places clearly allowed the demands of the story to modify the history; and they seldom give much sign of being aware that the mythical elements in their story, for example, the creation, the 'fall' of Adam and Eve, or the bodily ascension of Christ, were any less factual than the genuinely historical elements.

Modern readers cannot make such a mixture of myth and more or less accurate history their own in the way the original writers did. As Canon Bezzant put it, the story 'has been so shattered that the bare recital of it has the aspect of . . . travesty'. He added:

> Known facts of astronomy, geology, biological evolution, anthropology, the comparative study of religions, race and genetical and analytic psychology, the literary and historical criticism of the Bible, with the teaching of Jesus and the moral conscience of mankind, have banished this scheme beyond the range of credibility.[17]

The difficulty which the biblical story presents to a modern reader, it will be noted, does not arise simply from its character as story. It may well be that any account of the ultimate significance – or even of the ultimate insignificance – of life must take the form of a story of some sort. The Marxists have their story and the humanists have theirs; there can be no objection to the modern Christian having his story too. The point is that it must be *his* story, doing full justice to all the types of knowledge about the present and the past to which Canon Bezzant refers.

It must also be emphasized that to say we cannot make the biblical story our own as it stands is not for a moment to deny that we can learn a great deal from it. Indeed no one would be likely to call himself a Christian unless he believed that the biblical story has almost inexhaustible truth to disclose. The question with which sociology confronts theology is precisely the question how the biblical story is to be used in helping us to see what the modern Christian story must be; and it is in this context that we can often get light from the use our Christian predecessors have made of the Bible in constructing their various stories, even though they were usually unaware that their story and the biblical story were not identical.[18]

There seem to be at least two ways in which the biblical story cannot be used by the modern Christian. He must not attempt to exempt certain passages of the biblical story from their status as parts of the story, absolutize them as if they were timelessly valid and culturally unconditioned, and then seek to weave them together as they stand in the hope that *that* will produce the modern Christian story. Biblical passages simply cannot be treated in that way. For example, the New Testament claim that 'Jesus is the Christ' got its very meaning from its context in the biblical story as a whole.[19] If such a formula is taken over direct as part of the modern Christian story, it will inevitably take on new meaning and then questions will arise what that meaning is and whether the formula is the best way of expressing it.

Secondly, once the character of the biblical writings as basically story is recognized, it will be seen to follow that there can be no question of extracting '*the* meaning' of it in any exclusive sense. For if there is one thing on which all modern literary critics and students of comparative mythology are agreed, it is the impropriety of attempting to extract from a myth or drama or story something which can be stated in alternative words and claimed as 'the meaning' of it. What modern literary critics and students of mythology seek to do through their studies is not to isolate '*the* meaning' of what they are studying but to leave it more meaningful than it was before they went to work. Biblical exegetes will have to learn to do the same. Working against successive cultural backgrounds, they can be relied on to discover ever new depths of meaning in the text. This will be of inestimable help to the dogmatic theologian, but it remains true that the task of discovering the appropriate story in which to body forth the relations of God and the world for the contemporary world will always remain a creative and subjective, or inter-subjective, one requiring radical trust in the guidance of God. However excellent and profound the work of biblical exegetes, the task will never become one of stating or drawing out *the* meaning of the text.

If anyone feels inclined to object that such a conclusion would rob the Christian faith of the future of any generally agreed content, let him consider the strength of many a literary critical consensus and how it is achieved. A recent writer on modern biblical study writes as follows:

> Isn't the real situation much more like that of literary criticism? The critic looks more closely at a text than others have done, brings new ideas to bear from a wider experience, and points out what the rest of us have overlooked. But in the end our agreement is necessary. As Dr Leavis once pointed out, the characteristic critical judgment takes the form 'This is so – isn't it?' Where something authentic has been said, the rest of us eventually answer 'Yes, of course'.[20]

One is reminded of Leonard Hodgson's often repeated claim that the characteristic theological judgment should be of the form 'This is how I see it; can you not see it like that too?' Certainly it looks as if dogmatic judgments in the future will have to take some such form and abandon any claim to demonstrative status.

10

New Testament Interpretation in an Historical Age[1]

Just over a dozen years ago I prefaced the Introduction to a commentary on St Mark's Gospel with the question 'Why should a Gospel be supposed to need a commentary?'[2] As the succeeding paragraphs made clear, my question reflected a problem with which I had wrestled in the course of writing the book, and with which I imagine every New Testament commentator has to wrestle, namely the question: What is an interpreter of the New Testament – or for that matter any biblical critic or scholar – seeking to do? So far as he aims to go beyond the satisfaction of simple antiquarian curiosity and bring his readers contemporary enlightenment of some sort, how should he conceive and set about his task?

At first sight, the question itself may seem an odd one. It may seem obvious what the commentator's task is, namely to make clear to his readers the meaning of his text, or at any rate to supply the background information in the light of which they can discover it for themselves. But here as so often, the occurrence of the word 'meaning', particularly when it is preceded by the definite article, is a warning-signal of the presence of confusion. What is meant by 'the meaning' of a text in this sort of connexion?

Let us begin our answer by taking the example of a scholar setting out to comment on the sacred book of some ancient religion which has long since ceased to have any adherents. How will he set about his task? No doubt he will provide a modern translation of the original and add notes where they are necessary in order to make clear the precise flavour and connotations of words or phrases more fully than the translation could do by itself. Then he will describe historical events alluded to or presupposed in the text, and he will also describe the habits, institutions, presuppositions and mental preoccupations of the adherents of the religion, so that his readers may not only understand the historical allusions but, more important, get some idea of how the various beliefs, ritual practices and ways of behaving referred to in the text seemed to the original writer and readers to hold together as a single coherent religious system. To use Collingwood's language, our commentator will seek to help his readers to think the thoughts of the religion's adherents after them, to enter imaginatively, so far as may now be possible, into what it would have been like to adopt the approach to gods, men and the rest of the environment, described or demanded in the text. When he has done that to the best of his ability, when he has shown what the text meant to its writer and original readers, he will feel that he has fully discharged his task of explaining 'the meaning'.

Much the same thing will be expected of the New Testament commentator, but in his case, at any rate if he is a Christian, there will be a further demand. It will be assumed not only that the text had a meaning for its original readers but that, in a measure at least, that meaning is still capable of being appropriated today. The presumption will be that when the stance towards God and the world suggested in the text has been properly interpreted, it will prove capable of adoption in whole or part by modern readers, even if some modifications are required in the process. The New Testament commentator is expected to make clear where and in what sense the text is still applicable, and what modifications, if any, are necessary.

He is thus set a twofold task. My point is neatly illustrated for me by a well-known modern American commentary on the Bible in twelve volumes known as *The Interpreter's Bible*.[3] This work, which covers the entire text of the Bible, has the same format throughout. At the top of each page is a modern translation of a portion of the text and this is followed by notes from a biblical scholar designed to make clear what it meant, in the sort of way just described. A black line is then printed across the page and in the space below it another expositor seeks to make clear how the meaning of the passage as expounded by the biblical critic may be appropriated by modern Christians. A number of those who have reviewed the series have expressed doubts about the wisdom of dividing the work between two sets of scholars, but none, so far as I know, has doubted the propriety of the enterprise as such.

Yet it is, I believe, this twofold nature of his task which gives rise to many of the problems with which the modern commentator wrestles. Scholars often have an uneasy feeling that the two parts of the task are not readily combined, or even that they are downright incompatible. What I should like to do is to examine this suspicion, and investigate whether it has any basis, and if so, what should be done about it. The best approach, I think, may be a genetic one. I shall ask how each of the two tasks, or parts of the task, has come to be regarded as part of what a biblical commentator is expected to do.

So far as the first part of the task is concerned, there is in one sense nothing essentially novel about it. In 1773, for example, Dr Johnson observed that 'all works which describe manners, require notes in sixty or seventy years, or less'.[4] Nevertheless I want to maintain that in the form in which it imposes itself upon the commentator today, there is an important element of novelty in it and that this arises, as I implied by my title, because he is doing his work in an historical age.

To clarify that I must explain what I mean by describing ours as an historical age. In one sense of course every age since the emergence of *homo sapiens* has been an historical age; every age occupies some period of history. It is also true that men of every age must be, and are, concerned about what happened in the ages preceding their own; but by calling our age an historical age I do not mean to suggest that we are more concerned about the past than our predecessors were; in one sense at any rate, I am not at all sure that we are,[5] although, as we shall see, our approach to the past is more sophisticated and more accurate.

What I have in mind is more like what Germans often have in mind when they use the word *Historismus*. It is like what I think Nietzsche meant when he said that in the nineteenth century mankind developed, or recognized, a sixth sense, the historical sense; or what R. G. Collingwood meant when he wrote that 'The really new element in the thought of today as compared with that of three centuries ago is the rise of history'.[6]

What is chiefly in mind here is that modern man is aware in a way that his predecessors have not been of the historically conditioned character of all human experience, speech and institutions. We are acutely aware that human life as lived in history is always life lived in the context of some particular cultural grouping. For every individual, no matter how original, what it means and feels like to be a human being and live a human life is to a large extent controlled by the presiding ideas of the cultural community to which it is his destiny to belong.

We see the full significance of that when we recognize that each cultural grouping is the embodiment of a peculiar set of presiding ideas – what is sometimes called the Law of its culture – and as a result has its own distinctive attitude to everything in heaven and earth. A further point is also important in this connexion. Although in fact cultures vary very considerably in the character of their sensibility and of their presiding ideas, the members of a cultural community are – or at any rate have been until recently – almost entirely unaware of the contingent character of the cultural Law which moulds their outlook and all their institutions. To them the absolute validity of these ideas seems as much part of the givenness of things as the proximity of the nearby mountains or the periodic flooding of the local river.

T. E. Hulme put the point like this:

> There are certain doctrines which for a particular period seem not doctrines, but inevitable categories of the human mind. Men do not look on them merely as correct opinion, for they have become so much part of the mind, and lie so far back, that they are never really conscious of them at all. They do not see them, but other things *through* them. It is these abstract ideas at the centre, the things which they take for granted, that characterize a period. There are in each period certain doctrines, a denial of which is looked on by the men of that period just as we might look on the assertion that two and two make five. It is these abstract things at the centre, these *doctrines* felt as *facts*, which are the source of all the other material characteristics of a period. . . . In order to understand a period it is necessary not so much to be acquainted with its more defined opinions as with the doctrines which are thought of not as doctrine but as FACTS.[7]

These doctrines felt as facts lie *so* far back that not only do they pass unrecognized by those who hold them, they underlie and colour every element in a culture – its language, its science, its morals and politics, its rituals and religious beliefs, in fact its

entire way of understanding, and attempting to cope with, reality. It follows that to members of a cultural community the various elements in their culture appear to hang together as interde-
pendent parts of a coherent system; no one element makes full
sense, or can be fully understood, except in the context of all the
other elements. As Ernst Troeltsch put it, every culture is in a real
sense a totality, *eine Totalität.*[8]

When one or more of the doctrines felt as facts by a particular
community come to be called in question – and the reasons why
this happens are by no means fully understood as yet – the
connections, associations and implications which before seemed
to bind the various elements of a totality together with a certain
inevitability, become problematic. Gradually a new culture
grows up, based on different presiding ideas; and those who look
at the old culture from the standpoint of the new one find themselves asking why their predecessors believed and acted as they
did, and how they succeeded in thinking of their total outlook as
coherent; for they themselves can no longer make sense of reality
or unify it in the same ways. To borrow two comparatively trivial
examples from Professor Butterfield, we nowadays have difficulty in understanding why it seemed self-evident to everyone
for centuries that the heavenly bodies must be made of materials
totally different from any familiar to us on earth or how the most
acute medieval thinkers found it consistent with their idea of
justice to deny that the clergy could ever be amenable to the
ordinary law of the land just like everyone else.[9]

As we shall see, attention to questions of this sort can be
rewarding and enlightening, but those who ask them are subject
to a standing temptation, and yielding to it is the supreme treason
in this field. The temptation is to answer the questions, not in
terms of the cultural assumptions of the original community
but in terms of the questioner's own assumptions. Warning
examples are the grievous misunderstanding of eighteenth-
century politics by nineteenth-century historians who, as Butterfield puts it, 'knew no better than to read the activities of 1760
in the light of the politics of 1860'; or the writings of the
theologians who, according to Father Nicholas Lash, 'regularly
misinterpreted the decree of the Council of Trent as a result of
reading it through post-Tridentine spectacles' and so seriously
misled the Roman Catholic church for centuries.[10]

Closely connected with this characteristic of an historical age is another. Accounts of historical events and cultures which reach us from the past are coloured by the cultural attitudes and assumptions of those from whom they emanated, and so we can never accept them at their face value. We have to treat them as a court of law treats the statements of witnesses, as raw material for its own verdict. We have to compare and contrast these accounts, to cross-examine them, making allowances for the doctrines felt as facts at the time when they originated, and so arrive at our own verdict, an account consonant with integrity in our cultural situation.

It requires no special perspicacity to see that all this poses considerable problems for a religious tradition which claims, as the Christian tradition has been accustomed to do, that the essential truth of things was revealed once for all in the context of the life, outlook and institutions of one particular cultural community. What are those who live under other cultural laws to make of that revelation? To that question some of the most perceptive theologians of our time are addressing themselves and I cannot hope to make any direct contribution to the general debate in this essay. My aim is the more modest one of asking some questions about how the New Testament scholar may best prepare himself to make his contribution.

For there can be no doubt that his work is affected. At first sight it might seem as if religious attitudes and beliefs were exempt from the cultural pressures and particularities I have been describing. God, if he exists, is unchanging, and what he has done in the past he has done; there is a certain satisfying irreformability about past actions, human or divine. The briefest reflection, however, will show that this will not do. It is agreed in all religions that we cannot speak literally about God. Where the supernatural is concerned, language can only be used non-literally or metaphorically, and the meaning a term conveys when used metaphorically is controlled by the meaning it has when used literally. If God is described as father, for example, the meaning will depend on the literal understanding of fatherhood, and that varies widely from culture to culture; for instance, the emphasis may be on the act of begetting or on the way the child is treated, once begotten. For this and allied reasons, religion is not an entirely transcultural phenomenon. Language and beliefs about God in any community are inextricably tied in with its language and beliefs about everything else. Thus Professor J. S. Dunne can state unequivocally that 'any concrete formulation of a religion . . . has to integrate it with a culture', and his book *The City of the Gods* is one of those which has gone a long way towards demonstrating the point empirically.[11]

Indeed, recent developments in religious anthropology serve to illustrate and reinforce the point. At least up till the end of the last century anthropologists commonly studied religion as a transcultural phenomenon; at any rate they took such religious phenomena as magic or witchcraft, provided a general definition of each, listed examples from a wide variety of religions and then tried to formulate a general theory of how men came to believe and engage in such practices. In this century, however, intensive fieldwork such as that of Malinowski among the Trobriand Islanders or Evans-Pritchard among the Azande has led to a marked change of attitude. It has become clear that a community's religious beliefs and practices can only properly be understood and appreciated in the context of that community's total outlook and life-situation. Religious beliefs and practices bear a specific meaning and are justified in relation to a particular religious community and its universe by discourse, and *only* in that relation. Some words of Mr Don Cupitt about religious beliefs and practices are apposite. They are, he says, 'different in different societies, and each one must be explained in terms of its own setting-in-life'. Whatever may have been the case in the past, he goes on, today 'we are more likely to hear it said that belief in God can only be accurately discussed with reference to a specific case, where what counts as God, as belief, and as the criterion of right belief have had assigned to them the definite value proper to them in a particular community. The Muslim, for example, is not talking about God in a general . . . way, but about the God-whose-prophet-is-Muhammad, the One God whose revelation of his will is embodied in Islamic religious Law. That is, by "God" the Muslim means the One who is known and served only through the study of a certain sacred book, and certain practices . . . He does *not* suppose that true belief in the one True God, Allah, is abstractable from this very detailed context. The context is essential.'[12]

So far as there is truth in all this, its implications for the interpreter of the New Testament will be obvious enough. He is bound to reflect that in virtually every respect the culture of New Testament times differed widely from any culture to which he is likely to belong in the modern West. Whatever the subject – science, morality, medicine, genetics, psychology, astronomy, demonology – the assumptions will have been almost completely different. If, therefore, it is true, as we have seen it is, that every concrete formulation of a religion must be integrated with a particular culture, then the more fully he probes the New Testament formulation of the Christian faith, the more fully he will show it to be integrated with an alien culture, and the more difficult it will be to represent it as a faith which can be integrated, in anything like its original form, with a culture *toto coelo* different such as our own. You see why he feels as he does about the two sides of his task.

It is scarcely necessary for me to add that I appreciate and sympathize fully with his predicament, because I have already explained how I have felt the full force of it myself. Nevertheless, the more I reflect on the matter, the more I am inclined to feel that the dilemma is an unreal one and the anxiety unnecessary.

In order to justify that feeling I must now turn to the second part of the New Testament interpreter's task as it is commonly understood. What are we to make of the assumption that the religion of the New Testament as uncovered by a modern New Testament critic should be, broadly at least, capable of adoption by a modern Christian as it stands?

Once again I shall adopt a genetic approach. Although it means going well beyond the bounds of any competence I can claim, I venture to suggest that this assumption is not one which derives from the nature of Christianity as such and is therefore valid in all cultural situations, but that it is a highly contingent assumption which, as it stands, derives from the particular circumstances of the Reformation.

In the Christian centuries before the Reformation the religion which originated in the New Testament events received a variety of concrete formulations as a result of being integrated with a variety of cultures. The various systems of belief and practice which resulted diverged so far from New Testament faith and practice that they would no doubt have caused a good deal of eyebrow-raising among New Testament Christians, even if they had been accepted by them as recognizably Christian. These divergences, however, were scarcely recognized by Christians of the patristic and medieval periods, and caused them little embarrassment for a number of reasons. No doubt they assumed a general congruence between their faith and practice and those of New Testament times, but then their outlook was extremely un-historical in the sense in which I am using the word historical, and they were therefore unaware of the scale of the anachronism involved in their assumption.

We must also remember that for all the Christians of these periods the Bible was supplemented by an authoritative tradition which considerably modified the picture of primitive Christianity which would have emerged from the New Testament taken by itself and studied historically.

Thirdly, their habit of interpreting the Bible in allegorical and other non-literal ways gave them wide scope for manoeuvre when it came to deciding what was, or was not, in line with New Testament Christianity.

Finally, the patristic and medieval periods were relatively homogeneous philosophically, at any rate in the sense that all thinkers adopted the *philosophia perennis* in one or another of its fairly closely related forms. As a consequence, they assumed that anything which seemed to them to follow logically from the New Testament was an inescapable logical implication of the text *sans phrase*. They were unaware that in an area as complex as this, what passes as an inescapable logical conclusion depends on the character of the particular cultural Law under which the deduction is made.

So if we leave aside a few such relatively isolated figures as the so-called Anonymous of York, we may say that in this period the relation of contemporary faith and practice to the teaching of the New Testament gave rise to no very acute problems; but the situation changes sharply at the Reformation. Whatever we may think of their reasons, the Reformers were led to deny that the Christianity in which they had been brought up was the genuine article. Since the recognized religious authorities of the age – Popes, Councils, Schoolmen – were against them in this contention, their only recourse was to appeal to the one recognized authority they believed was on their side, namely the text of scripture.

It certainly *was* on their side to the extent that when studied in its literal – or as they would have put it, grammatical or historical – sense, and independently of most of the traditions, it compelled recognition that medieval Catholicism was a very different thing from New Testament Christianity; and no doubt the Reformers were right in detecting various abuses in the church of their day. Where I want to suggest that they were wrong, from our point of view, was in supposing the medieval Christianity, or indeed the Christianity of any post-New Testament period, *ought* to be, or could be, identical with the New Testament faith. In fact the Reformers did not make quite that claim. For one thing they recognized the need for some variations as the result of historical developments, and they also retained the medieval belief that the major deductions made from the New Testament by the councils of the early centuries were inescapable corollaries and timelessly valid implications of it. It was, I imagine, this sort of thing that the Thirty-nine Articles of the Church of England had in mind when they asserted of Holy Scripture that 'whatsoever is not read therein, *nor may be proved thereby*, is not to be required of any man, that it should be believed as an article of the Faith'. Similarly, Luther shows that for him the findings of the early fathers were an integral part of the true faith when he writes in his short catechism: 'I believe that Jesus Christ, very God, born of the Father in eternity, and also very man, born of the Virgin Mary, is *my* Lord, who has redemmed *me*, a lost and damned man, and has won and delivered *me* from all sins, from death, and from the power of the devil . . .'[13] This, Luther's *pro me*, also shows, incidentally, what a travesty of his position it would be to suggest that he regarded acceptance of the tenets of the New Testament, even the most slavish, as constituting a Christian. Christian discipleship was *sola fide*, and *fides* embraced far more than that. Nevertheless, the acceptance of the entire New Testament teaching in its original meaning, so far as that could be determined, was for the Reformers the necessary condition of salvation. Just as nothing which was not read in, or proved by, scripture could be proclaimed as an article of faith, so belief in everything which *was* read in, or could be proved by, scripture was demanded of every Christian. Everyone knows of the attempts made at the Reformation to base even the *minutiae* of liturgy and church order on the precise New Testament model.

To characterize this attitude on the part of the Reformers as an error from our point of view implies no condemnation. It is easy to see in retrospect how such an attitude was natural enough in the circumstances. Theirs was still an essentially un-historical age and their outlook, for all its undoubted differences from that of New Testament times, was still close enough to it for their attitude to appear plausible. Their societies were still non-industrial, non-mechanized societies, with methods of agriculture, means of communication and an outlook on natural science not radically different from those of their predecessors; and their horizons, so far as concerns matters of astronomy and cosmology, chronology, psychology, demonology, medicine and the rest, were not all that wider than those of the biblical writers. It is wise to bear in mind in this connexion the striking observation of Dr Charles Galton Darwin, that culturally 'London in 1750 was far more like Rome in AD 100 than like either London or Rome in 1950'.[14]

By the time the thought of the Enlightenment gave rise to doubt whether the entire religion of the New Testament was compatible with a modern outlook, historical study had advanced sufficiently to be able to suggest what seemed a possible *modus vivendi*. The authority of the New Testament writers rests on their status as witnesses to Jesus. Very well, then, let it be assumed that because of their relatively primitive cultural stage – you notice the modern historical outlook beginning to appear – they were, quite unwittingly, imperfect witnesses. Let their evidence be subjected to historical cross-examination – the modern outlook again – and it would emerge that the real Jesus, the Jesus of History, as he came to be called, was reflected only distortedly in their pages and had in fact been a figure whose teaching and example could well be taken over exactly as they stood by men of the Enlightenment and subsequent periods. In this particular – and of course, attenuated – form, the Reformation principle that a faith appropriate for contemporary man was to be found just as it stood in the pages of the New Testament was the central plank in the liberal protestant platform right down to the early years of this century.

What has happened since then is that the searchlight of a much more fully developed historical method has been turned on the New Testament accounts of Jesus and as a result several things have become clear.

First, that the historical truth about him cannot be known with anything like the fullness claimed by nineteenth-century liberal scholars.

Secondly, that their supposed knowledge of him rested largely on their having yielded to the historian's arch-temptation, that of reading a story from one culture through the spectacles of another.

Thirdly, that so far as the real Jesus can be discerned, he, like the New Testament witnesses to him, belongs essentially to the culture of his time and place; there is no real reason to think that the outlook of the historical Jesus will have been such as to be any more immediately acceptable today than that of, let us say, the historical Paul.

A whole epoch of New Testament study may be said to have come to an end when Father Tyrrell realized in the early years of this century with regard to Harnack that, as he puts it, 'The Christ [he] sees looking back through nineteen centuries of Catholic darkness, is only the reflection of a Liberal Protestant face, seen at the bottom of a deep well', and Albert Schweitzer wrote at about the same time 'Jesus of Nazareth will not suffer himself to be modernized. As an historic figure he refuses to be detached from his own time . . . the historic Jesus and the Germanic spirit [i.e. the *modern* German spirit] cannot be brought together except by an act of historic violence which in the end injures both religion and history'.[15] No scholar today supposes that New Testament Christianity as it stands is a possible religion for modern Western man, or that the character, conduct and beliefs of Jesus, even if we knew far more about them than we do, could constitute as they stand the content of a modern faith.

In view of all that, it might perhaps have been expected that all attempts to find a modern faith more or less ready-made in the pages of the New Testament would have been dropped. As Schweitzer put it: Jesus 'has no answer for the question, "Tell us Thy name in our speech and for our day" ';[16] but in fact the Reformation tradition has been carried on in another form, also attenuated, but attenuated in a different way. It has been widely claimed in the last half-century or so that in one thing at least the New Testament writers were objectively right, right in a way valid for all cultural situations, namely in claiming that the career of Jesus constituted a unique divine intervention in history, that is, an intervention qualitatively different from any other intervention in the whole history of the universe whether by way of providence or grace. Indeed, acceptance of the occurrence of such an intervention in and through Jesus has been made the *articulus stantis aut cadentis ecclesiae*.

Although the claim has been more or less universal, it has been made in varied forms, the variations centring mainly on two questions: first how the career of Jesus can be *known* to have constituted such an intervention; and secondly what the intervention achieved.

With regard to the first question, theologians in the Lutheran tradition have tended to say that the New Testament events can be recognized as a unique divine intervention *sola fide*. Just as it was only through supernatural illumination, responded to in faith, that the earliest Christians recognized the truth of what they saw, so it is only by faith, usually granted through preaching, that the truth can be recognized today. It follows that the scope of historical and linguistic work on the New Testament text is strictly limited. However competently carried out, it can never by itself disclose the supernatural character of the events it studies, any more than actually seeing those events disclosed it to the faithless among the contemporaries of Jesus. It is only as a consequence of the gift of faith that a New Testament commentator will be able to recognize the true meaning of his text or pass it on to his readers, though the application of his historical and linguistic skills may be able to clarify, deepen and give greater precision to, the faith-insight, once granted.

On any such view, the two sides of the commentator's task are sharply distinguished, and the primary qualification for a commentator is the possession of faith. To it his historical and linguistic activities are essentially subordinate; if, for example, they were to lead him to an interpretation of the text incompatible with that of faith, he would be told: 'You obviously do not possess faith, or you would see things in another light'. What the light would be will depend on the perspective of the speaker. If he is a Barthian, for example, he will assume the work God was doing through the New Testament events was basically what patristic and Lutheran orthodoxy has always assumed; if he is a disciple of Bultmann on the other hand, God's action, though mythologically described in the New Testament, will be taken to have been the making possible of 'authentic' human existence in an existentialist sense.

Such a position is clearly logically invulnerable. If a scholar claims that the meaning of certain past events has been supernaturally revealed to him and that any historical reconstruction of those events incompatible with this revealed meaning is *ipso facto* shown to be mistaken, there can be no arguing with him. In a country like this, however, where philosophers put so high a value on empirical verifiability, such logical invulnerability may not be altogether a recommendation; and certainly this position is radically un-historical. Historical investigation can have little, if any, part to play in determining which of the interpretations alleged to be revealed is the right one; and in many of its forms this position has the added disadvantage that it posits a trans-cultural interpretation of God's unique intervention. Barth in particular demands that a modern Christian should work with categories which belong to fifth-century and sixteenth-century cultures and have no natural link with the rest of his *Weltanschauung* – are indeed irresolubly paradoxical within it. Moreover a position such as Barth's involves doing what we have seen to be contrary to modern historical practice – taking a past generation's account of its own times more or less entirely at its face value.

Partly for these reasons, the approach in England has for some time been significantly different. Here there has been little tendency to subordinate historico-critical study of the new Testament events; rather such study has been relied on to reveal and confirm the unique character of the events. The assumption has been that if the interpreter does his work in a judicious and unprejudiced fashion, the picture of events which will emerge will demand interpretation in categories which are broadly those of the New Testament – or at any rate will make such interpretation highly plausible. The picture will be such that only the categories of the New Testament, and ultimately those of credal orthodoxy, will do justice to it.

Of recent years at any rate, English scholars have agreed that not all the history and interpretation contained in the New Testament can be accepted today; but the claim has been maintained that if the investigation is carried on in a moderate and judicious way, there will be found to be what Professor H. E. W. Turner calls 'an adequate dovetail' between the New Testament interpretation 'and the ascertainable facts'.[17]

It is important to be clear just what and how much is here being claimed. In the nineteenth century, English scholars such as Lightfoot, Westcott and Hort, or William Sanday in Oxford, put forward what amounted to a full-scale appeal to history. They argued that unless the reality of a unique divine intervention of the sort claimed in the New Testament was accepted, it was impossible to make historical sense of events in first-century Palestine. In particular they argued that unless Jesus had literally and physically risen from the dead, it was impossible to account for the complete change of attitude on the part of his disciples in the four or five days after the crucifixion.

Despite the superficial similarity between this and some of the things said by Professor Moule in the correspondence between him and Mr Cupitt published in the periodical *Theology* two or three years ago,[18] few English scholars today attempt to maintain such a position. Indeed they would be hard put to it to do so in view of the fact that so many highly competent historians – the great majority of modern historians in fact – find it possible to offer an account of the rise of Christianity which seems to them and most of their readers perfectly plausible and yet has no recourse to any miraculous resurrection or unique divine intervention. Accordingly, in the hands of such theologians as Professor Turner, or the late Dr Alan Richardson, the character of the argument has altered. It is now conceded that it is possible to make some sort of sense of the New Testament events without recourse to the occurrence of a special divine intervention; but it is suggested that reconstructions which do this rest on positivistic and sceptical presuppositions which are arbitrary, not particularly plausible, and by no means demanded by incontestable facts or discoveries. The argument is that on the basis of other presuppositions at least equally plausible and equally compatible with integrity even in an historical age, the most natural reconstruction of the New Testament evidence is broadly that of the New Testament itself.

Such a position is not to be lightly dismissed, but on the other hand it could only be called an appeal to history in a somewhat Pickwickian sense. It is in fact a defensive posture and it is obvious where its motivation lies: in a determination to maintain the Christian faith combined with a conviction that faith stands or falls by the occurrence of a unique, once for all, divine intervention in New Testament times.

Now this last assumption – that Christianity stands or falls by belief in a unique incarnation – has begun to be subjected to questioning on doctrinal and philosophical grounds. In this country, for example, it has recently been questioned in various ways by such scholars as Mr Cupitt, Professor Wiles, Dr Anthony Dyson and Father Harry Williams.[19] What I should like to see would be New Testament scholars subjecting it to like questioning in their own sphere. This would mean their forswearing all apologetic attempts to show that the New Testament evidence is compatible with this or that dogmatic belief, and simply setting out to explore the nature of New Testament Christianity in the same impartial spirit in which Malinowski investigated the religion of the Trobriand Islanders or Evans-Pritchard that of the Azande.

I am aware that as soon as I say that I shall be accused of begging the entire question. It will be pointed out that impartial, or what Strauss called presuppositionless, interpretation of the New Testament is impossible. My critics will say that if the possibility of any genuinely unique occurrence is ruled out in advance, primitive Christianity is bound to be found a natural religion, in principle of the same sort as the religion of the Trobriand Islanders or the Azande.

Such criticism, however, would misunderstand what I have in mind. Scholars working as I desiderate would not rule out *any* possibility *a priori*. They would simply behave as characteristic representatives of an historical age, assuming as a working hypothesis the truth of its presuppositions, including its assumption, at any rate in Barraclough's modified form,[20] that all past events form a single causally interconnected web and that no event occurs without this-worldly causation of some sort. They would then see how far it is possible to do justice to the evidence of the New Testament without going beyond those assumptions. They could, after all, plead that Occam's razor cuts as cleanly in historical study as in any other sphere, and that entities such as unique interventions ought not to be multiplied beyond strict necessity. In this case some such occurrence may in the end prove inescapable, but not unless and until its necessity has been clearly demonstrated. No other procedure could really claim to be an appeal to history.

What would concern me above all is that these scholars should avoid the historian's temptation. I would have them be scrupulously careful to see that all New Testament language and ideas were interpreted in their own context. Remember Mr Cupitt's words 'the context is essential'. I am not of course advocating the 'intentionalist fallacy' or suggesting that no meaning may be attributed to a text beyond what its original author consciously intended; but for our purposes it is essential that the presuppositions in the light of which the text is interpreted should be the doctrines-felt-as-facts by first-century men, and not by the fathers, the Reformers or people of our time. This would mean, for example, that New Testament accounts of the past had to be read in the light of the fact that people's attitudes to accounts of the past used to be very different from what they are today. As late as the Renaissance, a painter could quite happily represent the Emperor Constantine, let us say, or King David dressed as a Renaissance prince, surrounded by Renaissance courtiers and framed in a perspective of Renaissance buildings. There was no intention to deceive; the intention was simply to make clear that what a Renaissance prince was in *his* day – a wise, powerful and generous leader of his people in peace and war – King David and the Emperor Constantine had been in theirs. That was the primary aim: to represent people and events of the past in such a way as to bring out what was believed to be their true significance, natural and supernatural.

Our scholars would also have to be clear that where they were interpreting the word *theos* in the New Testament, for example, the reference was to Yahweh, the God of the Jews, as understood in the first century, and not to the God of the Schoolmen or the modern philosophical theologian. Similarly, all New Testament talk about sacrifice would have to be interpreted in the light of the doctrine felt by the author to the Hebrews as a fact too obvious to need justification: that remission of sins is simply impossible without the shedding of some blood.[21] The aim would be to show what sort of a unity the various ideas and practices formed in the eyes of New Testament Christians and then how, when belief in the end of the world failed to justify itself, the remaining beliefs

formed a different sort of unity for Christians of the fourth and
fifth centuries.

It would be idle to speculate very much about the results of
such an approach because I do not believe such an approach has
ever been made in any systematic or sustained way. It would for
example, involve co-operation with anthropologists, sociologists, psychologists and experts in the comparative study of religions on a scale not hitherto contemplated, though a work such
as J. M. Hull's recent book on the Lucan writings, for example,
shows that the penny is beginning to drop.[22]

I confess I should not be altogether surprised if those who
adopted such an approach concluded that, while the events of
Jesus' career were such as to demand interpretation in terms of a
unique – indeed literally final – divine intervention *given the
presuppositions of certain circles in first-century Jewish culture*, they
might not have seemed to demand such interpretation given
different cultural assumptions, for example to a modern Western
observer if such a one – twentieth-century presuppositions and
all – could be carried back to first-century Palestine on some
magic carpet or infernal time machine. It may be worth adding
that if that were the conclusion, it would not necessarily rob the
events of their profound religious significance. It would still be
possible to see the God whose hand is everywhere behind the
first-century events which launched the early Christians into a
relation with himself so intimate and vivid, that, given their
presuppositions, they were led to posit a final and decisive intervention on his part to account for it. And it would be possible to
interpret their sense of intimate and vivid relationship with God
as having been exactly what it seemed to them to be.

However, I must leave all such matters on one side in order to
deal with one further question. If scholars approached the New
Testament in the way I suggest, would they have any positive
contributions to make beyond satisfying our antiquarian curiosity? I believe they would, and the place from which I should begin
to develop a justification for my belief, had I the time, would be
from the argument of Professor J. S. Dunne's remarkable recent
book *The Way of All the Earth*. In that book the author points out
how large a part is played in our spiritual progress, both individual and corporate, by the process he describes as 'passing
over', that is, passing over to, and living again, earlier periods of

our own lives, individual and corporate, and the lives of other groups and other ages. I am convinced that whatever form Christianity has to take if it is to be properly integrated with any modern culture, its adherents will always find it necessary and enriching to pass over to the rock from whence they were hewn, the faith and experience of New Testament Christianity, just as they will also want to pass over to the faith of the Fathers, the Schoolmen and the Reformers. Professor Dunne writes: 'Whenever a man passes over to other lives or other times, he finds on coming back, some neglected aspect of his own life or times which correspond to what he saw in others. Passing over has the effect of activating otherwise dormant aspects of himself'.[23] Exactly what the benefits will be it is impossible to specify, certainly in the space at my disposal, especially as Professor Dunne himself writes that 'each time a man passes over into God he can see worlds that have never been seen before. If such experience of God is finite, then no man has seen all there is to see'.[24]

One thing, however, is certain; if this process of passing over to primitive Christianity is to be truly enriching, it must be genuinely the Christianity of the New Testament to which we pass over. Some words of the American literary-critic Lionel Trilling are apposite at this point:

it is [he writes] only if we are aware of the reality of the past as past that we can feel it as alive and present. If, for example, we try to make Shakespeare literally contemporaneous, we make him monstrous. He is contemporaneous only if we know how much a man of his own age he was; he is relevant to us only if we see his distance from us. Or to take a poet closer to us in actual time, Wordsworth's Immortality Ode is acceptable to us only when it is understood to have been written at a certain past moment; if it had appeared much later than it did, if it were offered to us now as a contemporary work, we would not admire it. . . . In the pastness of these works lies the assurance of their validity and relevance.[25]

That exactly expresses what I want to see – New Testament Christianity displayed in its pastness, with its various doctrines, rituals and commandments exhibited in the sort of unity they seemed to form in the context of first-century cultural assumptions. Such a reconstruction would not be easy, if only because in the case of the New Testament we have for the most part the myth without the ritual, a very misleading thing to have, as any student of religions will tell you.[26]

Certainly such a reconstruction is not available as yet. For all their genuinely good intentions,[27] Christian interpreters of the New Testament, because they believed themselves to be faced with a twofold task, have tried to face two ways, have halted between two opinions. They have been aware of the peril of modernizing Jesus and the early church, yet they have been loth to search them out in their full particularity and pastness for fear that in that form they would not speak directly to our condition. Thus they have interpreted New Testament accounts of the past as if they had been written by men who shared our attitude to the past; they have attributed to Jesus that essentially modern hybrid, 'realized eschatology'; they have read New Testament teaching on sacrifice, the wrath of God and the rest, as if they had been produced by men who shared our understanding of the Old Testament, the nature and demands of God and much else beside. They have discovered in the New Testament a degree of unity and homogeneity it does not possess. The result is that the Jesus, the Paul, the Mark, the John of these interpreters and commentaries have been what Professor Trilling calls them, 'monstrous' – figures that never were on sea or land.[28] Schweitzer rightly pointed out that the truly historical Jesus was bound to be 'to our time a stranger and an enigma', incapable of 'being made sympathetic and universally intelligible to the multitude by a popular historical treatment'.[29] Could that language be used of the founder of Christianity as pictured by C. H. Dodd[30] or of the existentialist Jesus of Bultmann and his followers, with his very twentieth-century refusal to furnish any credentials or to make any messianic claims? Are not these woefully hybrid figures, precisely the products of reading an ancient text through modern spectacles?

At least the approach I call for would go as far as it is possible to go in making New Testament Christianity in its genuine pastness available to us, so that we could 'pass over' to it. Something of the significance of that is hinted at in the following words from R. G. Collingwood's *Autobiography*, 'if what the historian knows is past thoughts, and if he knows them by re-thinking them himself, it follows that the knowledge he achieves by historical enquiry is not knowledge of his situation as opposed to knowledge of himself, it is a knowledge of his situation which is at the same time knowledge of himself. In re-thinking what somebody else thought, he thinks it himself. In knowing that somebody else thought it, he knows that he himself is able to think it. And finding out what he is able to do is finding out what kind of a man he is.'[31]

11

The Genealogy in St Matthew's Gospel and its Significance for the Study of the Gospels[1]

My title would be misleading if it suggested that the principle aim of this essay was to throw light on the various vexed questions which beset the detailed exegesis of Matthew 1.1-18 – the precise meaning of *biblos geneseōs* or of *genesis* in verse 18, the reasons for the inclusion of the four women, the meaning of the omission of the fourteenth name in the third section of the genealogy and so on.

Our concern will be rather different, and perhaps I could express the difference provisionally like this. I shall be asking not so much: what are we to *make* of Matthew's genealogy, and of the rest of the gospel material in the light of it? but rather: What are *we* to make of the genealogy and so of the rest of this material? What can Matthew 1.1-17 be expected to mean for us or do for us today? What can they say to us? There is one answer which is given implicitly by almost all ordinary readers, who simply skip the genealogy, and which has also been given by many scholarly readers, namely that it has nothing to say to us at all. Thus Bishop Barnes, for example, could declare roundly of the genealogies in both Matthew and Luke, 'it is now generally agreed that they are valueless'.[2] Today, however, few serious students of the New Testament will agree with that. Modern exegetes will retort sharply that whatever the eventual judgment on the historicity or probative force of these verses may be, they at least have the value, the very considerable value, of helping us to understand better the mind of St Matthew and so some of the beliefs and attitudes of the earliest Christians.

This retort is the more significant because it is now generally accepted that the *first* task of the New Testament scholar is to 'feel his way', as the Germans put it (*Einfühlung*), into the mind of the author he is studying. The issues here were put with characteristic trenchancy by Dr Austin Farrer in a Hulsean sermon he preached many years ago at Cambridge about St Mark. I should like to protest, he said, 'at a manner of interpreting the evangelists which neglects, and attempts to destroy, their living individuality. . . . We make haste to shoulder him [*sc.* Mark] out of the way, that we may lay our hands upon an impersonal and disjointed mass of tradition, which he is supposed to have had in his desk, or in his memory. We pull the Marcan mosaic to bits, and then it is amazing how free we find ourselves to reconstruct the ikon of Christ according to enlightened principles, whether it be scientific probability or transcendental Neo-Calvinism that lies most near our hearts.' On the positive side he goes on, 'We are not concerned to reconstruct St Mark as a missionary priest or a husband and father, or as anything save the author of a gospel. The only Mark we want is the Mark who became, for an unknown number of days and hours, the inspired act of meditating and writing this book. We want nothing but his mental life, and of his mental life no more than is enclosed between the first verse of his first chapter and the eighth of his sixteenth. If this is a whole, living, personal and continuous mental act, and I can touch it, then I can touch a vital and significant part of that web of life which made up the substance of Christian origins; and from it my thought can spread to other connected parts of the web. . . .'[3]

Vintage Farrer that, and as such a thought over-stated! In practice it is not so easy to separate Mark the evangelist from Mark the man in his other capacities. Nevertheless the general point is well taken and if so, if what we are after in the first instance is the 'mind' of the evangelist, in this case Matthew, what better starting-point than his own starting-point, the exordium of his gospel? It is now generally agreed that the first two chapters of the gospel form a sort of prologue to the rest, and of this prologue the first pericope will be not the least important. In the case of Mark, Luke and John, H. J. Cadbury, R. H. Lightfoot and others have shown the importance of a right understanding of the opening section for a right understanding of the gospel as a whole and Wilhelm Michaelis in his commentary on Matthew seems to have established that the same is true of him. Indeed the matter is simply one of the psychology of authorship. According to the traditional interpretation of what Euphorion and Panaetius say, Plato drafted and redrafted the opening passage of the *Republic* innumerable times before he was satisfied that he had the appropriate opening for his work. Plato may have been a perfectionist of unusual intensity, but every writer takes care to get things right in his opening sentences; no one begins a book with a passage he regards as insignificant or expects his readers to skip.

Although the principle is sound, its application in Matthew's case is somewhat disappointing because it is not easy to be sure how exactly he meant his opening pericope to be understood, and a variety of interpretations of it have been offered. The reasons for this uncertainty and variety are worth a moment's reflection. Whether it was J. A. Turretini in the eighteenth century, or some earlier writer, who first explicitly advised his fellow Christians to read the New Testament books as if they were ordinary writings, the advice contained far-reaching implications. For it has come to be realized, and is still recognized, despite the protest of the so-called 'new critics', that in the case of an 'ordinary' book emanating from an earlier culture, reading it seriously involves setting it against the background of the cultural *milieu* in which it was written. We have to enquire into the assumptions and presuppositions, and also the conventions as to style, imagery, word-usage and the like which the author shared, partly consciously and partly unconsciously, with his contemporaries and immediate predecessors. His work roots, as it were, in that soil, and only as the product of that soil can it be properly interpreted in the first instance, whatever further meaning may legitimately be found in it subsequently. The most sensitive exploration of the sort of thing involved known to me is that by the American critic Rosemond Tuve in her book *The Reading of George Herbert*,[4] but New Testament scholars need no instruction in this matter from a critic in the field of English literature. It is arguable that they were originally responsible for suggesting the type of approach Professor Tuve advocates, and they have certainly followed it in connexion with all the New Testament writings, including Matthew 1.1-17.

The results, however, have been rather perplexing and even

perhaps paradoxical. W. D. Davies in one of his books quotes T. S. Eliot as asserting that to understand any situation we must know its *total* setting, and he comments: 'This is also true of any document we have to study, and it is especially true of the documents of the New Testament.'[5] He is absolutely right, even if the ideal is never completely attainable in practice, and it is a pity that New Testament scholars have not paid more heed, but tended, at least in recent years, to confine their background studies to Old Testament, or at any rate, Jewish sources. In the case of Matthew's genealogy, for example, no study of it known to me makes any serious attempt to look at the general background; and yet even a nodding acquaintance with the relevant literature is enough to show that in all pre-modern – and indeed some modern – societies the genealogy has been a standard medium of propaganda, a way of demonstrating the true status or character of some individual or group. That is documented to cite only a few scholars, by Professor Ian Cunnison for the Luapula tribe in Central Africa, by Dr Emrys Peters and Professor Dorothy Emmet for the Bedouin Arabs, by Professor J. H. Plumb, among others, for the Pharaohs, the Memphite priests and the Sumerian kings, by Sir Steven Runciman for the Ottoman dynasty in Turkey in the fourteenth and fifteenth centuries and by Sir Thomas Kendrick even for the Welsh-Tudor monarchs in England as late as the first half of the sixteenth century.[6] These and other authors also make clear how the process normally worked. The genealogist started – or was paid to start – with a preconceived notion of the true status or character of his subject and framed the genealogy accordingly. An acquaintance with the facts in this broader area will at least predispose us in favour of Loisy's comment on the Lucan and Matthaean genealogies: 'Les généalogies ont été créés pour servir d'argument; elles ne contiennent en réalité q'une assertion.'[7]

Of that more later; meanwhile, if we want to know *what* exactly Matthew's genealogy asserts and how it purports to get there, then certainly we must look at the more immediate background, and it is here, as so often with the New Testament, that our difficulties begin. For the New Testament authors are among the most unselfconscious of writers, and, apart from the Old Testament, give little direct hint as to their backgrounds or assumptions. Consequently it is often possible with perfect plausibility to set their writings against different backgrounds and so arrive at very different interpretations of them. So far as Matthew's genealogy is concerned, it is now generally agreed that the immediate background is the Old Testament and, still more, the studies of it by the early rabbis and their predecessors. These . latter have been described by one modern scholar as 'the vast continent of the rabbinical sources'[8]; as you will know, they are voluminous in the extreme, and often very difficult either to interpret or to date; and even where they clearly belong to the post-Matthaean period in their present form, they often contain material which may be old enough to have formed part of Matthew's *milieu*. It is therefore possible for different scholars to point to different areas and traditions within this material as the background of various elements in the genealogy, and so to arrive at very different conclusions. Possibly some of you are not aware of the extent of the problem. Apart from the lengthy discussions in all the commentaries, there is a considerable periodical literature on Matthew's genealogy and it is discussed in the course of many monographs. And the book of 1969 by the American scholar Marshall Johnson, entitled *The Purpose of the Biblical Genealogies*, is in effect a full-scale, book-length discussion of Matthew 1.1.-17.[9]

I venture to labour the point because it seems to me one of general application. You might well think that there could not be much doubt about the interpretation of a simple list of names extending to only sixteen verses in all, but if so, you would be wrong. There are in fact a number of uncertainties. To deal with only one, the question why Matthew took the unusual course of including the names of women – no less than four women – in his list: Marshall Johnson distinguishes at least four different types of answer, each supported by a number of considerable scholars. It is true that Professor Krister Stendahl, in an article published in 1960, comes down firmly in favour of one of these answers and states categorically: 'that this is the only possible interpretation has been demonstrated beyond doubt . . . by Renée Bloch'.[10] Yet nine years later Marshall Johnson gave reasons for thinking that Mlle Bloch's account was not in fact the true story, or at any rate the whole story, and wrote of her explanation, 'The inclusion of the four women demands a more explicit explanation'.[11] What biblical scholars have got to accept, it seems to me, is the, admit-

tedly rather paradoxical, fact that the very increase in our knowledge and improvement in our techniques of investigation mean,
certainly in the short run, and very probably in the long run, that
we are less, rather than more, sure about the exact meaning of
many biblical passages. If that is true, it is a truth which I commend for reflection especially by those of you who have occasion
to use the Bible 'normatively' or are training to do so, whether as
clergy or teachers. How often is the Bible used normatively in the
course of preaching or teaching by those who are apparently
unaware that the interpretation they are commending as
authoritative is uncertain at best and at worst has been rendered
improbable or untenable by scholarly work with which they are
unacquainted. As Dr Ward Gasque has written recently, 'The
number of New Testament scholars who are aware of the complexity of the problems which face them in their study is few
indeed'.[12]

Matthew's genealogy affords only a rather trivial, and, as we
shall see presently, imperfect, example, but there are many more
perfect examples which are less trivial. Anyone familiar with the
relevant literature knows, for example, how very uncertain is the
background, both historical and interpretative, of the Lord's
Prayer; and on a wider scale the book by W. D. Davies on the
Sermon on the Mount, from which I have quoted, provides a
useful object-lesson. Is Matthew's gospel as a whole deliberately
structured on a five-fold pattern centring on the five main discourses, with a view to representing the gospel as the new Law of
the new Israel and Jesus as the new Law-giver? After an exhaustive study of this and similar questions extending over 480 long
pages, in the course of which he investigates the plausibility of
setting each section against the various backgrounds which have
been suggested for it, Davies is forced to conclude that only a
tentative answer is possible; and anyone who takes the trouble to
follow him through the countless nicely balanced questions he
has had to confront will recognize how right he is to be tentative –
and may indeed think that he would have done well to be more
tentative still; and that example is only one chosen at random out
of almost innumerable others. Just recall, for example, the uncertainty about the meaning of the stories of Jesus' baptism or
transfiguration or of the feeding of the five thousand or the
ceremony at the Last Supper.

After all that, I hope it will not seem too much of an anti-climax if I say that in broad terms the meaning of Matthew's genealogy is clear enough. You will all know what Matthew does: he traces Jesus' ancestry in lineal descent from Abraham through David and Zerubbabel. He seeks in this way to show that Jesus fulfilled at least some of the necessary conditions for being regarded as the 'seed' promised to Abraham (see Gen. 12.7 and Gal. 3.16) and also the messianic Son of David many Jews were expecting – his claim to be the latter being strengthened by the fact that his descent from David passed through Zerubbabel, the great leader of the revived post-exilic Israel. Obviously in seventeen verses the evangelist could not go further and show that Jesus fulfilled all the *necessary* conditions for messiahship, still less that he fulfilled the *sufficient* conditions; that was left over for the remainder of the gospel.

At least one other thing, however, Matthew did do in his genealogy which he regarded as extremely important; we can be sure of this because he more or less tells us as much in so many words. In verse 17 he explicitly points out that according to his list, the number of generations from Abraham to David was precisely fourteen, and so was the number between David and the deportation to Babylon, and the deportation and the time of Jesus, respectively. (I leave aside the problem that on the most plausible interpretation of the most likely form of the text as we have it, the third period contains only thirteen names; Matthew clearly intended, or understood, it to contain fourteen.) Whatever the *precise* background or significance of the number symbolism here – and the question is a much disputed one – Matthew clearly attached great significance to it, and there can be little doubt what, in broad terms, that significance was. I can hardly improve on W. D. Davies's statement of it. 'The genealogy', he writes, 'is an impressive witness to Matthew's conviction that the birth of Jesus was no unpremeditated accident but occurred in the fullness of time and in the providence of God, who over-ruled the generations to this end, to inaugurate in Jesus a new order, the time of fulfilment.'[13] As Matthew saw it, history was under the direct and detailed control of the divine providence, and in the providential scheme the call of Abraham, the accession of David and the Babylonian exile and return were pivotal points of great significance. The significance was revealed by their being separated in each case by exactly the sacred number of fourteen generations; and it was therefore to be expected that when a further fourteen generations had elapsed, as it had exactly by the time of Jesus' birth, the time would have arrived in the divine providence for a further and even more significant – or rather for the final and ultimately significant – event to occur. The genealogy had already shown that Jesus had several of the characteristics of the messianic saviour; the fact that he was born precisely at the moment when that saviour was to be expected greatly enhanced the probability that he was in fact the saviour in question. The genealogy thus witnesses to two further important theological convictions: the implicit conviction that history is continually subject to the sovereign hand of God, so that his faithful people have no ground for fear, and the explicit conviction that the time of Jesus' birth was precisely the moment when it could have been foreseen that 'the time was fulfilled and the Kingdom of God would draw near'. Once that is grasped, there will be no doubt that the Matthaean genealogy is a theologically highly-charged document and that the Jewish-Christian church members to whom it was most probably directed[14] will have drawn much comfort and edification from it. As G. A. Buttrick says, 'the genealogy unfolds the treasure of the good news'.[15]

All of which makes it the more incumbent on us to ask an idiot-boy question at this point, the question namely: How did Matthew know all this? The question is clearly an important one because Matthew's belief in the divine government of history, for example, obviously depended in part on his belief in the balanced set of 3×14 generations; but it is a question which immediately brings us face to face with the problem of the almost total inconsistency and incompatibility which is pretty well universally agreed nowadays to exist between the genealogies in Matthew and Luke. (See e.g. the treatments of the matter by Frs J. L. Mackenzie and C. Stuhlmueller in the modern Roman Catholic *Jerome Biblical Commentary*.[16] The relatively conservative Protestant scholar Joachim Jeremias, who possesses an unrivalled knowledge of the relevant historical circumstances and who advances some *very* modest claims for the authenticity of a few of the later names in the Lucan genealogy (claims, incidentally, which would not be accepted by the majority of his New Testa-

ment colleagues), makes no serious attempt to argue for any
historical basis for the Matthaean list.[17] It may well be true, as
Jeremias suggests, that, especially in Jerusalem, some non-
priestly families of the period kept a record of their ancestry for
some generations back, for various legal and ritual purposes, but
he himself makes no attempt to suggest that any such record in
the family of Joseph underlies Matthew's list of names. Marshall
Johnson speaks for the overwhelming majority of New Testament scholars when he writes that 'the N.T. genealogies do not
come from the earliest strata of the gospel tradition', that they are
not 'the result of accurate genealogical records' and that 'the use
of the genealogical *Gattung* in Judaism renders it highly improbable that either [Matthew's or Luke's] list preserves the
family records of Joseph'.[18]

If then Matthew had nothing which we should regard as
authentic genealogical information to go on, how did he draw up
his genealogy? So far as the first two groups of names and the first
two names in the third group are concerned, he seems to have
drawn them from the LXX, mainly from I Chronicles 2-3, supplemented, or interpreted, by Ruth 4.18-22 and possibly Haggai
1.1 – an intelligible enough procedure if you believed, as presumably Matthew did, that the Old Testament was inerrantly
accurate on all matters, including matters genealogical. It is also
intelligible that the descent from David was traced through
solomon, rather than through Nathan, as in the Lucan genealogy. In II Samuel 7, David was promised by God that his descendant should rule his people and it was natural to suppose that it
was from the kingly line, descended through Solomon, that this
descendant would spring. Matthew may even have meant to
suggest that the glory which had departed from Israel with the
cessation of the kings at the Exile, was now restored in fullest
measure.

When we come to the last eleven names in the third list, the
vital names which specifically link Jesus with the acknowledged
kingly line in Israel, we are completely in the dark. The most that
can be said with certainty is that all the names mentioned occur in
one context or another in the late Old Testament writings, that
three of them are known to have been current among the Jews in
Egypt in New Testament times, but that there is not enough
evidence to show whether they were current in Palestine in

Matthew's day. Jeremias, it is true, writes: 'It is hardly likely that the list in Matthew is a pure invention; in default of exact information he has used the material of another Davidic list.'[19] He gives no grounds for his statement, however, and it is hard to see what grounds he could have. If, as he himself agrees, the family of Joseph is unlikely to have preserved a pedigree of any great length, some early Christian must have made up this list and there seems to be no grounds for, or point in, ascribing the action to someone other than Matthew. In any case the point does not affect our argument, for if Matthew did not make up the list, he took it over from someone else, fully knowing it, as we shall see, for what it was.

Meanwhile, we may ask: if Matthew drew on the Old Testament because he regarded it as authoritative, how comes it that he felt free to deviate widely from it in the way he does, for example omitting four names from the list it gives and assigning Rahab to a date fully three hundred years later than that to which both the Old Testament and later Jewish tradition unmistakably and unanimously ascribed her? It has often been suggested that the absence of the names of three of the kings may simply have been accidental, the result of an error on the part of a copyist; in which case we should presumably have to say that the balanced numerical structure which so impressed the evangelist was fortuitous and factually baseless. Although this suggestion of a scribal mistake is not without plausibility on palaeographical grounds, to suggest that such a symbolic numerical structure was simply the result of an accident surely stretches our credulity rather far, and we may notice that if we accept it, we shall have to suppose that Matthew cared so little about accuracy in such matters that he did not know, and did not bother to check, whether the numbers he regarded as so significant were really derived from the Old Testament. Particularly in view of the facts about Rahab, of which Matthew *must* surely have been aware, it seems better to assume that the omission of the three names was deliberate, especially as we know that artificial interpretations of the Old Testament genealogies which strained the evidence, were quite common in rabbinic circles in Matthew's time. One of the best known of these, which also uses the list of names in Ruth 4.18-22, is so pertinent that it is worth quoting. It comes from Exodus Rabbah on 12.2, the words to Moses and Aaron: 'this month shall be unto you the beginning of months', and the relevant part runs as follows:

> just as the month has thirty days, so shall your kingdom last until thirty generations. The moon begins to shine on the first of Nisan and goes on shining till the fifteenth day, when her disc becomes full: from the fifteenth till the thirtieth day her light wanes, till on the thirtieth it is not seen at all. With Israel too, there were fifteen generations from Abraham to Solomon. Abraham began to shine. . . . When Solomon appeared, the moon's disc was full. . . . Henceforth the kings began to diminish in power. . . . With Zedekiah . . . the light of the moon failed entirely. . . .[20]

The force of such rabbinic parallels is much strengthened if Johnson and other scholars are right in arguing that other peculiarities of Matthew's genealogy reflect contemporary rabbinic concerns and practices. In particular Johnson puts up an interesting case for thinking that Matthew's inclusion of four women, and his choice of the four women he includes, are related – almost certainly deliberately – to debates which we know to have been current at the time in rabbinic circles.

The widely held view is therefore probably to be accepted according to which Matthew's list is an artificial one arrived at by a sort of midrashic use of the Old Testament. As Johnson puts it: 'Both of the lists [i.e. those in Matthew and Luke] fall into the category of Midrash, which has a homiletical and hortatory function, and thus may be considered part and parcel of the tendency towards historification of "non-historical" materials. . . . In Matthew this midrashic quality emerges most clearly. The genealogy has become a means of structuring history which finds its closest parallels in similar schemes that appear in the apocalyptic literature. This structure serves to communicate the author's deep sense of eschatological fulfilment. . . .'[21]

Such statements are by now commonplace, and most of us already accept them, or are perfectly willing to do so. What I want to suggest is that we usually do it without stopping to consider sufficiently all that it implies. Put in the abstract scholarly language I have just quoted, the point seems innocuous enough, but I ask you to consider for a moment its implications for our primary concern in this essay, the discovery of the mind of the evangelist, of the nature of that spell of mental activity which constituted the composition of his gospel. In this context it makes little difference whether he composed the genealogy himself or took it over without demur from others, for in either case he must have been aware of the clashes and inconsistencies it appears at least to involve. Will he not have been conscious, for example, that on any normal human reckoning, or indeed on that normally pre-supposed in the Old Testament, the thirteen names in the third section of his genealogy would not have *begun* to fill the period of nearly six hundred years they are supposed to cover? It may be that he was not aware of it – it is always dangerous to judge men from other cultures by the standards of one's own – but it is perhaps significant that where he has thirteen generations, Luke has nineteen. In any case, Matthew cannot have been unaware of the *prima facie* inconsistency between his tracing of Jesus' descent through Joseph in his first pericope and the virgin-birth story contained in his second. It is significant for what we have been saying that he gives no clear hint, or at any rate nothing which constitutes a clear hint for a modern reader, of how he thought the two pericopes should be reconciled. Of the many suggestions that have been made on the subject so far, the best is probably that of Krister Stendahl, who thinks that 1.18 was meant retro-spectively and intended as a bridge verse; and that verses 19–25 were intended by the evangelist not primarily as a birth narrative in the way that has usually been supposed, but as an account of how God engrafted Jesus into the Davidic line, through the agency of Joseph directed by an angel, just as he had earlier engrafted into the Davidic line some of the non-Davidic figures mentioned in the genealogy. On this showing Matthew's first two pericopes are virtually two parts of a single whole.

Assuming, as we surely may, that Matthew was an honest man, and not a deliberate deceiver, and that he intended his genealogy as a serious and accurate account of the past,[22] we must ask what it would have been like in all the circumstances to be able to write as he did without loss or lack of integrity. What frame of mind will have been involved?

In detail I do not profess to have the answer to that question, even if it is in principle answerable. To answer it would need, at the minimum, a length of time and a really intimate knowledge of the workings of the rabbinic mind which I – and probably most of you – do not have. Suffice it for now if we recognize that, what-ever exactly the frame of mind may have been, it will have been one quite alien to our experience. G. E. P. Cox quite rightly says in his commentary that 'the Jewish character of the genealogy and its purpose are foreign to our minds'.[23] Nearly all of you will probably have read enough of the rabbinic writings to be aware how totally unconvincing a large proportion of their argumentation seems when judged by our standards of logic. So much so that translators and interpreters of rabbinic writings frequently have to insert words into the text in square brackets in order to make what the rabbis deemed a valid argument even intelligible, let alone cogent, to our minds. It is interesting in this connection to find Dr L. Finkelstein, an authority on the rabbis, writing à propos one rabbinic argument: 'This may seem a weak argument for the authenticity of a tradition; but antiquity was apparently prepared to be impressed by it. So impressive indeed was this argument, that in the Gospel of Matthew, the early Christian apologist, directing his argument against the Pharisees (and also the Sadducees) adopted a similar claim for Jesus, and traced his genealogy back to Abraham in a series of three chains of fourteen links each (Matt. 1.17).'[24]

If we attempt to characterize the frame of mind briefly from a *logical*, as distinct from a psychological, standpoint, perhaps we may say that what the rabbis and Matthew were saying in effect was: 'Given our understanding of how things are now, the past *must have* been of such and such a character.' Matthew was saying: 'Given that Jesus was in fact the Davidic saviour, then this is how things must have fallen out in the past, and this is what the Old Testament must originally have said and meant.' Thus, according to Yehezkel Kaufmann, 'after the Babylonian Exile the tradition grew that messiahs were sons-of-David not because they were descended from David, but were sons-of-David because they were messiahs'.[25] To put it thus baldly is inevitably to misrepresent. Professor Amos Wilder speaks of 'imaginatively objectifying' contemporary beliefs, Krister Stendahl talks of 'the tendency to *describe* what was originally *believed*', and we have already seen how Marshall Johnson speaks of 'the tendency towards the historification of "non-historical" materials'.[26] The following quotation also seems to me illuminating, although it refers explicitly to early medieval, rather than biblical, thinkers and writers. It comes from a book on church history by one of our most distinguished medievalists, Sir Richard Southern. 'The primitive age had few records, but it had clear ideas of the past. These ideas were based on accumulated traditions, legends, pious fabrications, and above all on a reluctance to believe that the past is largely unknowable. Hence even learned and critical men easily believed that the past was like the present. Documents were therefore drawn up in which the theories of the present were represented as the facts of the past . . . the authors believed that they enforced truths which could not be abandoned without grave danger to their souls.'[27]

Without meaning to suggest that the outlook of New Testament writers was at every point like that of early medieval thinkers, I venture to hope that all that may set you thinking about the mind, or frame of mind, of the author of Matthew's gospel. We will not quarrel over the possibility that the first two chapters are an addition to an originally shorter gospel. That once popular hypothesis is now largely discredited, mainly through the efforts of those who have worked on the prologue and shown that its concerns and *motifs* are those of the gospel as a whole. Even if this suggestion is adopted, however, it remains true that the frame of mind we have outlined was that of the redactor of the gospel in the form in which we have it, and we have no particular grounds for supposing that those responsible for the material he utilized were of any different mind.

So I am brought to one of the main things I want to say. If what we really have in 1.1-17 is what Matthew thinks *must have* occurred in the past, given his present situation, may not the same be true of other pericopes in his gospel? So long as we remember that we are confining ourselves simply to an abstract, logical analysis of what Matthew was doing, and not attempting to probe the workings of his mind psychologically, or discover what it felt like to be Matthew, may we not suggest that what he was saying in some of the pericopes in the body of the gospel amounts to something like this: Given my understanding of my position now as a member of a community created, forgiven, instructed and watched over by Christ, things in the days of his flesh, must have fallen out thus and so? Put like that, it sounds far too individualistic. No doubt it was usually the community's beliefs rather than his individual view that Matthew was transmitting. In any case please do not misunderstand me: I am not suggesting that Matthew's mind worked in connexion with every

pericope in the way it seems to have done with the opening
pericope. That it did work in some such way for the rest of the
prologue is fairly widely agreed. So far as the rest of the gospel is
concerned, the work of scholars such as Riesenfeld and Gerhards-
son must be given its full weight. I am only suggesting that in the
case of any pericope Matthew's mind *could* have worked in this
way, and that given his background and cultural *milieu*, it would
have been perfectly natural for it to do so. My point is simply that
if anyone says to you: 'the evangelist would never have made up
such and such a story or altered the tradition in such and such
ways', you must always bear in mind that the evangelist about
whom this claim is made was the author, or at least the willing
transmitter, of 1.1-17 and the rest of the prologue. And the point
of some of my earlier remarks was to make clear that we cannot
attempt to shrug off the genealogy as trivial or hardly integral to
the gospel. On the contrary, it is the exordium of the whole work
and, as such, the author will have lavished a good deal of care on
it; it must therefore be taken very seriously as an indication of the
way his mind worked.

There that particular matter must be left if I am to have time to
allude even briefly to another, much wider, question to which the
genealogy gives rise. Those who write about Matthew 1.1-17
often betray, even if only involuntarily, a sense of regret that the
passage does not stand up better to being judged by modern
standards of historical and genealogical accuracy. Quite apart
from the fact that such an attitude implies the lack of a truly
historical, or historicist, perspective – why, after all, *should* a
writing emanating from a first- or second-century Jewish *milieu* in
the middle-east, stand up to criticism by the quite different standards of twentieth-century Western Europe? – it surely raises the
following question.
   Suppose that by some unexpected turn of the wheel of fortune
you and I became convinced that Matthew was right and that
Jesus was, beyond any peradventure, descended from Abraham
through David and Zerubbabel. Even suppose that *per impossibile*
– or at any rate *per improbabilissimum* – we became convinced that
his descent was structured in three lots of fourteen generations,
each beginning with one of Matthew's high moments, what
difference, if any, would it make to our beliefs? I will not ask

whether we should be convinced thereby that Jesus was indeed the looked-for messianic figure because, as we have seen, even Matthew did not expect the genealogy alone to produce *conviction* on the point; but should we even be more predisposed to believe it?[28]

That is a question you must all answer for yourselves. So far as I and several people with whom I have discussed it are concerned, it would make no difference to our beliefs at all. If that should be the case with you too, you would surely have to ask the further question *why* it is the case. It is presumably not for the sort of reasons which might have prevented a contemporary of Matthew from being convinced. It is not, for example, that you share beliefs of a messianic sort generally similar to Matthew's, except for holding, let us say, that what God had in mind was to raise up a messiah from the house of Levi, rather than from the house of David; or that what he planned was to send the messiah, not 14×3 generations after Abraham but 11×7 generations after creation, as Luke perhaps intended to suggest, or anything of that sort.[29] The reason would rather be that you no longer share the general outlook and assumptions which both Matthew and Luke took for granted; you no longer think God ever intended to begin the closure of world-history 42 generations after Abraham or even that his purposes require what Vögtle calls 'the special conception attested from the time of Daniel onward, that the will of God is manifested in a secret, established numerical period-ization of world events'.[30] Such a way of conceiving God and his workings is foreign to your modern Western-European outlook. You no longer inhabit a universe of discourse in which messianic claims of the traditional sort make sense.

In his book *The Death of Christ* the American scholar Dr John Knox has a passage which I find very thought-provoking. In it he describes an occasion when a New Testament scholar was discussing with a colleague the difficulties he found in supposing that Jesus ever regarded himself as Son of Man. In response to some of the difficulties he voiced, the colleague countered, 'But suppose he *was* the Son of Man?' Knox comments, 'I find such a question very hard to deal with, not because of what it asks for, but because of what it seems to presuppose. It seems to ascribe to the "Son of man" objective and personal reality. It seems to assume that there was, and is, a Son of man. But what does the phrase "Son of man", in the context of apocalypticism (and no one can deny that context in many of the Gospel statements) really designate? Must we not say that it stands for an idea, or an image, in the minds of certain ancient Jews? One can trace to some extent the beginnings and development of this idea or image in Jewish culture. But do we for a moment suppose that it is the name of any actual person – that the Son of man in fact exists or ever existed?'[31]

If this attitude to the Son of Man is justified, the same sort of attitude must presumably be adopted towards the title Son of David and the other titles of Jesus in the New Testament which may be described as messianic in the broad sense of the term. If so, what prospect opens up?

Our immediate subject is Matthew's genealogy, so let us begin from that. As we have seen, its essential purpose is to vindicate a messianic status for Jesus. If Professor Knox is right, we should have to say, not only what we have already said, that the evidence on which the genealogy rests is inadequate by our standards to justify acceptance of it as historically accurate, but also that the belief it bodies forth – that it 'objectifies imaginatively', as Amos Wilder might say – is itself not something we can take over as it stands. And should we not have to say something else as well? If Matthew's genealogy, with its precise structure of three lots of fourteen generations, is not historically trustworthy, it constitutes in itself no evidence of God's sovereign control of history. It is of course evidence of Matthew's, and the early church's, *belief* in God's sovereign and detailed control of history, but that is something quite different and raises the question of the nature and solidity of its justification.

I think you will agree that *if this passage were to prove typical of many others in the gospels*, what we have been saying would constitute a formidable and thought-provoking agenda for the New Testament exegete, and indeed the doctrinal theologian, to ponder. You may, however, feel that in spite of my suggestion that the exordium to a work is likely to prove characteristic, and indicative of its writer's mind and way of proceeding, Matthew 1.1-17 is in fact an uncharacteristic passage which raises questions that do not arise, at any rate to anything like the same extent, in connexion with other passages in the gospels.

You may well be right, and in any case you will of course want

to decide for yourselves. May I, however, just to start you thinking, make certain points? The aim of vindicating a messianic
status for Jesus is one which Matthew's genealogy shares with a
large number of other passages in the New Testament; if there
should prove to be anything in Professor Knox's point of view,
then in that respect, at any rate, what applies to Matthew's
genealogy would apply equally to all these other passages.
Perhaps the problems in this area can be illuminated a little if we
indulge for a moment in the following fancy: suppose that by
some magic device you and I, with all our modern Western
attitudes, standards and knowledge, could be enabled to go back
and stand in Matthew's sandals as he stood preparing to write the
first seventeen verses of his gospel. Faced with the data, indeed
with the whole situation, which led him, coming as he did from a
first-century Jewish-Christian background, to compose his
genealogy, it seems clear that we should not have been moved to
make those claims, or probably indeed *any* claims, about Jesus'
ancestry; nor should we have wished to make messianic claims
for him, at any rate in the sense of the word messianic which
Matthew shared with Jews and Christians of his day. What
claims, either natural or supernatural, should we have been
moved to make? It is often suggested that that is the question we
should ask. The issue is posed, for example, in the form: 'What
must the truth be now if people who thought as they did put it
like that?' In the case of Matthew's genealogy, however, I see no
way of answering such a question; we do not even know enough
about the data and situation by which Matthew was faced at that
point to know whether *on that basis* we should have wanted to
make any claim at all.

How far then does the same thing apply to other passages in
the gospels? Here there is – quite legitimately – a wide divergence
of opinion, and my concern in this essay is only to see that the
question is asked and fully faced. Suppose that you – exactly as
you are now – were faced with the situation or the data which led
Matthew to write the stories in the rest of his prologue, or indeed
the later part of his gospel as a whole, which led Mark to write his
accounts of the stilling of the storm and the Gerasene demoniac,
or Luke his account of the events on the road to Emmaus, what
account of the past would you be led to give and what claims for
Jesus would you be led to advance?

My concern is not so much with the details of any historical or theological claims you might make, as with the prior question whether you feel you are in a position to make any claims at all on the basis of the material now available; but I should be very sorry to end a lecture in memory of T. W. Manson of all people on anything which sounded like a negative note. It is a fairly open secret that in my view the sort of questions I have in mind can be answered only to a very limited extent in the case of a good deal of the gospel material, and it would be idle to deny that the very novelty of the resultant situation sometimes makes it appear somewhat daunting.

Yet I do not find it daunting in any absolute sense. The case of Professor John Knox seems to me a very significant one in this connexion. As those of you who are familiar with his writings will know, in spite of his views about the culturally conditioned character of the messianic and allied categories in the New Testament, his awareness of all that has sprung from the life and activity of Jesus, and his experience of reconciliation and communion with God in the community which resulted from that life and activity, compel him to assign to them a vitally important part in human history and indeed in the providence of God and the history of our salvation.

If I understand the situation correctly, two points must be specially noticed here. The first is that Knox must be free to understand and expound the significance he finds in Jesus in his own way, that is, in terms and categories which are as consonant with his modern Western outlook as messianic categories were consonant with the outlook of Matthew's time and place. The second point is that in discovering what these terms and categories should be, he will take account of what has happened since New Testament times as least as much as of what happened before. In one of his books he speaks of 'a new community in which are found a new forgiveness, victory and hope', and he says that the existence of this community 'is a matter of empirical knowledge in the Church'.[32] In view of that, the question which constantly engages him is what the activity and significance of Jesus must have been that his life should have given rise to such a community as the vehicle of such an experience.

If I am right in what I have been saying, in asking that question Dr Knox is following closely in the footsteps of the New Testament writers. They constantly, though no doubt unselfconsciously, asked some such questions, and a great deal of what they wrote was written to convey their answers to it. Very often their answers were cast in the form of historical, or purportedly historical, accounts because, as we have seen, it was natural in their cultural circumstances to objectify one's beliefs imaginatively, to 'historify . . . non-historical materials', 'to *describe* what was originally *believed*'.[33]

But if that is the way Dr Knox approaches the matter – and I certainly approach it in some such way myself – that does not in the least mean that either he or I attach diminished importance to the New Testament, and the detailed exegesis of it, whether for religious or any other purposes. Our difference from others, if there is one, lies in the perspective from which, and the expectations with which, we approach the text.

Our starting-point is a relationship with God in his church now. We recognize that, if it is a genuine relationship with God, it can never be fully articulated in human terms, but such articulation of it as we can achieve must be an account in our own terms of our response to the divine initiative; we certainly do not expect to be able to borrow from the very different culture of New Testament times categories and modes of articulation which can serve our turn just as they stand. The situation is rather that our relationship to God is so central for us that we cannot rest content until it informs and controls the whole of our lives in every area and at every level. In the attempt to see that it does so, we are constantly seeking for help, and where is it more natural to look than to the accounts of relationships between men and God given in the New Testament?

Because we approach the matter from this perspective we are not greatly troubled if the New Testament exegete cannot uncover in detail the historical facts behind the various New Testament accounts; and, as I say, we do not expect him to be capable of the impossible feat of expounding New Testament categories in such a way as to make them immediately acceptable to us. Indeed, we become suspicious if he claims to be able to do so. It is such claims on the part of a scholar like C. H. Dodd, for example, that seem to us, welcomed though they have been by many, to be the least satisfactory part of his remarkable work.

What we ask of the New Testament exegete is that he should

uncover as far as possible the beliefs and experiences of relationship with God of which the various New Testament
theologies and accounts of the past are the expressions and
historifications. We want to be able, by an appropriate 'sus-
pension of disbelief', to enter into those beliefs and relationships,
to think the thoughts, and experience the experiences, of the
New Testament Christians after them. We appreciate that we
shall never be able to do that fully, and in any case that we cannot
make those beliefs and experiences our own as they stand; we
recognize that they will remain 'incapsulated' elements in our
modern experience, to use Collingwood's term. Nevertheless we
have been convinced, most recently by the brilliant writings of
Father J. S. Dunne,[34] that it is possible to 'pass over', as he puts
it, into the faith and way of life of another culture in such a way
that one returns to one's own time and culture with one's outlook, faith and understanding deepened and broadened in ways
which may not be specifiable, even after the event, but which are
no less vitally important for that. We ask the New Testament
exegete to help us to pass over into the beliefs and relationships
with God witnessed to in the New Testament, not in the belief
that they were necessarily better than our own, but in the faith
that they will prove complementary to our own, revealing to us
new insights, new dimensions of relationship with God, and also
gaps, lacks and superficialities in our present relationship both
with God and men which, once they are revealed, must, and can,
be dealt with in our own terms.

If I return in conclusion to St Matthew's genealogy it is to
emphasize that if we approach such a passage in the ways I have
just been describing, none of the very real problems I have been
raising with regard to it need be seriously or ultimately daunting.
There is in principle no difficulty about our thinking St Matthew's
thoughts in such a passage after him and entering deeply, for
example, into his sense of God's sovereign control of history.
Perhaps I can make clear something of the value I see in that if I
cite once again a passage which I frequently find myself quoting
from R. G. Collingwood's *Autobiography*: 'If what the historian
knows is past thoughts, and if he knows them by rethinking them
himself, it follows that the knowledge he achieves by historical
inquiry is not knowledge of his situation as opposed to knowledge of himself, it is a knowledge of his situation which is at the

same time knowledge of himself. In rethinking what somebody else thought, he thinks it himself. In knowing that somebody else thought it, he knows that he himself is able to think it. And finding out what he is able to do is finding out what kind of a man he is.'[35]

Notes

Introduction

1. *Central Society of Sacred Study*, Leaflet 205, April 1951, pp. 7-15.
2. 'The Gospels and the Life of Jesus', *Theology*, vol. LIX, 1956, pp. 97-103.
3. See below p. 194 n. 2.
4. Appreciation of the importance of sociology in this connexion came largely as a result of reading, and talking to, the American theologian, Professor John Knox, a scholar to whom I am deeply indebted in a number of ways.

1. The Order of Events in St Mark's Gospel – an Examination of Dr Dodd's Hypothesis

Originally published in Dennis Nineham (ed.), *Studies in the Gospels*, Blackwell 1955, pp. 223-40.

1. Now published in his *New Testament Studies*, Manchester University Press 1953.
2. For example, Professor Vincent Taylor in his book, *The Foundation of the Gospel Tradition*, Macmillan 1933, second edition 1935, Dr G. S. Duncan in his book, *Jesus, Son of Man*, Nisbet 1948, and Professor A. M. Hunter in his book, *The Work and Words of Jesus*, revised edition, SCM Press 1973.
3. Here, of course, it is not possible to speak confidently, but examples would appear to be: E. F. Scott, in *The Validity of the Gospel Record*, Nicholson & Watson 1938, Professor Harvie Branscombe, *St Mark*, Moffatt Commentaries, Hodder & Stoughton 1937, and perhaps Professor D. M. Baillie in his book, *God was in Christ*, Faber & Faber 1956.
4. C. H. Dodd, *The Apostolic Preaching and its Developments*, Hodder & Stoughton 1936; new edition 1950, p. 86 n. 1.
5. It would be interesting to know why Professor Dodd felt precluded from using it.
6. This argument Professor Dodd subsequently stated in much greater detail, notably in *The Apostolic Preaching and its Development*.
7. Though this is, of course, notoriously uncertain in the case of I Cor. 11.23.
8. That is, in the case of Mark's gospel 14.1 to the end.

9. K. L. Schmidt, *Der Rahmen der Geschichte Jesu*, Berlin 1919. The quotation is from Professor Dodd's own masterly résumé of the book.

10. The Man with an Unclean Spirit, Simon's Wife's Mother, General Healing in the Evening and the Lord's Departure to a Desert Place. The third of these approximates to the character of a *Sammelbericht*.

11. The Storm, the Gadarene Swine, Jairus's Daughter and the Woman with the Issue of Blood.

12. The Feeding of the Multitude, the Voyage and the Landing (cf. also 8.1-10).

13. E.g. καὶ ἐκεῖθεν ἐξελθόντες, 9.30; κἀκεῖθεν ἀναστάς, 10.1.

14. This point may be clearer if set out as follows: Let *a,b,c,d,e,f,g* . . . be a series of *pericopae* in St Mark's gospel as we have it, and suppose that *d* seems topically irrelevant in its present position. Mark may have drawn it and *c* together from a source in which they appeared in company with a quite different set of *pericopae*, thus: *u,v,w,c,d,x,y,z*. In *that* context they may have had topical relevance to each other and to surrounding *pericopae*. There is thus no evidence that the basis of connexion in the source was historical rather than topical. It is not difficult to think of a context, for example, in which Mark 10.2-12 was grouped on a topical basis with 10.13-16, and possibly with 10.17ff. as well.

15. Parallels could be quoted from ancient authors.

16. As it happens, Professor Lightfoot himself provides a good example of the sort of thing envisaged in connexion with the very *pericope* we have been discussing (Mark 10.2-12 on divorce). In his book, *The Gospel Message of St Mark*, Oxford University Press 1950, he suggests reasons why Mark may deliberately have put this *pericope* in its present position *out of purely topical considerations* (p. 114 text and note).

2. *Eye-witness Testimony and the Gospel Tradition · I*
Journal of Theological Studies, n.s., vol. IX, pt 1, April 1958, pp. 13-25.

1. The substance of what follows has been read, in rather different forms, to more than one theological society and conference; I should like to take this opportunity of thanking the members of the various groups concerned who have helped me to clarify my thoughts by their searching, but always sympathetic and constructive, comments and questions.

2. On this see further note 30 below.

3. Vincent Taylor, *The Formation of the Gospel Tradition*, Macmillan 1933; reissued 1953, pp. 41-3; see also p. 107.

4. Acts 1.21-22. It is true that the word used here is μάρτυς, and that μάρτυς has wider connotations than αὐτόπτης, covering as it does, most of what we mean by 'bearing witness'. But the qualifications for the μάρτυς in this passage seem to show that here at least μαρτυρία was felt necessarily to involve αὐτοψία, and that also appears to be the implication in other passages in Acts.

5. Acts 10.39 and 41.

6. John 19.35. Cp. also 21.24.

7. I John 1.1-3.

8. *Apud* Eusebium, *HE*, iii.39.

9. A. M. Farrer, *A Study in St Mark*, A. & C. Black 1951, Oxford University Press, New York 1952.

10. To mention only one reason, it is difficult on any other view to account for the very close formal similarity between St Mark's gospel and admittedly the traditional material in St Matthew and St Luke.

11. H. J. Cadbury, *The Making of Luke-Acts*, 1927, reissued SPCK and Allenson 1958, p. 23.

12. R. H. Lightfoot, *The Gospel Message of St Mark*, Oxford University Press 1950, pp. 104-5.

13. Taylor, op. cit., p. 38.

14. Cp. for example, J. Schniewind, *Das Evangelium nach Markus* (NT Deutsch), p. 42: 'Grade des sehr Ungünstige, das über den Führer der ersten Gemeinde berichtet wird, kann nur auf Petrus selbst zurück-gehen'. The whole section at this point in Schniewind is a good example of the sort of argument discussed above.

15. See *Journal of Theological Studies*, vol. XXV, p. 226 and also his commentary on Mark in *A New Commentary on Holy Scripture*, ed., C. Gore, H. L. Goudge and A. Guillaume, SPCK 1928.

16. Schniewind, op. cit., p. 65: 'Die starke Gemütsbewegung Jesu (wie 1.41, 43, 8.12, 8.33, 11.15ff. bei Mt. und Lk. nicht erwähnt) entspricht der Unmittelbarkeit und Kraft der Marcus-Erzählung'.

17. Taylor, *The Gospel According to St Mark*, Macmillan 1952, p. 185.

18. Op. cit., p. 192. These examples are chosen from an almost inex-haustible supply in many commentaries.

19. For example by Dibelius.

20. In this precise form I owe this point to a conversation with Dr H. J. Cadbury.

21. It may be of course that the vivid details were already incorporated in the tradition as it reached Mark, but in that case they afford no evidence for the direct influence of eye-witnesses *at the Markan stage of the development*.

22. Taylor, *The Formation of the Gospel Tradition*, p. 40.

23. The point may be illustrated by reference to Professor Dodd's suggestion that Mark derived his knowledge from an outline account of the Lord's career preserved in the church's tradition. (See ch. 1 above where this view is examined at length, and the reference to the original *Expository Times* is given article p. 187 and note 1 above.) If this sugges-tion could be accepted, then Mark's knowledge of the order of events would be no evidence for the impingement of eye-witness testimony on the tradition at the Markan stage. In fact Professor Dodd's outline account would be, as it were, an extra form in the form-critics' repertoire, to put alongside paradigms, *Novellen*, and the rest. It would be a

medium, hitherto overlooked by scholars, through which *history*, but not the direct testimony of the eye-witness, exercised a control on Mark's gospel.

24. Vincent Taylor, *The Life and Ministry of Jesus*, Macmillan 1954.

25. A. M. Hunter, *The Work and Words of Jesus*, SCM Press, revised edition 1973.

26. H. E. W. Turner, *Jesus, Master and Lord*, Mowbray 1953; second edition 1954.

27. A. I. Polack and W. W. Simpson, *Jesus in the Background of History*, Cohen & West 1957.

28. See Lightfoot, *The Gospel Message of St Mark*, pp. 33-4.

29. In his book *The Problem of History in Mark*, SCM Press 1957.

30. It may be as well to underline the last four words and to point out that even the form-critics, for all the weight they attach to impersonal factors in modifying the tradition, do not deny the vital importance of eye-witness testimony in connection with the *origin* of the tradition. Even Bultmann, generally regarded as the most negative of form-critics, found enough material that went back ultimately to eye-witnesses to form the basis of his book, *Jesus*, Berlin 1926, ET, *Jesus and the Word*, Nicholson & Watson 1935, Scribner's Sons 1958. At any rate the origin of the tradition in eye-witness testimony is assumed in this essay, which is simply concerned with the questions how, when, and to what extent such testimony continued to control the tradition in the later stages of its development.

3. Eye-witness Testimony and the Gospel Tradition · II

Journal of Theological Studies, n.s., vol. IX, pt 2, October 1958, pp. 243-53.

1. For a discussion of Dr Farrer's argument see above, p. 27.

2. See Vincent Taylor, *The Formation of the Gospel Tradition*, p. 39.

3. Lightfoot, *History and Interpretation in the Gospels*, Hodder & Stoughton 1935, pp. 68-9. He follows Wellhausen.

4. Lightfoot, *The Gospel Message of St Mark*, p. 24.

5. Sir Edwyn Hoskyns and Noel Davey, *The Riddle of the New Testament*, 1931, 1936 edition pp. 86ff.

6. *The Gospel According to St Mark*, p. 192.

7. It is possible that at certain points (e.g., 3.24 though see Barrett ad loc.) John is consciously correcting the historical information given in the earlier tradition. But this explanation will hardly account for the main features in which he differs from the synoptics, for example the long hieratic discourses about the Lord's own person and work which he substitutes for the pithy sayings and parables about the Kingdom of the synoptic gospels.

8. C. K. Barrett, *The Gospel according to St John*, SPCK 1955, p. 117.

9. If C. F. Evans is right about Luke's reasons for his ordering of his

material in 9.51ff. (see *Studies in the Gospels*, ed., D. E. Nineham, Blackwell 1955, pp. 37ff.) we have another striking example here.

10. Barrett, *St John*, p. 115.

11. Leonard Hodgson, *For Faith and Freedom*, 1956–57, SCM Press 1968, vol II, pp. 69-70.

12. Origen, *Commentary on St John's Gospel*, x.4. The last part of the quotation is as follows in the original: σώζομενου πολλάκις τοῦ ἀληθοῦς πνευματικοῦ ἐν τῷ σωματικῷ, ὡς ἄν εἴποι τις, ψεύδει.

13. J. P. Gabler, quoted from C. Hartlich and W. Sachs, *Der Ursprung des Mythosbegriffes in der modernen Bibelwissenschaft*, Tübingen 1952, p. 67: 'Es liegt in dem Charakter des Orientalers, eine Begebenheit nie nackt zu erzählen, sondern so, wie er sich dachte, dass es dabei zugegangen oder die sie erfolgt sein möchte. Räsonnement war immer in Geschichte eingeschlossen, und wurde selbst als Faktum d dargestellt; weil der Orientaler sichs gar nicht denken könnte, dass etwas anders vorgefallen sein könnte als er sichs gerade vorstellte. *Das Faktum und die Art, sich das Faktum zu denken, floss bei dem Morgenländer in Ein unzertrennliches Ganze zusammen*. . . . Tatsachen von eigenem Urteil darüber zu unterscheiden, war nicht die Sache des Orientalers: sondern die Begebenheit und das Räsonnement darüber floss in ein Ganzes bei seiner Erzählung zusammen.' A good deal of the discussion in this book is of interest in relation to our subject.

14. Ibid.

15. Cp. II Cor. 5.16, a text which is apt to receive too little attention in this discussion. See Johannes Weiss, *Paul and Jesus*, Berlin 1909, ET, Harper 1909, for conclusive evidence that the words κατὰ σάρκα qualify the verbs, and not the noun and the pronoun.

16. In his 'Theology Occasional Paper', *The Purpose of Acts*, now reprinted in the collected volume of papers, *Early Christianity*, Greenwich, Connecticut 1954.

17. The interpretation of Acts 18.24ff. is too uncertain for us to be able to build very much upon the passage. But if it if it implies that Apollos was only imperfectly informed about the events dealt with in the gospel tradition, it is a very significant piece of evidence. For if a Christian teacher, a man of education and zeal (Acts 18.24-25) had found it difficult to discover the full truth about the Lord's life, from eye-witnesses or any other source, perhaps some of the form-critics' contentions are not quite as 'absurd' as Dr Taylor holds them to be. See above, p. 24.

4. *Eye-witness Testimony and the Gospel Tradition · III*
Journal of Theological Studies, n.s., vol. XI, pt 2, October 1960.

1. See ch. 2 above, pp. 25–6ff.

2. No doubt Paul's epistles reveal a greater acquaintance and concern with the events of Jesus' earthly life than was at one time allowed, and

the work of such scholars as Hoskyns and Davey, Scott and Dodd has very properly redressed the balance; but the findings of these scholars must always be viewed in perspective, as Professor Brandon rightly insists – see *The Fall of Jerusalem and the Christian Church*, 1951, SPCK ²1957, pp. 3-4.

3. Cp. Luke 24.26-28; Acts 1.8(?), 22; 2.32; 3.15; 5.30-32; 10.41; 13.31; and see R. P. Casey in F. J. Foakes Jackson and Kirsopp Lake (eds), *The Beginnings of Christianity*, 5 vols, New York and London 1920-33, re-issued Eerdmans 1966, vol. v, note V, where he writes, for example: '. . . the emphasis is laid on the testimony about Jesus, *and especially his resurrection*. . . . The qualification of a μάρτυς in Luke-Acts is that he should be one of those fore-ordained of God to see the *risen* Jesus, and so an eye-witness *of the Resurrection*' (p. 32, italics mine).

4. The significant resemblances between Luke 1.1-4 and the proems of contemporary history books have often been noted and discussed. Cp. especially H. J. Cadbury in Jackson and Lake, *The Beginnings of Christianity*, vol. ii, pp. 489ff., who says (p. 490): 'The form of the preface should be considered in the light of contemporary Hellenistic literature', and in his note on αὐτό-ται (p. 498) remarks that 'Luke is following a convention of historians in urging the intimate connexion of himself and his associates with the facts themselves'. He quotes Polybius, iii.4.13, and in his note on αὐτόπται (p. 498) remarks that 'Luke is following a note deserves careful study in connexion with our inquiry.

5. A partial exception to this must be made in favour of some discussions which have originated in America, the most recent being ch. iii of Professor W. N. Pittenger's *The Word Incarnate*, Harper & Row, and Nisbet 1959. Even this, however, is very brief and general, so far as our particular question is concerned. See further note 25 below.

6. It is worth noticing in that connexion how largely the idea of the imitation of Christ in the modern sense is lacking from the New Testament. When Paul wants a practical example for his correspondents to follow, he normally quotes himself and his fellow missionaries – e.g. I Cor. 4.16 and 11.1; Phil. 3.17 and 4.9; cp. also Heb. 6.12. The nearest we come in the New Testament to an exception is in I Peter; see E. G. Selwyn's discussion in the commentary on *I Peter*, Macmillan 1946.

7. John Knox, *The Death of Christ*, Collins 1959.

8. See above pp. 6ff.

9. In his *Apologie pour l'Histoire, ou Métier d'Historien*, ET under the title *The Historian's Craft*, Manchester University Press 1954, from which all subsequent quotations from Bloch in this essay are taken.

10. Op. cit., pp. 134-5, from which the passage quoted below is also taken; italics mine.

11. T. A. Roberts in his *History and Christian Apologetic*, SPCK 1960, p. 17. Readers of this book will recognize how closely I have studied it, and especially this section of it; perhaps I should add that I am not wholly convinced of the justice of all Dr Roberts's criticisms of Collingwood.

12. The quotation is from Collingwood, *The Idea of History*, Oxford University Press, p. 257, cited, not quite accurately, by Dr Roberts.

13. Ibid., p. 256.

14. Bloch, op. cit., p. 101.

15. F. H. Bradley, *The Presuppositions of Critical History*, 1874, reprinted as the first item in vol. 1 of his *Collected Essays*, Oxford University Press 1935.

16. A phrase of François Simiand designed to emphasize that the modern historian is by no means confined for evidence to written matter, let alone to explicitly historical documents.

17. Bloch, op. cit., pp. 63-4.

18. This possibility of knowing about the general environment of Jesus' life is vitally important for the kind of knowledge of him claimed as possible in this essay, if only as making intelligible the terms in which he understood and expressed himself; see further Professor John Knox, *Jesus: Lord and Christ*, Harper & Row 1958, e.g. pp. 7-8.

19. J. M. Robinson, *A New Quest of the Historical Jesus*, SCM Press 1959. See especially pp. 66-72.

20. Ibid., p. 69; the further quotation is from pp. 69-70.

21. Collingwood, *The Idea of History*, p. 281.

22. Pittenger, op. cit., pp. 26-7.

23. For some remarks on how this increasing insight is reflected in the gospels see R. H. Lightfoot, *History and Interpretation in the Gospels*, Hodder & Stoughton 1935, e.g. pp. 24, 81ff., 91.

24. Cp, e.g. John 2.22; 12.16 16.14.

25. Since completing this essay I have carefully re-read the three short works by Professor John Knox now published in the single volume *Jesus: Lord and Christ*. Had I the chance to elaborate the point of view adumbrated in these essays, I should want, to a larger extent, to follow the lines he has laid down.

5. *Wherein Lies the Authority of the Bible?*

Originally published in L. Hodgson *et al.*, *On the Authority of the Bible*, SPCK 1960, pp. 81-96.

1. This essay contains the substance of a lecture delivered at Sion College, London in Advent 1958. In view of the inevitable constraint on time, the lecture was deliberately limited to a critique of certain views on the subject which, though widely current at the time, seemed to me to have been rendered untenable by contemporary cultural developments. Since this gave the lecture a rather negative tone, I added a brief account of what seemed to me the most promising positive approach to the matter; this account was too sketchy and informal to bear reprinting here.

In connexion with several points, particularly on pp. 63 and 69-70, I should like to express my indebtedness to some unpublished work by the Rev. Graham Neville, on which I have been allowed to draw.

2. I am aware that this formulation of the matter begs an important question. There are those who, in interpreting these events as revelatory, emphasize, not so much their being acts of God in a special sense, as the providential presence of witnesses inspired to see and proclaim the events of their time as originating in the will of God. In many ways I myself sympathize with this interpretation; but as the question was not immediately relevant to this discussion, I have deliberately begged it here.

3. See e.g. C. C. J. Webb, *Problems in the Relation of God and Man*, Nisbet 1911. Leonard Hodgson, *For Faith and Freedom*, SCM Press 1968, vol. I, ch. iv.

4. I use quotation marks because this phrase itself is a question-begging abstraction.

5. Dr Hodgson formulates the question in slightly different ways in several of his books. See e.g. *For Faith and Freedom*, vol. I, pp. 87-8.

6. C. Smyth, *Church and Parish*, SPCK 1950, p. 159.

7. In the course of the lecture I did not have time to develop this point, but it is one which deserves, and needs, to be developed fully. It should not be supposed that the idea of a multiple sense of scripture was a peculiarity to Origen and a few like-minded eccentrics; in one form or another it dominated practically all patristic and medieval exegesis, and most protestant exegesis in the period before the rise of the 'critical' study of the Bible.

8. C. S. Lewis, *De descriptione temporum*, now published in *They Asked for a Paper*, Bles 1962.

9. Charles Galton Darwin, *The Next Million Years*, Hart-Davis 1952, p. 49.

10. The words 'biblical theology' have been applied to a variety of views, and it is a pity that the Lambeth Report does not define more precisely how it understands the term.

11. The Lambeth Committee Report suggests the use of the category of *drama* to supplement and illuminate the other categories employed by biblical theology. For a critique of this suggestion, see *The York Quarterly*, November 1958, pp. 4-5.

12. Hodgson, *For Faith and Freedom*; see vol. I, p. 78.

13. Ibid., vol. I, p. 76.

14. A. M. Farrer, *The Glass of Vision*, Dacre Press 1948.

6. History and the Gospel

The London Quarterly and Holborn Review, April 1967, pp. 93-105.

1. A. T. Hanson (ed.), *Vindications*, SCM Press 1966.
2. W. R. Farmer, C. F. D. Moule and R. R. Niebuhr (eds), *Christian*

History and Interpretation, Cambridge University Press 1967, pp. 199-222.

3. Now printed in *They Asked for a Paper*, Bles 1962, pp. 9-25.

4. See e.g. his *Christianity and History*, Bell 1949, p. 12.

5. For the significance in this connection of the differences in method between Holmes and Poirot, see Collingwood, *The Idea of History*, Oxford University Press 1946, p. 281.

6. Collingwood, op. cit., p. 256.

7. Martin D'Arcy, *The Nature of Belief*, London 1931, and *The Sense of History*, Dublin 1958. See especially the latter, pp. 55-7.

8. H. E. W. Turner, *Historicity and the Gospels*, Mowbray 1963.

9. Collingwood, op. cit., p. 281.

10. E. Fuchs in the *Zeitschrift für Theologie und Kirche*, 1956, p. 229.

11. Kierkegaard, *Philosophical Fragments*, 1936, Princeton ²1962, p. 130.

12. See for example his *Criticism and Faith*, Hodder & Stoughton 1953, p. 32, or his *The Church and the Reality of Christ*, Collins 1963, pp. 9ff.

13. Cf. his book, *Old and New in Interpretation*, SCM Press 1966.

7. *The Use of the Bible in Modern Theology*

A lecture originally delivered in the John Rylands Library on Wednesday 7 May 1969 and published in *Bulletin of the John Rylands Library*, vol. 52, no. 1, Autumn 1969.

1. S. J. Case, *Jesus through the Centuries*, University of Chicago Press 1932, e.g. p. 339.

2. J. K. S. Reid, *The Authority of Scripture*, Methuen 1957, p. 139.

3. Ibid., p. 268.

4. Ibid.

5. Ibid., p. 130.

6. H. Cunliffe-Jones, *Authority of the Biblical Revelation*, James Clarke 1945.

7. O. Chadwick, *From Bossuet to Newman*, Cambridge University Press 1957.

8. Helen Gardner, *The Limits of Literary Criticism*, Oxford University Press 1956, pp. 60-1.

9. R. P. C. Hanson and R. H. Fuller, *The Church of Rome*, SCM Press 1948, p. 95.

10. Ronald Knox, *The Belief of Catholics*, Unicorn Books 1939, p. 167.

11. C. C. Morrison, *What is Christianity?*, Willet Clark & Co., Chicago and New York 1940, e.g. p. 191.

12. C. H. Dodd, *The Authority of the Bible*, Nisbet 1929; Fontana ed. 1960.

13. A. B. Come, *An Introduction to Barth's Dogmatics for Preachers*, SCM Press 1963, p. 219.

14. Morrison, op. cit.

15. Karl Barth, *Church Dogmatics*, T. & T. Clark 1936 edition, I/1 (trs. G. T. Thomson), pp. 111f.

16. *Church Dogmatics*, I/1, p. 117.

17. Sir Edwyn Hoskyns, *Cambridge Sermons*, SPCK 1938, p. 70. For Coleridge cp. S. T. Coleridge, *Confessions of an Inquiring Spirit*, ed. H. St. J. Hart, A. & C. Black 1956, pp. 42–3. Eg., 'Whatever *finds* me, bears witness for itself that it has proceeded from a Holy Spirit'.

18. Since writing these words I have come across the following in the so-called 'Dutch Catechism' of the Roman Catholic Church (ET, *A New Catechism*, Search Press 1967, new edition with supplement 1970, p. 478): '. . . this is . . . the place to say something which should be understood as said at many other places of this book. It is that this catechism tries to expound clearly the living truth of faith. But there is more force, life, truth and authenticity in the pages of the Bible. *The pages of the Bible seem to glow with the warmth of faith, experience and divine revelation, with the warmth of Jesus' own words. Very often the Bible does not explain – it simply impinges on one, in the way that life itself makes its impact.*' (Italics mine.)

8. Schweitzer Revisited

1. Albert Schweitzer, *The Quest of the Historical Jesus*, A. & C. Black 1910, third edition 1954.

2. See Schweitzer, *My Life and Thought*, ET 1933, Allen & Unwin 1954, British Publishers' Guild, 1955, edition, p. 116.

3. *The Quest*, p. 84. It was perhaps with some half-conscious recollection of that passage that R. H. Lightfoot once remarked in conversation: 'If those who pay lip-service to Schweitzer would only read him, half the unnecessary books which now get written about the New Testament would never see the light of day.'

4. It is interesting, for example, to compare Schweitzer's discussion of Jesus' teaching in the 'little Apocalypse' (Mark 13) with the treatment of the same subject by such more recent English scholars as C. H. Dodd in the *Journal of Roman Studies*, XXXVII, pp. 47-54; T. W. Manson, *Sayings of Jesus*, SCM Press 1949, pp. 329-30; Vincent Taylor, *The Gospel According to St Mark*, Macmillan 1952, p. 512 and J. A. T. Robinson, *Jesus and His Coming*, SCM Press 1957, p. 122. And C. H. Dodd's last book *The Founder of Christianity*, Collins 1971, seems vulnerable to almost all the criticisms Schweitzer levelled against earlier writers.

5. *My Life and Thought*, p. 109.

6. A title devised specially for the English version. The title of the original German would translate *From Reimarus to Wrede*. See pp. 122–3 below for the significance of that.

7. Lest the account given above should convey a one-sided impression, it may be well to quote some words of Professor C. F. Evans: 'So far from its being the case, as is commonly supposed, that the modern

methods of historical investigation were first perfected outside the field of theological studies, and were then applied, perhaps somewhat reluctantly, to the study of the Bible and Christian history, the opposite is nearer the truth. The pioneers in the field of textual criticism, Richard Bentley and Carl Lachmann, graduated in their science not upon classical texts, but upon the text of the New Testament and, perhaps significantly, Bentley never produced his text because he found the conditions so much more complex in the study of the New Testament than in the study of classical texts. When Wilamowitz dedicated his Homeric Studies to the Old Testament scholar Julius Wellhausen he greeted him as the pioneer of that method of rolling back the history of the transmission of the text which he himself was now using. Methods evolved within the heart of Christian studies, in order to enable theologians to handle the problems presented by their own subject matter, have contributed greatly to the specifically modern study of history in general.' 'The Inspiration of the Bible', *Theology*, vol. LIX, January 1956, p. 11.

8. For a brief discussion of that question by the present writer, see D. E. Nineham (ed.), *The Church's Use of the Bible*, SPCK 1963, pp. 154ff.

9. See Marc Bloch, *The Historian's Craft*, Manchester University Press 1954, pp. 134-5, and see above p. 52.

10. See e.g. *Quest*, pp. 40-3 and other parts of Chap. IV for some striking examples. It is noteworthy that so comparatively modern a scholar as Vincent Taylor felt compelled to adopt this sort of rationalizing position with regard to a number of gospel incidents. See his commentary on St Mark, e.g. p. 452 (on Mark 11.1-25) or p. 538 (on Mark 14.12-16).

11. *Vermittlungstheologie* and 'the mediating school' are phrases sometimes used in a restricted sense to describe a particular group of scholars of whom Dorner, Rothe and Bunsen are perhaps the best known. Schweitzer, however, is by no means alone in using it in a much wider sense.

12. In a slightly different context, Professor W. R. Farmer points out how B. H. Streeter fell into that trap; see *The Synoptic Problem*, Macmillan 1964, pp. 144ff. The treatment of Luke 1.46 in the NEB could possibly be another example.

13. Cf. *The Death of Christ*, Collins 1959, ch. 2.

14. It is of course true that a concern for the authenticity of the traditional picture can sometimes be very useful heuristically in so far as it sharpens the eye for flaws in theories which would discredit it.

15. For K. G. Bretschneider see p. 85; the rationalists found John congenial because of the relatively small part the miraculous plays in it.

16. Quoted in *The Quest*, p. 125.

17. His two-volume commentary which was published posthumously in 1908 seems to have been written principally between 1883 and 1887; but there is reason to think that it represents his views right up till the time of his death in 1901. See his son's prefatory note, p. vi.

18. For this language and some interesting remarks about it see E. C. Hoskyns, *The Fourth Gospel*, Faber & Faber 1947, pp. 26ff.

19. It was presumably another relic of orthodox sentiment which made so many of them feel that though Jesus was not divine in the traditional sense, he must, as a human being, have displayed a quite outstanding degree of originality. Schweitzer speaks of 'the obsession of the fixed idea that it was their mission to defend the "originality" of Jesus'. See J. Knox, op. cit., pp. 44ff, and for a fuller discussion by the present writer, *The Use and Abuse of the Bible*, Macmillan 1976, pp. 13f., and *The Myth of God Incarnate*, ed. John Hick, SCM Press 1977, pp. 193f.

20. For example, he writes: 'Schenkel . . . knows the most secret thoughts of Jesus and is therefore no longer bound to the text' (p. 206) and on p. 220, with reference to a group of liberal scholars, 'these ingenious psychologists never seemed to perceive that there is not a word of all this in Mark'. Schweitzer says the same sort of thing about Wernle, Oskar Holtzmann, von Soden, Kalthoff and De Jonge and it is, alas, not difficult to think of more recent writers about whom he would speak at least as strongly!

21. One example may be quoted, from p. 200, where Schweitzer writes: 'this portrait is fixed from the first, being determined by the mental and religious horizon of the (eighteen-) sixties'. The 'mental and religious horizon of the nineteen-sixties' was very different, but it is difficult not to picture Schweitzer muttering in this connexion, 'Plus ça change, plus c'est la même chose'. See also pp. 203, 208, 307, 310, 314, 324 and 330.

22. In the light of more recent discoveries concerning the Judaism of Jesus' time, failure to set him against the background of his period has less excuse; that it nevertheless persists is shown, for example, by the fact that H. J. Cadbury needed to write his important book *The Peril of Modernizing Jesus*, Macmillan, New York 1937, new edition SPCK 1962, and by the general failure to come to terms with it.

23. *The Kingdom of God and Primitive Christianity*, A. & C. Black 1968, mainly written during the years 1950 and 1957. Cf. also the epilogue he contributed to E. N. Mozley's *The Theology of Albert Schweitzer*, A. & C. Black 1950, and his preface to the sixth edition of his own book, published in the same year.

24. It was along these lines that Schweitzer interpreted such passages as Mark 10.45 and Mark 14.24 (parallel to Matt. 20.28 and Matt. 26.27-28) and also the clause in the Lord's Prayer 'bring *us*' (i.e. Jesus' followers in contrast to Jesus himself) 'not to the test' (Matt. 6.13). Schweitzer may well have been right in interpreting the whole of the Matthaean version of the Lord's Prayer along eschatological lines, p. 387 and also cf. *The Mystery of the Kingdom of God*, A. & C. Black 1914, pp. 124, 118-9 and 146.

25. In his German introduction to the latest German edition (Silben-stern, Taschenbuch Verlag, München and Hamberg 1966), vol. I, p. 12. Incidentally, had modesty permitted, Schweitzer might have given

his book what from his point of view would have been a more optimistic title: *From Reimarus to Schweitzer*!

26. See now the (abbreviated) English translation by S. G. F. Brandon, *The Formation of Christian Dogma*, A. & C. Black 1957.

27. From the foreword of his book *Die Bedeutung der neutestamentlichen Eschatologie für die neuere protestantische Theologie*, 1935. Readers who try to estimate how Schweitzer fared by his own test will probably conclude that *in certain respects* he does pretty well. See further below.

28. Associated specially with the names of Rudolf Otto and C. H. Dodd.

29. Cf. also, from p. 335, 'there is (in contrast to Wrede's position) the eschatological solution which at one stroke raises the Marcan account as it stands, with all its disconnectedness and inconsistency, into genuine history. . . . *Tertium non datur*'.

30. *The Kingdom of God and Primitive Christianity*, A. & C. Black 1968, p. 71, a page which documents all the statements made above.

31. Cf. *My Life and Thought*, p. 50, 'the eschatological interpretation of the life of Jesus put an end to all need to doubt the credibility of the gospels of Mark and Matthew. It showed that their reports of the public activity and the death of Jesus follow a faithful tradition which is reliable even in details'. In particular Schweitzer's position is heavily dependent on the authenticity of Matthew's account of the sending out of the Twelve (Matt. 10.5ff.) and of the visit of the disciples of John the Baptist (Matt. 11.2ff.).

32. See p. xiv of the English version of Schweitzer's preface to the 1950 edition of the *Quest* for his own recognition of this.

33. The lack of recognition has been interestingly exemplified in the last few years when the liturgical revisers of the various English-speaking denominations proposed for use a modern and, so far as it goes, fairly accurate version of the Lord's Prayer; great surprise was evinced in many quarters that Jesus should have recommended a form of prayer not immediately intelligible, or unsable as it stands, in the later twentieth century. If Schweitzer's understanding of the prayer is correct, the problem is still more acute than is generally recognized.

34. For Schweitzer's own recognition of this, cf. his striking words, 'the recognition of the claims of eschatology signifies for our dogmatic' a burning of the boats by which it felt itself able to return at any moment from the time of Jesus direct to the present' (p. 285).

35. *My Life and Thought*, p. 53.

36. Ibid., pp. 54-6 for these quotations.

37. See also Schweitzer's treatment of the matter in E. N. Mozley, op. cit., pp. 104ff.

38. See Hans Jonas, *Augustin und das paulinische Freiheitsproblem*, Göttingen 1930, 2 Auflage 1965, p. 82, cited from J. M. Robinson, op. cit. p. 20.

39. It is a great pity Schweitzer did not develop the strong negative

criticism he brings against the attempt of Wobbermun to distinguish the merely historical Jesus (*der historische Jesus*) from the historic Jesus (*der geschichtliche Jesus*). This 'play of artificial distinctions', he says, 'achieves absolutely nothing', and there can be little doubt that he would have wanted to apply to much of the work of the Bultmann school and of other contemporary German theologians his further words, 'What is essential above all things is that theology employs simple language. Be your speech yea yea, nay nay. Whatsoever is more than these cometh of the Evil One'! (*Geschichte der Leben-Jesu-Forschung*, 1966 edition, vol. ii, pp. 520-1).

9. A Partner for Cinderella?
Originally published in Morna Hooker and Colin Hickling (eds), *What about the New Testament? – Essays in Honour of Christopher Evans*, SCM Press 1975, pp. 143-54.

1. Published by Durham University in 1960 under the title *Queen or Cinderella*.

2. Ibid., p. 6.

3. Ibid., p. 22.

4. Of course the word 'exclusive' in that sentence is extremely important, as the work of a philosophical theologian such as Ian Ramsey showed.

5. The reader's indulgence is asked in advance for the number of very broad generalizations this paper will be found to contain. The excuse for them must be the need for brevity, and it is hoped that none of them would be found on detailed examination to need so much qualification as to destroy the validity of the argument. A case in point is what is said below about the relative homogeneity of the philosophical position presupposed by patristic writers.

6. See note 5 above.

7. Or at least of that form of it which appealed most to the exegete doing the work.

8. As the latest critical edition of Anselm's works (that by F. S. Schmitt, OSB, Nelson 1946+) makes clear, the title *Cur Deus-Homo* is best taken as meaning: why there needed to be a God-man. See Schmitt, II, 6ff., and cf. J. McIntyre, *St Anselm and his Critics*, Oliver & Boyd 1954, p. 117.

9. Gore's kenoticism does not prevent his doctrine of the incarnation from being 'traditional' in the sense relevant to our argument.

10. See e.g. Peter L. Berger, *Invitation to Sociology*, Penguin Books 1966, pp. 79-80.

11. Just how widely is something still not sufficiently recognized by many theologians. The point is developed further in my book *The Use and Abuse of the Bible*, especially chs 1 and 3. See also p. 194 n. 8 above.

12. So far as bypassing Q is concerned, Albert Schweitzer put the point

with characteristic vividness in his description of the nineteenth-century approach to the figure of Jesus. 'It loosed the bonds by which He had been riveted for centuries to the stony rocks of ecclesiastical doctrine, and rejoiced to see life and movement coming into the figure once more, and the historical Jesus advancing, as it seemed, to meet it.' Schweitzer, however, almost alone among his contemporaries, recognized the full dimensions of the problem. He went on: 'But he does not stay; He passes by our time and returns to His own' (*The Quest of the Historical Jesus*, ET A. & C. Black 1910, p. 397).

13. Cf. Martin Kähler's reaction against what he described as 'the papacy of the scholars' (*The So-called Historical Jesus and the Historic, Biblical Christ*, ET Fortress Press 1964, e.g. pp. 109ff.).

14. Cf. C. C. Richardson, *The Doctrine of the Trinity*, Abingdon Press 1958; W. Norman Pittenger, *The Word Incarnate*, Harper & Row, and Nisbet 1959; E. Fromm, *The Dogma of Christ*, Routledge & Kegan Paul 1963.

15. A fact attested independently by the literary critic Ian Robinson when he wrote recently, *à propos* the appreciative attitude of the translators of the Authorized Version towards earlier translators: 'For them the earlier versions were a guarantee, a sort of communion of saints, inspiring them, as ever, to the salvation of souls' (*The Survival of English*, Cambridge University Press 1973, p. 61).

16. See H. G. Gadamer, *Wahrheit und Methode*, Tübingen 1960.

17. *Objections to Christian Belief*, D. M. MacKinnon and others, Constable 1963, p. 84.

18. See p. 135 above.

19. In which, for example, the anointing or 'christing' of kings and priests was the accepted way of signalizing God's choice and appointment of them. Apart from that, as one scholar has remarked, the Greek phrase *ho christos* might well have been taken to mean 'the person who has just had a bath' – for it was mainly in connexion with bathing that Greeks anointed themselves!

20. Father Laurence Bright, OP, in a letter to *The Times*, 18 June 1974.

10. New Testament Interpretation in an Historical Age

Originally published under the same title by Athlone Press 1976.

1. The text of the Ethel M. Wood lecture delivered at London University on 4 March 1975.

2. D. E. Nineham, *The Gospel of St Mark*, Penguin Books 1963, p. 15.

3. *The Interpreter's Bible*, Abingdon Press, New York and Nashville 1961-7.

4. Boswell's *Life of Johnson*, ed., Birkbeck Hill 1887, vol. ii, p. 212.

5. See e.g. J. H. Plumb, *The Death of the Past*, Macmillan 1969.

6. Friedrich Nietzsche, *Werke in Drei Bänden*, Hanser 1966, ii, pp. 686-7;

R. G. Collingwood, *The Idea of History*, Oxford University Press 1946, p. 209.

7. T.E.F. Hulme, *Speculations*, Routledge & Kegan Paul 1949, pp. 50-1.

8. Cp. B. Malinowski, *Argonauts of the Western Pacific*, Routledge 1922, latest edition 1972, p. xvi: 'One of the first conditions of acceptable Ethnographic work certainly is that it should deal with the totality of all social, cultural and psychological aspects of the community, for they are so interwoven that not one can be understood without taking into consideration all the others.'

9. Sir Herbert Butterfield, *The Discontinuities between the Generations in History: Their Effects upon the Transmission of Political Experience*, Cambridge University Press 1972, pp. 5-6; and cp. Malinowski, op. cit., p. 176, 'Nothing is so misleading . . . as the description of facts of native civilizations in terms of our own'.

10. Butterfield, op. cit., p. 7; Nicholas Lash, *Change in Focus*, Sheed & Ward 1973, p. 42.

11. J. S. Dunne, *The Way of All the Earth*, Sheldon Press 1973, p. 126; *The City of the Gods*, Sheldon Press 1973.

12. The quotations, and some of the ideas in the section preceding them, are taken from an extremely interesting, but so far unpublished, broadcast talk entitled 'Justification of Belief in God'. For examples of the sort of work referred to see Malinowski, op. cit., and E. E. Evans-Pritchard, *Witchcraft, Oracles and Magic among the Azande*, Oxford University Press 1937.

13. Article VI. For the Luther quotation see H. Bettenson, *Documents of the Christian Church*, Oxford University Press 1946, p. 288.

14. Charles Galton Darwin, *The Next Million Years*, Hart-Davis 1952, p. 49.

15. The Tyrrell quotation is from *Christianity at the Crossroads*, published posthumously Longmans Green 1909, p. 44. For Schweitzer see *The Quest of the Historical Jesus*, A. & C. Black 1910, third edition 1954, pp. 310-11.

16. Ibid.

17. H. E. W. Turner, *Historicity and the Gospels*, Mowbray 1963, p. 25. See also p. 33.

18. See *Theology*, vol. LXXV, October 1972, pp. 507-19.

19. See e.g. M. F. Wiles, *The Remaking of Christian Doctrine*, SCM Press 1974; A. O. Dyson, *Who is Jesus Christ?*, SCM Press 1969; H. A. Williams, *Poverty, Chastity and Obedience*, Mitchell Beazley 1975. Now see also *The Myth of God Incarnate*, SCM Press 1977.

20. See Geoffrey Barraclough, *History in a Changing World*, Blackwell 1956, e.g., pp. 4-5.

21. Hebrews 9.22.

22. J. M. Hull, *Hellenistic Magic and the Synoptic Tradition*, SCM Press 1974.

23. Dunne, op. cit., p. 180.

24. Ibid., p. 226.

25. Lionel Trilling, *The Liberal Imagination*, Mercury Books, London 1964, p. 186.

26. The difficulty mentioned is only one aspect of a wider difficulty which is succinctly expressed by Sir Herbert Butterfield: '. . . there exist . . . subtle and delicate differences, some of them in the realm perhaps of presuppositions – things not always avowed, indeed things which men do not always know to quarrel about, such ideas and assumptions being so much part of the air that one breathes. They are things that the men of 1600 shall we say . . . do not have to explain to one another, and the result is that they do not always get into the historian's evidence'. Op. cit., p. 6. That is, not only do the presuppositions and ideas of the New Testament writers often pose problems for us when we know them; in many cases we do not even know what their underlying ideas and assumptions were. Cp. also the discussion of the *'inponderabilia'* in Malinowski, op. cit., ch. 1, § VII.

27. In view of some of the plain speaking which follows, I should like to emphasize the last four words. I am far from wishing to suggest that any of those referred to have had any conscious intention other than that of discovering and communicating the truth to the very best of their ability.

28. Cp. Malinowski, op. cit., p. 157. 'This error is due to the same cause which lies at the bottom of all our misconceptions about people of different cultures. . . . If you measure [a man] by moral, legal or economic standards . . . essentially foreign to him, you cannot but obtain a caricature in your estimate.'

29. Schweitzer, op. cit., p. 397.

30. E.g. in his surely much over-praised book *The Founder of Christianity*, Collins 1971. In fairness to Dodd it should perhaps be added that the substance of this book was embodied in lectures delivered as early as 1954; that, however, cannot mitigate criticism of the basic methodological flaws it exhibits.

31. R. G. Collingwood, *Autobiography*, Penguin Books 1944, p. 78.

11. *The Genealogy in St Matthew's Gospel and its Significance for the Study of the Gospels*

Bulletin of the John Rylands Library, vol.58, no.2, Spring 1976, pp.421-44.

1. The Manson Memorial Lecture delivered in the University of Manchester on 20 November 1975.

2. E. W. Barnes, *The Rise of Christianity*, Longmans Green 1947, p. 72.

3. A. M. Farrer, *A Celebration of Faith*, Hodder & Stoughton 1970, second edition 1972, p. 41.

4. Rosemond Tuve, *The Reading of George Herbert*, Faber & Faber 1952.

5. W. D. Davies, *The Setting of the Sermon on the Mount*, Cambridge University Press 1964, p. 191.

6. See e.g. Ian Cunnison, *History of the Luapula*, Rhodes-Livingstone Papers xxi, Oxford University Press 1951; Dorothy Emmet, *Function, Purpose and Powers*, Macmillan 1958, pp. 14-15 and the unpublished paper there mentioned; J. H. Plumb, *The Death of the Past*, Macmillan 1969, e.g. pp. 29-30; Steven Runciman, *The Fall of Constantinople*, Cambridge University Press 1969, pp. 29f.; T. D. Kendrick, *British Antiquity*, Methuen 1970, especially pp. 35ff., though the whole of the earlier part of the book is interesting in this connection.

7. Loisy, *Les Évangiles Synoptiques*, Chez l'auteur, Ceffonds 1907, i. 329.

8. Davies, op. cit., pp. 184-5.

9. Marshall Johnson, *The Purpose of the Biblical Genealogies*, Cambridge University Press, Society for New Testament Studies, Monograph Series, no. 8.

10. *Beiheft zur ZNTW*, xxvi, 1960, pp. 94ff.; see especially p. 101.

11. Johnson, op. cit., p. 156. Cf. his own explanation on pp. 159ff.

12. Ward Gasque, *A History of the Criticism of the Acts of the Apostles*, J. C. B. Mohr 1975, p. 308.

13. Davies, op. cit., p. 73.

14. For a different view see Johnson, op. cit., p. 255.

15. In *The Interpreter's Bible*, Abingdon, Nashville 1951, vol. VII, p. 252.

16. *The Jerome Biblical Commentary*, Geoffrey Chapman 1968.

17. Cf. Jeremias, *Jerusalem in the Time of Jesus*, SCM Press 1967, pp. 290ff.

18. Johnson, op. cit., p. 254.

19. Jeremias, op. cit., pp. 294-5.

20. Soncino translation, pp. 196ff.

21. Johnson, op. cit., p. 254.

22. It is surely difficult to suppose, as is done by T. H. Robinson for example in his Moffatt Commentary on Matthew, Hodder & Stoughton 1928, p. 3, that Matthew did not *intend* his genealogy to be taken as an account of what had actually happened in the past.

23. G. E. P. Cox, *St Matthew* (Torch Bible Commentaries), SCM Press 1952, p. 29.

24. For the reference see Davies, op. cit., p. 304, n. 1 and p. 302, n. 1.

25. Kaufmann, 'The Messianic Idea', *El Ha'ayin*, v, 1961, quoted by W. F. Albright and C. S. Mann, *Matthew*, Doubleday & Co. 1971, p. 2.

26. Stendahl, art. cit., p. 94, italics mine; Johnson, op. cit., p. 254; cf. Davies's comment on the Mishnah, 'by itself the evidence from the Mishanh on historical matters is always uncertain, because of the possibility that it is imaginatively coloured and creates a past which never existed', op. cit., p. 283, n. 1.

27. R. W. Southern, *Western Society and the Church in the Middle Ages*, Penguin Books 1970, pp. 92-3.

28. The same sort of point is made in Johnson, op. cit., pp. 144-5, a passage which was not in mind when the above was first written.

29. On the uncertainties about the correct text and interpretation of Luke's genealogy see the commentaries; also J. Jeremias, op. cit., pp. 292f., and Johnson, op. cit., pp. 231ff.

30. See Anton Vögtle, *Biblische Zeitschrift*, ix, 1965, pp. 36-68.

31. John Knox, *The Death of Christ*, Collins 1959, pp. 71-2.

32. Ibid., p. 159.

33. See above p. 177.

34. See especially his book *The Way of All the Earth*, Sheldon Press 1973.

35. R. G. Collingwood, *Autobiography*, Penguin Books 1944, p. 78.

Index of Names

Euphorion, 168
Evans, C. F., 134, 191, 197
Evans-Pritchard, E. E., 151, 160, 203

Farmer, W. R., 195, 198
Farrer, A., 8, 27, 73, 74, 101, 167, 191, 195, 204
Febvre, Lucien, 53
Finkelstein, L., 178
Foakes Jackson, F. J., 193
Fromm, Eric, 141, 202
Fuchs, E., 196
Fuller, R. H., 98, 196

Gabler, J. P., 44f., 192
Gadamer, H. G., 142, 202
Gardner, Helen, 97, 196
Gasque, Ward, 171, 205
Gore, Charles, 76, 138, 201

Hanson, A. T., 76, 195
Hanson, R. P. C., 98, 196
Harnack, A. von, 124, 126, 156
Hart, H. St J., 196f.
Hartlich, C., 192
Heenan, John, Cardinal, 104
Hick, John, 198
Hickling, C. J., 201
Hodgson, Leonard, 44, 63, 66, 73, 74, 101, 102, 105, 141, 144, 192, 194, 195
Holtzmann, H. J., 117, 120
Holtzmann, O., 199
Hooker, Morna, 201
Hort, F. J. A., 159
Hoskyns, Sir Edwyn, 40, 110, 191, 193, 199
Hull, J. M., 162, 203
Hulme, T. E. F., 148, 203
Hunter, A. M., 2, 26, 35, 121, 188, 191

Jeremias, J., 173f., 205, 206
Johnson, M., 170, 174, 176, 178, 205, 206

Johnson, Dr Samuel, 148
Jonas, H., 132, 200
Josephus, 193

Kähler, M., 202
Kaufmann, Y., 178, 205
Keats, John, 5
Kendrick, T. D., 169, 204
Kierkegaard, S., 88f., 106, 196
Knox, John, 52, 77, 90, 101, 119, 181, 182ff., 185, 188, 193, 194, 198, 206
Knox, R., 98, 196

Lachmann, C., 197
Lake, Kirsopp, 193
Lascelles, Mary, 97
Lash, Nicholas, 149, 203
Lewis, C. S., 69, 70, 75, 195
Lightfoot, J. B., 121, 159
Lightfoot, R. H., 2, 3, 30, 36, 40, 85, 110, 159, 167, 189, 190, 191, 194, 196
Lohmeyer, E., 34
Loisy, A., 2, 110, 169, 204
Luther, Martin, 97, 154

McIntyre, J., 201
Mackenzie, J. L., 173
MacKinnon, D. M., 4, 202
Malinowski, B., 151, 160, 203, 204
Mann, C. S., 205
Manson, T. W., 2, 184, 197
Manson, W., 2
Melanchthon, Philipp, 7
Michaelis, Wilhelm, 167
Morrison, C. C., 108, 196
Moule, C. F. D., 159, 195
Mozley, E. N., 199, 200

Neil, W., 95
Neville, G., 195
Newman, John Henry, 110
Niebuhr, R. R., 195
Nietzsche, F. W., 148, 202
Nineham, D. E., 192, 198, 202

Index of Subjects

Allegory, 68, 96, 153
Anamnesis, 109
Anthropology, 70, 151
Apocalyptic, 123-6, 176, 182
Apocryphal Gospels, 34
Apostles, 83
Atonement, 100
Authority, 67f., 94f., 109

Barth, hermeneutics, 95, 157
    View of modes of revelation, 108f.
    see also, das Nichtige
Bible,
    a priori assumptions about, 69, 83
    Authority of, 110
    Exegesis of, 68, 101
    Images in, 73f.
    Meaning of, 94ff., 135, 139, 142, 144
    Roman Catholic view of, 92, 197
    as Word of God, 96
    see also, 'Dogma of Normativeness'
'Biblical Theology', 71f., 140,
    see also, Kerygma
Bultmann, demythologization, 101, 132, 140
    Hermeneutics, 95, 157f.
    see also, Vorverständnis

Canon, 110, 135
Christ, of faith, 45, 59, 86, 129
    'Imitatio Christi', 52
    -event, 107

    see also, Jesus, Historical Jesus
Christianity, traditional, 67f.,
    see also, Orthodoxy
Christian Socialism, 138
Christology, 106f., 131
Creation, Doctrine of, 137
    -mythology, 67
Cultural assumptions, 80, 126
    Tacit assumptions, 163, 169, 204
Cultural change, awareness of, 69f., 77, 116, 135
Cultural conditioning, 43, 65, 130, 142, 155, 168, 184
Cultural totality, 149f., 169

Demythologization, 101, 132,
    see also, Bultmann
Doctrines, 91
    Development of, 110, 125
    'Felt as facts', 148, 150, 161
'Dogma of Normativeness', 92, 104, 110, 171
Doublets, 39

Einfühlung, 167
Enlightenment, 155
Eschatology, 67, 122-32
    De-eschatologization, 125
    Konsequent-eschatologisch, 124
    'Realized eschatology', 125, 164
Existentialist theology, 119, 132, 140f., 164; *see also*, Bultmann
Eye-witness testimony, 8, 24-60, 78, 117